THE FEAR OF THE LORD

THE FEAR OF THE LORD

Essays on Theological Method

Michael Allen

LONDON • NEW YORK • OXFORD • NEW DELHI • SYDNEY

T&T CLARK
Bloomsbury Publishing Plc
50 Bedford Square, London, WC1B 3DP, UK
1385 Broadway, New York, NY 10018, USA
29 Earlsfort Terrace, Dublin 2, Ireland

BLOOMSBURY, T&T CLARK and the T&T Clark logo are trademarks
of Bloomsbury Publishing Plc

First published in Great Britain 2022
Paperback edition published 2023

Copyright © Michael Allen, 2022

Michael Allen has asserted his right under the Copyright, Designs and
Patents Act, 1988, to be identified as Author of this work.

For legal purposes the Acknowledgments on p. 201 constitute
an extension of this copyright page.

Cover image: Vlad Georgescu/Getty

All rights reserved. No part of this publication may be reproduced or transmitted
in any form or by any means, electronic or mechanical, including photocopying,
recording, or any information storage or retrieval system, without prior
permission in writing from the publishers.

Bloomsbury Publishing Plc does not have any control over, or responsibility for,
any third-party websites referred to or in this book. All internet addresses given
in this book were correct at the time of going to press. The author and publisher
regret any inconvenience caused if addresses have changed or sites have
ceased to exist, but can accept no responsibility for any such changes.

A catalogue record for this book is available from the British Library.

Library of Congress Cataloging-in-Publication Data
Names: Allen, Michael, 1981- author.
Title: The fear of the Lord : essays on theological method / Michael Allen.
Description: London ; New York : T&T Clark, 2022. | Includes index. |
Identifiers: LCCN 2021029027 (print) | LCCN 2021029028 (ebook) |
ISBN 9780567699275 (hb) | ISBN 9780567699688 (paperback) |
ISBN 9780567699282 (epdf) | ISBN 9780567699305 (epub)
Subjects: LCSH: Theology–Methodology. | God (Christianity) | LCGFT: Essays.
Classification: LCC BR118 .A4345 2022 (print) | LCC BR118 (ebook) | DDC 231–dc23
LC record available at https://lccn.loc.gov/2021029027
LC ebook record available at https://lccn.loc.gov/2021029028

ISBN:		
	HB:	978-0-5676-9927-5
	PB:	978-0-5676-9968-8
	ePDF:	978-0-5676-9928-2
	ePUB:	978-0-5676-9930-5

Typeset by Integra Software Services Pvt. Ltd.

To find out more about our authors and books visit www.bloomsbury.com
and sign up for our newsletters.

CONTENTS

Preface: "The Fear of the Lord Is the Beginning of Wisdom"	vi
Chapter 1 "IN YOUR LIGHT DO WE SEE LIGHT": THE FUTURE AND THE PROMISE OF THEOLOGY	1
Chapter 2 LIVING AND ACTIVE: THE EXALTED PROPHET IN THE EPISTLE TO THE HEBREWS	15
Chapter 3 THE CREATURE OF THE WORD	29
Chapter 4 DIVINE TRANSCENDENCE AND THE READING OF SCRIPTURE	49
Chapter 5 SYSTEMATIC THEOLOGY AND BIBLICAL THEOLOGY	73
Chapter 6 ON APOCALYPTIC THEOLOGY	103
Chapter 7 DISPUTATION *FOR* SCHOLASTIC THEOLOGY: ENGAGING LUTHER'S 97 THESES	117
Chapter 8 DOGMATICS AS ASCETICS	135
Chapter 9 THE CONTEMPLATIVE AND THE ACTIVE LIFE	155
Chapter 10 REFORMED RETRIEVAL	171
Chapter 11 RETRIEVAL AND THE PROPHETIC IMAGINATION	185
Acknowledgments	201
Index	202

Preface: "The Fear of the Lord is the Beginning of Wisdom"

"The fear of the LORD is the beginning of wisdom" (Ps. 111.10). Proverbs 2.5 goes further to suggest that this fear—a reverential fixation upon the one true God—comes by accepting and storing, turning and applying, calling out and crying, looking for and searching after the very Word of God. Such actions deserve our effort, because that "fear of the Lord" is the very foundation of all wisdom. "Beginning" speaks not only of wisdom's inception but of its perpetual foundational bedrock. That watchword of theological practice and of all Christian existence serves also as an intellectual axiom. In recent years, theology has been tempted by many other things, manifesting fear of much else beside the Lord. Yet theocentrism cannot be left behind as if it were merely an initial posture or an inception point. Christian theology, if it is to be true to its name, must always manifest fear of the one living and true God.

These chapters seek to reflect on the task of theology and to do so in a way that maintains that Godward focus and seek to practice that fear. Five areas in particular have garnered my attention at greater length in recent years: the implications of Trinitarian and Christological doctrine for the promise of theological practice, the scholastic or systematic shape of Christian doctrine, the ascetical or spiritual character of Christian doctrine, theological exegesis or theological interpretation of Scripture and its relationship to both biblical and systematic theology, and the promise of retrieval or *ressourcement* for Christian doctrine. Each chapter in this book addresses one or more of those areas of methodological concern. I should say a word about how each of those themes appears here and relates to my other writings.

First, theological practice needs to be described primarily in light of the work of the living and true God. While we will need to say much more about human agency and the like, we must begin and remain ever vigilant to keep our eye upon the presence and works of the triune God. My textbook on *Reformed Theology* begins with that as a hallmark of my own particular theological tradition, and my more recent work on future prospects for Reformed theology further addresses that concern.[1] In touching on various other doctrines (i.e., sanctification), I have regularly tried to maintain that Godward glance at all times, most recently by exploring the loss and need for theocentrism in Christian eschatology and ethics

---

1. *Reformed Theology* (Doing Theology; London: T&T Clark, 2010); and "Future Prospects for Reformed Theology," in *The Oxford Handbook of Reformed Theology* (ed. Michael Allen and Scott R. Swain; Oxford: Oxford University Press, 2020), 623-30.

in my small book, *Grounded in Heaven: Re-centering Christian Hope and Life in God*.[2] Here several chapters focus more specifically on why that's of methodological significance. "'In Your Light We See Light': The Future and Promise of Theology," "Living and Active," and "The Creature of the Word" each tend to those fundamental principles that are rooted in a catholic heritage and methodologically developed in some powerful ways in the Reformed tradition.

Second, scholastic and systematic theology has been much maligned in recent decades, often for putting God in a box and distorting the dramatic character of more occasional or narratival modes of thought. Yet the best historical studies of scholastic theology in its medieval and post-Reformation settings (both Roman Catholic and Reformed) show that concern for narrative and history doesn't wane with the turn toward more school-oriented genres of writing. Indeed, I have tried to argue constructively that systematic thought serves a unique role precisely in keeping our eyes upon the whole counsel of God and its interconnections (many of which, though not all, are narratival). I've argued elsewhere that our post-Christian moment in the contemporary West uniquely calls for the missionary importance of systematic theology, when we can no longer assume a Christian sense of many biblical loan words (i.e., love, freedom, power). Only systematic reflection will enable us to examine the overlapping and distinctive ways that Christians use such common language in Christian ways.[3] Here I tend to the importance of such scholastic and systematic work in "Disputation *for* Scholastic Theology," "On Apocalyptic Theology," and "Systematic Theology and Biblical Theology." (Essays in the companion collection, *The Knowledge of God: Essays on God, Christ, and Church*, will also take up this task overtly and at length: i.e., "Into the Family of God" and "Sources of the Self.")

Third, theology is hard intellectual work, but it cannot be any less spiritual and moral for so being. Theology directs itself to the importance of communion with the triune God and therefore occurs always within the economy of God's grace. Further, it demands not only intellectual but also moral and theological virtues for good execution. Therefore, the modern theological encyclopedia and the setting of theological study (mentally if not geographically) within the walls of the modern research university push against a more integrative approach to doctrine. I have been compelled to rethink the systematic or doctrinal task along older, classical lines whereby doctrine serves not only the spiritual life but specifically to mortify and vivify the intellectual commitments of the theologian. Theology involves self-denial, countermands idolatry, and thus needs wholehearted spiritual commitment. *Grounded in Heaven* explored the reintegration of an evangelical asceticism into Christian theology this side of the Reformation and the Neo-Calvinist movement. There is further need to explore the ways in which theology itself involves ascetical discipline by God's grace. "Dogmatics as Ascetics" and "The Contemplative and the

---

2. Grand Rapids: Eerdmans, 2018.

3. See *Sanctification* (New Studies in Dogmatics; Grand Rapids: Zondervan Academic, 2017), 44.

Active Life" serve to examine the way in which systematic theology or Christian dogmatics relates to that broader task of Christian intellectual discipleship by considering recent and medieval visions of that spiritual or moral component of theology.

Fourth, thinking theologically must be yoked to reading Holy Scripture, and any appropriate reading of Holy Scripture will have to read it for what it is: the living Word of God. The nature of scriptural hermeneutics and the connection between biblical exegesis and the task of Christian dogmatics both warrant attention. My first book (originally a dissertation) was a dogmatic treatise in Christology. It engaged in a wide-angle dogmatic analysis of varied topics of Christian theology and also narrow-angle theological interpretation of particular passages of Holy Scripture.[4] I've since edited a festschrift focused on *Theological Commentary* and coedited a reexamination of *Reformation Readings of Paul*.[5] Scott Swain and I have served as general editors of the T&T Clark International Theological Commentary series that has sought to advance theological interpretation of Scripture (often termed "TIS") in its disciplinary development by offering longer, more slowly fermenting commentaries on the whole Bible. I've turned recently to writing a biblical commentary: *Ephesians*.[6] "Divine Transcendence and the Reading of Scripture" and "Systematic Theology and Biblical Theology" each examine the character of theological reading of Scripture, pondering the relationship of divine revelation and human reading (in the former) or the disciplinary relationships of systematic theology and exegesis to biblical theology and TIS (in the latter).

Fifth, many theologians have observed that contemporary theology has suffered where it has failed to remain in deep and vibrant touch with its spiritual and intellectual heritage. Too often "the new" has dominated and "revision" has been the watchword. There have been decades when engagement of the tradition appears only for the sake of "doctrinal criticism." Sometimes that contemporary self-fascination with the present has traded under the supposed support of the Protestant and Reformed maxim, *sola Scriptura*. Scott Swain and I have published a manifesto, *Reformed Catholicity*, to commend the promise of retrieval or *ressourcement* for the sake of renewing recent theology.[7] Our *Christian Dogmatics* textbook has also gathered a range of compelling contributors whose various theological arguments each involve productive engagement upon that catholic

---

4. *The Christ's Faith: A Dogmatic Account* (T&T Clark Studies in Systematic Theology; London: T&T Clark, 2009).

5. *Theological Commentary: Evangelical Perspectives* (ed. Michael Allen; London: T&T Clark, 2012); and *Reformation Readings of Paul: Explorations in History and Doctrine* (ed. Michael Allen and Jonathan A. Linebaugh; Downers Grove, IL: IVP Academic, 2015).

6. *Ephesians* (Brazos Theological Commentary on the Bible; Grand Rapids: Brazos, 2020).

7. Michael Allen and Scott R. Swain, *Reformed Catholicity: The Promise of Retrieval for Theology and Biblical Interpretation* (Grand Rapids: Baker Academic, 2015).

heritage.[8] With my colleague Jonathan Linebaugh, I coedited a volume, *Reformation Readings of Paul*, that sought to challenge the so-called new readings of Paul that would suggest the Protestant Reformers were bad examples of exegetical care. Acknowledging fresh light that yet breaks out of God's Word in no way demands falsely rebuking ancestors for misreadings (not least when they being misread in such accusations); I've also tried to further that argument in portions of my books, *Justification and the Gospel* and *Sanctification*, addressing places where many luminaries in recent Pauline studies have castigated Luther and Calvin without actually engaging their own claims.[9] Here "Reformed Retrieval" commends the theological beliefs that make such *ressourcement* theologically and ecclesiastically productive (rather than simply parroting the principles of sociological or hermeneutical theory), while "Retrieval and the Prophetic Imagination" explores how retrieval theology actually helps keep the church more alert to the failures of the status quo.

Other topics deserve attention in a broad, systematic consideration of theological method. My future writing will tend not only to matters named here or addressed in other publications but also to those remaining matters of importance as yet unexplored by me. It remains my hope, however, that gathering these texts will satisfy demands of readers who regularly request various essays or articles scattered among many publications or journals. These are exploratory essays on the way toward that larger, later project, hopefully eliciting critical response that will benefit author as much as reader. More importantly, I hope that this volume manifests a consistent concern to practice the fear of the LORD, which is and ever remains the beginning of wisdom, whenever addressing one of these five categories of methodological concern. In that sense, I publish it as a book with a singular concern, unfolded in various movements.

* * *

This collection of essays and its sibling (*The Knowledge of God: Essays on God, Christ, and Church*) gather studies prepared over the course of the last fifteen years. I have resisted the urge to rewrite and refashion, modifying only by updating bibliographic references and correcting formatting or typos. My teaching assistant, Angel Roman-Diaz, helped with preparing the essays for production. My colleague, John Muether, prepared the index. I thank a host of publications for permission to publish here: *International Journal of Systematic Theology*, *Journal of Reformed Theology*, *Scottish Bulletin of Evangelical Theology*, *Reformed Faith & Practice*, *Themelios*, Blackwell Publishing, and Zondervan Academic. Various friends and colleagues read chapters on different occasions, and I have noted them

---

8. *Christian Dogmatics: Reformed Theology for the Church Catholic* (ed. Michael Allen and Scott R. Swain; Grand Rapids: Baker Academic, 2016).

9. *Justification and the Gospel: Understanding the Contexts and Controversies* (Grand Rapids: Baker Academic, 2013); and *Sanctification*.

where I can. I should especially highlight three people in particular: Wesley Hill, Jonathan Linebaugh, and Scott Swain, who contribute to my ongoing research and writing in all manner of ways. It remains a pleasure to work with Anna Turton and the Bloomsbury team and an honor to publish again with T&T Clark, now in their 200th year of publishing Christian theology.

Ascension Day 2021
Oviedo

Chapter 1

"IN YOUR LIGHT DO WE SEE LIGHT": THE FUTURE AND THE PROMISE OF THEOLOGY

Theology and the Future

The future is uncertain for so many things. Pundits and predictions fail left and right. The Scriptures should have prepared us for such: "Come now, you who say, 'Today or tomorrow we will go into such and such a town and spend a year there and trade and make a profit'—yet you do not know what tomorrow will bring. What is your life? For you are a mist that appears for a little time and then vanishes" (Jas. 4.13-14). The mist appears; then like vapor (the very "vanity of vanities" in Ecclesiastes) it vanishes. No, the future is not certain.

Yet the future is bright for theology. By theology I adopt a definition roughly similar to that of Thomas Aquinas, who believed this intellectual study to involve God and the works of God (or, otherwise put, all things in relation to God).[1] This kind of reflection has a promising future, where the complexities of modern life will need to be viewed in light of God's luminosity and the challenges of humanity will require consideration from the perspective of God's truth.

The path of theology in the future is not owing to the intellectual sophistication or moral fortitude of theologians. A scan of the theological field over the last several decades includes a number of movements or emphases that have come and gone (e.g., the death of God theology). There have been hopeless detours and hapless mistakes, and even the most faithful of theologians err in their listening and testifying to God's Word. Theology is always done East of Eden. The promise

---

1. See, e.g., Thomas Aquinas, *Summa Theologiae*, Volume 1: *Christian Theology* (trans. Thomas Gilby; Oxford: Blackfriars, 1964), 1a.1.7, reply; on the relation of thinking "about God" and "about all other things," see Gilles Emery, *The Trinitarian Theology of Thomas Aquinas* (trans. Francesca Aran Murphy; Oxford: Oxford University Press, 2007), 41–3, 413–15. Early creedal summaries of the faith included "two elements" that "remain constant," namely, the identity of God and the exposition of the works of God (in particular, the gospel narrative), according to Jaroslav Pelikan, *The Christian Tradition: A History of the Development of Doctrine*, volume one: *The Emergence of the Catholic Tradition (100–600)* (Chicago: University of Chicago Press, 1971), 117.

and potential of theology, then, cannot be premised on institutional vitality, academic sophistication, moral clarity, or ecclesial power alone.

The promise of theology follows from the electing love of the triune God. "How precious is your steadfast love, O God! The children of mankind take refuge in the shadow of your wings. They feast on the abundance of your house, and you give them drink from the river of your delights. For with you is the fountain of life; in your light do we see light" (Ps. 36.7-9). God is "the fountain of life"—"in his presence is fullness of joy; at his right hand are pleasures forevermore" (Ps. 16.11). The rest we find in God involves his illumining work that we might see and know both him and life in him: "you will show me the path of life" (Ps. 16.11); "in your light do we see light" (Ps. 36.9). God brings life and light to our world—humans have hope not only for existence but for knowledge being gained and truth being known.

The goodness of the triune God gives promise and a future to theology. It is of this glorious one that we say "in your light do we see light." The potential of human knowledge of God is entirely premised on the gratuity of God. We live in an *ek*-centric fashion, wherein we constantly receive life from the outside and live on borrowed breath. More specifically, we might say that we live in light of the resurrection of Jesus Christ. He is alive and luminous: in his light we do see light. As John Webster has reminded us: "He is that from which we move, not that towards which we strive; he is not that which we posit (rationally, experientially), but the one whose unqualified self-existence posits us."[2] This Word is "living and active".[3] Karl Barth spoke of him as "eloquent and radiant," reminding us that he compels with beauty, truth, and goodness.[4]

Not only does theology have a future because of the triune God but theology can help shape the human future more broadly. "Nature commends grace; grace emends nature."[5] The communicative presence of God brings grace, and this grace transforms or transfigures human creatureliness in its particularity and specificity. Herman Bavinck expands on this idea: "Human beings are in every respect dependent on the world outside of them. In no area are we autonomous; we live by what is given, i.e., by grace. But, reciprocally, we are made and designed for that

---

2. John Webster, "Resurrection and Scripture," in *Christology and Scripture: Interdisciplinary Perspectives* (LNTS 348; ed. Andrew T. Lincoln and Angus Paddison; London: T&T Clark, 2007), 141.

3. See Chapter 2 in this volume.

4. Karl Barth, *Church Dogmatics*, Volume 4: *The Doctrine of Reconciliation*, Part 3.1 (ed. G. W. Bromiley and T. F. Torrance; trans. G. W. Bromiley; Edinburgh: T&T Clark, 1961), 79. For astute and poignant reflections on the prophetic office of Christ, see John Webster, "'Eloquent and Radiant': The Prophetic Office of Christ and the Mission of the Church," in *Barth's Moral Theology: Human Action in Barth's Thought* (Grand Rapids: Eerdmans, 1998), 125-50.

5. Herman Bavinck, *Reformed Dogmatics*, Volume 1: *Prolegomena* (ed. John Bolt; trans. John Vriend; Grand Rapids: Baker Academic, 2003), 362.

whole world outside of us and connected to it by a whole spectrum of relations."[6] Theology points to the ways in which God's grace renews humans.

Theology does so instrumentally: serving as a prompt and aid to the church's testimony to the life-giving gospel of Jesus. It is Christian testimony in worship and witness that is the church's primary calling. Theology serves as a critical tool meant to render this testimony more faithful and, hence, effective. The distinction between first- and second-order language proves helpful here: while the praise and proclamation of the church is first-order language, the tools of theological analysis are second-order language meant to help critique and commend the church's primary calling.

A primary way in which theology will serve the church is by offering critique of idolatry. Nicholas Lash views doctrine in this way: "one of the principal functions of doctrine, as regulative of Christian speech and action, would be to help protect correct reference, by disciplining our manifold propensity toward idolatry."[7] Lash further identified this "stripping away of the veils of self-assurance by which we seek to protect our faces from exposure to the mystery of God' as the prompt for viewing theology as a critical practice."[8] Idolatry is nothing new—Israel of old and the *ekklēsia* of today are lured into its traps. Theological reflection serves as a prophetic check to this tendency of our religious culture and character.

Theology and Biblical Interpretation

We have seen that God's goodness is determined to fill all things with his glory (Eph. 4.10). God's sharing his life with us involves his shedding abroad the knowledge of his love. Thus, we have wonderful news to proclaim to the enslaved: because there is a living God revealed in Jesus Christ, there really can be life for those caught in the pangs of death. God not only promises such life, he sees fit to provide for our knowledge of this promise. The Lord not only acts but he speaks testimony about his deeds. In short: because Jesus is alive, theology has a future.

God's self-revelation has taken particular shape: among Israel, in Jesus of Nazareth, by his prophets and apostles. Dietrich Bonhoeffer was well aware of the need to consider God in his particularity:

> In Jesus Christ the reality of God has entered into the reality of this world. The place where the questions about the reality of God and about the reality of the world are answered at the same time is characterized solely by the name: Jesus Christ. God and the world are enclosed in this name ... we cannot speak rightly

---

6. Ibid., 501.
7. Nicholas Lash, "When Did the Theologians Lose Interest in Theology?," in *The Beginning and End of "Religion"* (Cambridge: Cambridge University Press, 1996), 134.
8. Nicholas Lash, "Criticism or Construction? The Task of the Theologian," in *Theology on the Way to Emmaus* (London: SCM, 1986), 9.

of either God or the world without speaking of Jesus Christ. All concepts of reality that ignore Jesus Christ are abstractions.[9]

Bonhoeffer knew full well the danger of fuzzy religion and natural theology unconstrained by Christological revelation and creedal convictions. He had seen the use of religious language in the Nazi propaganda, and so he was concerned that Jesus and the triune God shape our convictions and our very selves, rather than simply caring about our social formation according to the status quo of one's religious pedigree or dominant religious subculture. Terms like "kingdom," "hope," and "righteousness" have very particular meaning given by the Christian God. Human nature as well as divine being has been revealed in the face of Jesus Christ (Jn. 1.18). Like the disciples on the mount of transfiguration, then, we are summoned to "listen to him" (Mt. 17.5).

Now we turn to find sustenance in the Word of God. "The holy, Christian Church, whose only Head is Christ, is born of the Word of God, abides in the same, and does not listen to the voice of a stranger."[10] Jesus Christ is alive and he speaks through his prophetic auxiliaries; Jesus Christ is risen and he sanctifies by his Holy Spirit. The Epistle to the Hebrews offers a concluding benediction that is *apropos*: "Now may the God of peace who brought again from the dead our Lord Jesus, the great shepherd of the sheep, by the blood of the eternal covenant, equip you with everything good that you may do his will, working in us that which is pleasing in his sight, through Jesus Christ, to whom be glory forever and ever" (Heb. 13.20-21). Notice that the risen one is "the great shepherd of the sheep"—there is gospel in the present tense here: he tends the sheep; his Father equips for every good work; by him God works in us that which is pleasing to his Father. And this benediction sums up the spiritual exercise of listening to or (now) of reading this apostolic scripture: it is in this auxiliary or instrument that Jesus exercises his pastoral care for his sheep.

The Scriptures do not come to us bare; they are texts, but they are not mere texts. They have been sanctified by God for a specific calling; hence the tendency to refer to them as "Holy Scripture."[11] They function within a nexus of the triune God's communicative presence. In discussions of dogmatic prolegomena, theologians often speak of the principles of theology to express this communicative matrix. Herman Bavinck is illustrative. He speaks of three foundations or principles of theology: "first, God as the essential foundation (*principium essendi*), the source of theology"; "second, the external cognitive foundation (*principium cognoscendi*

---

9. Dietrich Bonhoeffer, *Ethics* (ed. Clifford Green; Dietrich Bonhoeffer Works 6; Minneapolis: Fortress, 2005), 54.

10. "The Ten Theses of Berne," in *Reformed Confessions of the Sixteenth Century* (ed. Arthur C. Cochrane; Louisville: Westminster John Knox, 2003), 49.

11. On language of the sanctification with respect to the nature of Scripture, see John Webster, *Holy Scripture: A Dogmatic Sketch* (Current Issues in Theology; Cambridge: Cambridge University Press, 2003), 5–41.

externum), viz., the self-revelation of God, which, insofar as it is recorded in Holy Scripture, bears an instrumental and temporary character"; "finally, the internal principle of knowing (*principium cognoscendi internum*), the illumination of human beings by God's Spirit."[12] He insists: "They may and can, therefore, never be separated and detached from each other. On the other hand, they do need to be distinguished."[13] God is the principle of being, and God's agency as "source of theology" functions in two ways: externally and internally. Christ speaks through his written Word, and the Holy Spirit illumines human reception of the same.

Perhaps no passage of Scripture so exemplifies this location of the Bible in the economy of grace as 2 Timothy 3–4. Oftentimes this text is quoted for what it says directly of the Bible: "All Scripture is breathed out by God and profitable for teaching, for reproof, for correction, and for training in righteousness, that the man of God may be competent, equipped for every good work" (2 Tim. 3.16-17). Taking Paul's reference to what we would now call the "Old Testament" Scriptures (*graphe*) as extended to the apostolic "New Testament" writings as well, theologians argue that this passage speaks of their inspiration and effectiveness. Notice, however, that the passage continues: "I charge you in the presence of God and of Christ Jesus, who is to judge the living and the dead, and by his appearing and his kingdom: preach the word" (2 Tim. 4.1-2). The emphasis upon the written Word comes in the midst of a declaration that Paul and Timothy exist "in the presence of God and of Christ Jesus." The scriptural embassy functions only in the administration of its sovereign speaker: the risen Christ. Because Christ is communicatively and redemptively present to us through these Scriptures, they are to be to us as a means of grace.

When thinking about God's work outside and inside us, it is helpful to reflect on our deep need. In an early letter Franz Kafka identified what we sorely lack and, if we are honest, should want:

> If the book we are reading does not wake us, as with a fist hammering on our skull, why then do we read it? Good God, we would also be happy if we had no books, and such books as make us happy we could, if need be, write ourselves. But what we must have are those books which come upon us like ill-fortune, and distress us deeply, like the death of one we love better than ourselves, like suicide. A book must be an ice-axe to break the sea frozen inside us.[14]

We need words of life. We require the burning coal placed to our lips and the transfigured glory presented before our very eyes. Like those who have traipsed

---

12. Bavinck, *Reformed Dogmatics*, Volume 1, 213 (see also 505, 580). See also John Webster, "The Domain of the Word," in *The Domain of the Word: Scripture and Theological Reason* (London: T&T Clark, 2012), 3–31.

13. Bavinck, *Reformed Dogmatics*, Volume 1, 214.

14. A letter from Franz Kafka (cited by George Steiner, *Language and Silence* (New York: Atheneum, 1970), 67.

through the temples of this age, we require a bath (baptism), a word (the Word of God), and a meal (the Eucharist). We need to be renamed, reclaimed, and resourced, and God provides for all these needs through his Word proclaimed and made visible in the sacraments. The key is that *God* does this: "For God, who said, 'Let light shine out of darkness', has shone in our hearts to give the light of the knowledge of the glory of God in the face of Jesus Christ" (2 Cor. 4.6).

The future of theology is pegged to its close tie with God's Word, because here God is present with all his sanctifying beauty. Here our desires and practices are recalibrated by God and to God. It is just this—our intentionality and our direction—that can go so terribly awry. Nicholas Lash has defined idolatry as taking many forms, yet "common to them all is setting our hearts on something less than God."[15] This takes shape in "getting the reference wrong: of taking that to be God which is not God, of mistaking some fact or thing or nation or person or dream or possession or ideal for our heart's need and the mystery 'that moves the sun and other stars.'"[16] Our problem is not to lack passion for the divine or a will to worship; our problem is an insistence in approaching God or the gods on our own terms and in our own way.[17]

A theology that will flourish constantly needs the presence of the communicative God. By his election Scripture is "the eternally youthful Word of God."[18] Scripture is that which is "living and active, sharper than any two-edged sword" (Heb. 4.12). Therefore, theology that will flourish must take the form of what John Webster has termed "biblical reasoning." Webster has distinguished between "exegetical reasoning" and "dogmatic reasoning," yet he argues that both are subsumed under this broader commitment to biblical reasoning.[19] Whether in the mode of specific exegesis of a given passage ("exegetical reasoning") or synthetic reflection upon the contours of the whole biblical canon ("dogmatic reasoning"), theology is a positive and not a *poietic* science; it is receptive, not creative. It follows God's revelation given to us now in Holy Scripture rather than fashioning its own object.

The rule and boundaries given to theology by God's Word are precisely what makes theology a free science. Karl Barth reminds us: "[T]his means that we shall be guided by the direction of Holy Scripture, that we shall not have to champion the thesis in our own strength or on our own responsibility, and that we may thus champion it without anxiety because it is not really exposed to the charge of arbitrariness." Theology is "guided" and, thus, it can be practiced "without anxiety."

---

15. Nicholas Lash, *Easter in Ordinary: Reflections on Human Experience and the Knowledge of God* (London: SCM, 1988), 258.

16. Lash, "When Did the Theologians Lose Interest in Theology?". 134.

17. Walter Brueggemann, "Foreword," *Journal for Preachers* 26 (Easter 2003), 1; see also Patrick D. Miller, *The God You Have: Politics, Religion, and the First Commandment* (Facets; Minneapolis: Fortress, 2004).

18. Bavinck, *Reformed Dogmatics*, Volume 1, 384–5.

19. On these terms, see John Webster, "Biblical Reasoning," in *The Domain of the Word: Scripture and Theological Reason* (London: T&T Clark, 2012), 129–32.

Barth expands further: "The distinctive thought-form of the Bible is not something which is discovered in that way; it is demanded, enforced and indeed created by that which is attested, namely, by the lordship of Jesus Christ Himself."[20] The risen Christ directs and demands, enforcing and creating life, by the instrument of his prophetic and apostolic word. When theology is practiced in this domain, his reign and his peace cast out all fear and anxiety.

Emphasis upon the agency of the risen Christ by and through his Holy Spirit does not undercut or downplay the empirical agency of men and women who pray, think, read, question, and so forth. Theology is done by humans. John Owen reminds us: "The Holy Spirit so worketh in us as that he worketh by us, and what he doth in us is done by us."[21] And the way in which we involve ourselves in this work is according to our humanity as such; again Owen is helpful: "That he acts nothing contrary unto, puts no force upon, any of the faculties of our souls, but works in them and by them suitably according to their natures."[22] Theological science is work, human work, that requires care, commitment, and the development of certain competencies. But it is work that is always the gift of another—the loving triune God of eternity—who shapes and sustains its exercise and endurance.

Renewal through Retrieval

Theology has a future, and theology's hope is premised upon its ever-fresh grace given in God's Word to which it attends. Theology—like every facet of the church's life—will live by grace alone or it will die. Knowing God's promise, however, the real question is not whether or not it will have a future but how it will receive the promised future which it has been pledged by God.

---

20. Barth, *Church Dogmatics*, Volume 4, 95–6. For further reflections on how freedom is found in boundaries, see Reinhard Hütter, *Bound to Be Free: Evangelical Catholic Engagements in Ecclesiology*, Ethics, *and* Ecumenism (Grand Rapids: Eerdmans, 2005), esp. 111–81.

21. John Owen, *Pneumatologia, or A Discourse Concerning the Holy Spirit* (Works of John Owen 3; repr. Edinburgh: Banner of Truth Trust, 1965), 204.

22. Ibid., 225. For further reflections on the nature of divine and human agency involved in theological work (or other historical events), see Antonie Vos and Eef Dekker, "Modalities in Francis Turretin: An Essay in Reformed Ontology," in *Scholasticism Reformed: Essays in Honor of Willem J. Van Asselt* (ed. M. Wisse, M. Sarot, and W. Otten; Leiden: Brill, 2010), 74–91; Kathryn Tanner, *Jesus, Humanity, and the Trinity: A Brief Systematic Theology* (Minneapolis: Fortress, 2001), 2–3. These reflections from Reformed theologians follow a broadly Augustinian and Thomist approach to providence. Thomas's own words are instructive: "During the whole of a thing's existence, God must be present to it, and present in a way in keeping with the way in which the thing possesses its existence" (Aquinas, *Summa Theologiae*, 1a.8.1, reply).

Over and again we are told that Christianity must change or die. Its metaphysics must be recast, lest it appear oppressive and narrow-minded, reducing the many to the one. Its liturgy must be rethought, or else it fails to communicate and compel contemporaries. Its polity must be reshaped, or else it will not be positioned to meet the pressing challenges of an increasingly mobile, fluid, interactive, flat world. Its moral commitments must be revised, or else it will find itself on the back end of societal reform and be likened unto the imperialists, misogynists, and racists. In these various ways, exemplified by everything from the emerging church to the revisionism of the mainline churches and not a few supposed evangelicals too, the future is to be seized by reinvention.

Yet there is another way: a path to renewal by means of retrieval. This path expresses greater doubt in our own ability to manipulate circumstances and creatively meet challenges. This path demonstrates deeper reliance upon the wisdom of those who have faced analogous situations in centuries past and on continents far away. This path sees its calling not only in terms of effectiveness in the present but in terms of faithfulness to the past.

The approach of seeking theological renewal by way of retrieval is based on the very example of Jesus and his apostles. If ever there were charismatic leaders fit to start *de novo*, it was those leaders who served at the very founding of the Christian church. Yet when one reads the apostle Paul's writings, it becomes immediately apparent that his arguments are shaped thoroughly by the scriptures of Israel and are cast in canonical terms precisely because Paul views himself as a thinker and practitioner ruled by *Torah*.[23] Similarly, the anonymous author of the Epistle to the Hebrews saturates his writing with lengthy exegetical forays. He cannot engage in Christology without addressing the Psalms (e.g., Psalm 110), and he does not articulate an atonement theology but by reflecting upon the promises of the fiery prophet (e.g., Jer. 31.31-34). Indeed, the very structure of his Epistle takes the form of a renewed Deuteronomy, wherein the scriptural matrix of the past is recontextualized for a new redemptive situation. Whereas Deuteronomy recontextualized the Mosaic law for the life in Canaan, Hebrews now recontextualizes the entire Old Testament for life this side of Jesus' exaltation and heavenly session.[24] A further scan of the apostolic writings (whether the use of Ezekiel and Daniel in the Apocalypse or the regular allusion to Exod. 3.14 in the Gospel according to John) would provide further evidence for this well-attested reality: the apostles administered their charismatic leadership by means of stewarding their scriptural past for the ecclesial present.

The New Testament provides other examples of biblical traditioning, wherein Scripture is the ultimate authority amid a number of lesser yet no less divinely

---

23. See especially Francis Watson, *Paul and the Hermeneutics of Faith* (London: T&T Clark, 2004); Richard B. Hays, *The Conversion of the Imagination: Paul as Interpreter of Israel's Scripture* (Grand Rapids: Eerdmans, 2005).

24. David M. Allen, *Deuteronomy and Exhortation in Hebrews: A Study in Narrative Re-Presentation* (WUNT 2:238; Tübingen: Mohr-Siebeck, 2008).

intended authorities meant to shape and sustain the faith and practice of the Christian community.[25] For instance, when Paul writes to young Timothy about his pastoral charge, he urges him not merely to follow in Paul's path but also to maintain a catholic heritage. It is no small thing that he does call Timothy to imitate him and to minister as he has done so (see 2 Tim. 1.8; 3.10-11); this itself shows that a mentor has genuine authority, and it manifests Paul, the apostle of freedom, willing to call Timothy to follow his authoritative example. Still more notable, however, is Paul's embrace of a wider pattern that both Timothy and he follow. "Follow the pattern of sound words that you have heard from me, in the faith and love that are in Christ Jesus. By the Holy Spirit who dwells within us, guard the good deposit entrusted to you" (2 Tim. 1.13-14; see also 1 Tim. 6.20). The deposit here, and explicitly in 1 Tim. 6.20, precedes Paul himself; he has been deposited or given this pattern just as much as has Timothy.[26] That which is to be guarded is not merely an object of study but a particular "pattern" of words. The church and her ministers, according to Paul, are committed not simply to a common conversational space or subject but to a particular approach in communicating and confessing it.[27] Paul not only notes this pattern of doctrine as something prescriptive—that which Timothy and he are to honor—but also as a pledge of God. I. Howard Marshall comments that 2 Tim. 1.12 has just insisted that the God whom Paul has believed is "able to guard until that Day what has been entrusted to me."[28] Paul expands on the way in which the triune God does guard this deposit entrusted to Paul (and now also, by extension, to Timothy) by pointing to the Holy Spirit in verse 14. The Spirit guards the apostolic deposit by

---

25. This paragraph and the next are taken from Michael Allen and Scott R. Swain, *Reformed Catholicity: The Promise of Retrieval for Theology and Biblical Interpretation* (Grand Rapids: Baker Academic, 2015), 71–94.

26. I. Howard Marshall with Philip H. Towner, *A Critical and Exegetical Commentary on the Pastoral Epistles* (ICC; London: T&T Clark, 1999), 726-7; cf. 676. On Paul's Gospel as related to earlier oral tradition, see Peter Stuhlmacher, "The Pauline Gospel," in *The Gospel and the Gospels* (ed. Peter Stuhlmacher; trans. John Vriend; Grand Rapids: Eerdmans, 1991), 156–66.

27. Donald Wood has registered concerns on this front about how too often emphasis upon catholicity and the exegetical tradition skates lightly over the binding and authoritative nature of its primary form—the church's creeds and confessions—in the interests of promoting an ongoing space for conversation (see "Some Comments on Moral Realism and Scriptural Authority," *European Journal of Theology* 18, no. 2 (2009), 151–3; see also Oliver J. O'Donovan, "The Moral Authority of Scripture," in *Scripture's Doctrine and Theology's Bible: How the New Testament Shapes Christian Dogmatics* (ed. Markus Bockmuehl and Alan J. Torrance; Grand Rapids: Baker Academic, 2008), 165–75). For further reflection, see "A Ruled Reading Reformed: The Role of the Church's Confession in Biblical Interpretation," in Michael Allen and Scott R. Swain, *Reformed Catholicity: The Promise of Retrieval in Theology and Biblical Interpretation Grand Rapids* (Baker Academic, 2015), 95–116.

28. Marshall, *A Critical and Exegetical Commentary on the Pastoral Epistles*, 714–15.

preserving its transmission and communication from one generation to the next (*à la* Ps. 145.4).

Some have suggested that this kind of portrayal of early Christianity might be termed "early Catholicism," a departure from the vibrant Paulinism of other New Testament writings. Without engaging that historiographic debate here, we can point to the continued emphasis in these pastoral epistles upon Scriptural authority as the final arbiter of Christian faith and practice.[29] "All Scripture is breathed out by God, and profitable for teaching, for reproof, for correction, and for training in righteousness, that the man of God may be competent, equipped for every good work" (2 Tim. 3.16-17). Thus, Timothy is to "preach the Word" (2 Tim. 4.2). The apostle Paul here envisions a ministry that focuses upon preaching the scriptures and yet doing so cognizant of a vibrant and ongoing interpretative tradition that serves to provide authoritative parameters for expositing those sacred scriptures. Scripture and tradition are not mutually exclusive here—the former generates the latter, while the latter serves the former. One is reminded here of Zacharias Ursinus's comments about how Scripture is meant to shape systematic theology, which then informs catechesis; this is the order of being and of authority.[30] At the same time, however, the order of knowing runs precisely the other way: one is catechized, then formed as a theologian, and finally capable of reading the Bible well.

The apostles not only point to the truth of Jesus and the life found therein but they demonstrate the way of Jesus. The path of the gospel is not one of innovation or ecclesial reinvention—charismatic or otherwise—but of biblical traditioning and inhabiting the catholic heritage of God's people. In other words, we not only entrust ourselves to the triune God or to Jesus specifically but entrust ourselves to the triune God, who in Christ has promised to provide for us through certain means. We live receptively, and that means that we submit ourselves to spiritual authorities, scriptural rules, and our catholic context.

This posture of receptivity runs against the tendencies of the modern and late modern (what is frequently termed the "postmodern") eras. By and large theology has been practiced in ways that run in a deistic manner. Indeed, the common moniker given to the theological or doctrinal task today—"constructive theology"—suggests the frequently *poietic* and anthropocentric nature of this intellectual calling. Humans construct a theology based on various assumptions, resources, and needs. Inventiveness and creativity are high values in this schema.

---

29. It is worth noting a recent argument that, without ever focusing upon this genetic or developmental question, nonetheless puts the lie to the argument that there was a marked shift toward an "early Catholicism." It does so from the other side, however, by highlighting the traditioned or catholic nature of earlier texts rather than arguing for the ecclesiastical mildness of certain later texts. See Edith Humphrey, *Scripture and Tradition: What the Bible Really Says* (Grand Rapids: Baker Academic, 2013), 27–34, 43, 136–7.

30. Zacharius Ursinus, *Commentary on the Heidelberg Catechism* (trans. G. W. Williard; Phillipsburg, NJ: Presbyterian and Reformed, 1985), 9.

Three centuries after Kant, his moral concerns about deference to religious tradition remain sturdy: dogma, orthodoxy, confessions, creeds—these all symbolize intellectual oppression in the wider cultural sphere.[31] This Kantian suspicion of the catholic past has affected biblical interpretation and theology.

Mark Bowald has argued that "most contemporary accounts of biblical hermeneutics are deistic."[32] In modern biblical criticism the interpreter is construed as one given the task of getting back behind the accretions: whether they are historical and contextual or ecclesiastical and imperialist. The role of the interpreter is to prosecute an excavation, peeling back layer upon layer to get to something more pristine. The process is premised, at least in theological rather than strictly religious studies contexts, on the notion that God acted there and then, and we have only to get back to these primal events.

In this chapter we have sketched a radically different approach to theology. We do theology always in the wake of God's agency, not merely in the past but in the present. We remember the wisdom of Jewish rabbis who always began their works on page two, cognizant that they spoke in the wake of God's communication. Yet we do not embrace this dependence as a strictly chronological count, as if God acted and now we respond. Theology depends upon grace at every moment. This is not unique to theology, of course, for all things hold together in Christ (Col. 1.15). But theology should express greater cognizance of this dependence than other human activities.

For theology to flourish it must regain its bearings as an exegetical discipline and a receptive practice. Our faith must be placed in the specific, particular ways wherein God promises to meet his people's needs. Theology must be centered on the means of grace: they are word-focused, ecclesially bounded, and missionally aimed. We will briefly reflect on each of these aspects

First, the means of grace for theology are word-focused, whether in terms of the reading and proclamation of the gospel itself or its visible demonstration in the practice of the sacraments. The scriptural writings are the authoritative auxiliaries of Christ's ongoing speech to the church; *sola Scriptura* is meant to honor the final authority of Scripture over other valid authorities in the Christian and churchly life. The 1559 French Confession of Faith portrays the role of *sola Scriptura* in the life of the church:

[I]nasmuch as it is the rule of all truth, containing all that is necessary for the service of God and for our salvation, it is not lawful for men, nor even for angels,

---

31. For his attack on traditioned reasoning (at least in its Christian form), see Immanuel Kant, "An Answer to the Question: What Is Enlightenment?" in *Practical Philosophy: Cambridge Edition of the Works of Immanuel Kant* (ed. Mary J. Gregor; Cambridge: Cambridge University Press, 1999), 17–22.

32. Mark Bowald, *Rendering the Word in Theological Hermeneutics: Mapping Divine and Human Agency* (Aldershot: Ashgate, 2007), 173. For further criticism of deistic approaches to biblical interpretation, see Bavinck, *Reformed Dogmatics*, Volume 1, 384–5.

to add to it, to take away from it, or to change it. Whence it follows that no authority, whether of antiquity, or custom, or numbers, or human wisdom, or judgments, or proclamations, or edicts, or decrees, or councils, or visions, or miracles, should be opposed to these Holy Scriptures, but, on the contrary, all things should be examined, regulated, and reformed according to them.[33]

There will be other authorities, councils, judgments, and wisdom, of course, and *sola Scriptura* is no denigration or denial of such realities.[34] But God exercises his ultimate sovereignty over all ecclesiastical and theological practices by means of his scriptural ambassadors: the apostolic and prophetic writings through which Jesus Christ addresses his people.

Second, the means of grace for theology are ecclesially bounded and, therefore, theological reflection does well to learn again from its ancestors the ways of life, lest it continue to flirt with the self-aggrandizing path to death. There are other authorities in the Christian life: there are preachers who proclaim the Word, there are pastors who administer the sacraments, and there are councils that govern the life and ministry of the church judicially and, one prays, theologically. One does not engage the Scriptures separate from this nexus of formative influence. The reader will be shaped, for good or ill, by their immediate context. Better to be cognizant of this cultural formation (both Christian and non-Christian and perhaps even outright anti-Christian) and to engage intentionally not only one's immediate ecclesial environment but the wider catholic context of the church.

Third, the means of grace for theology are missionally aimed. We will find that theology that seeks ecclesial renewal through catholic retrieval will be well placed to encourage the church's contribution to the future of humanity in its fullness. Whereas modern and late modern theology has tended toward narrowing focus, catholic theology has offered a much more holistic approach to the church's witness. "Theological research, we are now prepared to say, is devotion to exploring the reality which exists in the presence of God's name. It follows in the way, the trace, of the reality drawn in by this name."[35] All reality is so drawn in by this name— for it is the name of the majestic one—that theology will reach out in mission to address God's grace for and claim upon everything.[36]

---

33. "The French Confession of Faith (1559)," in *Reformed Confessions of the Sixteenth Century*, 145–6 (article V). See also "The Geneva Confession (1536)," in *Reformed Confessions of the Sixteenth Century*, 120 (chapter 1).

34. For engagement of misapprehensions (by friend and foe alike) of *sola Scriptura*, see Michael Allen and Scott Swain, "The Catholic Context of *sola Scriptura*," in *Reformed Catholicity*, 49–70.

35. Hans G. Ulrich, "*Fides Quaerens Intellectum*: Reflections Toward an Explorative Theology," *International Journal of Systematic Theology* 8, no. 1 (2006), 53.

36. For reflection on how theology addresses all reality without becoming a totalizing discourse, see Michael Allen, *Reformed Theology* (London: T&T Clark, 2010), 156–77.

Theology will only have its end when God so determines to fulfill his promises. Until then theology will live on borrowed breath. Such is not its misery, but its freedom and glory. To journey well and to serve the church (and, indirectly, the wider world) faithfully, it does well to move forward receptively: scripturally and catholically. Its dependence upon Christ alone must manifest itself in focused attention to the places where he exercises his authority (the apostolic writings) and ministers his grace (the people of God). If theology does so, then it will journey well into its ancient future and manifest its calling to be a form of "biblical reasoning" that serves Christian worship and witness.

Chapter 2

LIVING AND ACTIVE: THE EXALTED PROPHET IN THE EPISTLE TO THE HEBREWS

"In many times and in various ways" the Word attests our God and his instruction through the prophets (Heb. 1.1). Hebrews not only affirms the varied and voluminous character of God's speech but displays its flavor by engaging in myriad exegetical maneuvers. The text rarely argues apart from explicit scriptural analysis, and its argumentative moves range from the exemplarist to the typological to yet more narrow hermeneutical approaches. The catena of texts pulled together in 1.5-14 attest a Christocentric approach to exegesis of the Old Testament to be sure, yet that survey is matched by the later panoramic sketch of that first testament in 11.1-40 where the "great cloud of witnesses" (12.1) provides so many examples of living by faith, examples which are to be imitated.

The danger for theologians today comes in narrowing the contours of what it means for Hebrews to speak of God's prophetic speech of and by his Son (1.2). Too often this can take the form of a myopic focus on a supposedly Christ-centered hermeneutic wherein earlier biblical episodes are meant to point only unto a Christological resolution or fulfillment of something which Christ does outside us and in our place. Such readings are needful, appropriate, and beautiful, and Hebrews offers them aplenty. Such readings are also insufficient as a guide to the full panoply of ways in which the Word of God dwells richly in this sermon. We do well to see that speech of and by the Son also comes in a number of forms; even the seemingly exemplarist is no less Christological, at least not when considered in the light of 12.1-2. For Hebrews, Scripture charts many exegetical ways to and from the Christ.

Exegetical myopia can be matched by Christological narrowness and, I suggest, this can easily happen in Christian proclamation as well as in Christian theology and biblical interpretation. In this chapter I hope to prompt reflection on the broader scope and sequence of Christological teaching in Hebrews, so that we might be alerted to the varied ways in which the Son acts to make atonement for his people. While problems can settle in by failing to attend to the states of Christ's work (as in the revisionary approach of Karl Barth), much more common is the danger of fixing one's eye upon too narrow a span of his history of redemption.[1]

---

1. Karl Barth, *Church Dogmatics*, Volume 4: *The Doctrine of Reconciliation*, Part One (ed. G. W. Bromiley and T. F. Torrance; London: T&T Clark, 1956), 132–5. Barth's revision shifts the distinction of humiliation and exaltation away from a chronological sequence and toward dual aspects of the divine being understood dialectically.

In that regard, I will seek to bring into relief the significance of the exalted Christ's ongoing work not only as a priest serving like unto Melchizedek but also as a prophet who continues to send forth the Word of God in living and active form. My argument will first draw out some of the most salient ways in which Hebrews attests the place of the exaltation of Christ as a context for further agency and not merely an acknowledgment of accomplished activity. Then I will focus upon ways in which the exaltation of Christ is linked to the ministry of the Word of God, such that the teaching of Hebrews regarding Scripture can be appreciated as being more tightly tethered to the present action of the great prophet, even Jesus. Like a three-stranded cord, the threefold office of Christ serves to alert us to the ways he fills all the needs for delivering a sure salvation; that being the case, to depend solely on one strand (the cultic) in developing an atonement theology apart from the other two (the royal and the prophetic) will fail to affirm the wholeness and completeness of his salvific work. Hopefully this analysis will show the significance of the prophetic task of the exalted Christ for the saving of his people.

"Into Heaven Itself, Now" (9.24): The Exaltation of the Son in the Epistle to the Hebrews

"After making purification for sins, he sat down at the right hand of the Majesty on high" (1.3). With all its talk of sacrifice and of blood offered, Hebrews shouts a word of finality. "Once for all" (9.26; 10.11) hangs over that central section (in chs. 5-10) as a profound summary statement attesting the reality that there is now "no longer any offering for sin" (10.18). The immediate prompt for the sermon itself involves a need to understand the singularity of Christ's sacrifice which need not be repeated, lest the Hebrew Christians fall back into the rhythms of Jewish cultic worship again. Not surprisingly, then, the rhetoric of completion and finality lands so strongly. Yet Hebrews attests more, noting also the "again and again" character of the good news of this Son. He has gone "into heaven itself, now" on our behalf "to appear in the presence of God" (9.24).

The exaltation of Christ has been shown renewed attention in the work of David Moffitt, whose book *Atonement and the Logic of Resurrection in the Epistle to the Hebrews* has gestured toward the significance of resurrected life for the sake of Christ's ongoing priesthood.[2] He has presented four arguments in this vein. First, Hebrews 6.2 and 11.19 attest a confession that the resurrection of the dead is part and parcel of the Christian's hope: Abraham could expect a resurrection of

---

2. David M. Moffitt, *Atonement and the Logic of Resurrection in the Epistle to the Hebrews* (Supplements to Novum Testamentum 141; Leiden: Brill, 2011); see also idem, "Blood, Life, and Atonement: Reassessing Hebrews' Christological Appropriation of Yom Kippur," in *The Day of Atonement: Its Interpretations in Early Jewish and Christian Traditions* (ed. Thomas Hieke and Tobias Nicklas; Leiden, The Netherlands: Koninklijke Brill, 2012), 211-24.

the soon-to-be-slain child of the promise (11.19) and, likewise, "the elementary doctrine of Christ" includes, among other things, "the resurrection of the dead" (6.2).[3] Second, Hebrews 12.2 presents Jesus as the "author and perfector" of this faith. If Abraham and the others looked to resurrection, how much more the perfectly faithful one?[4] Third, Hebrews 5.7 identifies Jesus as one who prayed to him "who was able to save him from death, and he was heard."[5] Fourth, Hebrews 7.16 says that Jesus has become a high priest "by the power of an indestructible life" rather than by bodily descent from Aaron or the Levites. The argument of chapter 7 turns to Melchizedek rather than the Israelite priesthood as a paradigm for Jesus, highlighting, of course, the way in which this mediator from Salem lived forever (7.3, 8). Jesus has "arisen" in the likeness of Melchizedek (7.15): while this term could refer to simple elevation or assumption of office, the wider context points toward genuine resurrection, because chapter 7 emphasizes Melchizedek's service lasting forever, uses the verb "to arise," and references the "indestructible life" of Jesus, a term that seems to connote eternality or immortality.[6]

In light of these four points, the benediction of 13.20 is no mere appellation but a genuine reference to a discrete and explicit aspect of Hebrews' teaching: the "God of peace" has "brought again from the dead our Lord Jesus." To summarize thus far: Moffitt's first two points strongly show that Hebrews affirms the resurrection of the dead, broadly speaking, and his last two points suggest that Hebrews assumes or implicitly affirms the resurrection of Jesus specifically. Unfortunately neither is a direct reference, so one wonders how far we are from the recent commentators that Moffitt says he will correct: F. F. Bruce and William Lane, for example.[7] While I can affirm that Moffitt has shown the unlikeliness of what he calls the agnostic, the spiritual ascension, or the no resurrection approaches,[8] Moffitt seems to offer a lovely return to what Bruce, Lane, and others have argued: Hebrews largely passes

---

3. Moffitt notes that 11.35 confirms the place of the resurrection of the dead in the Christian faith: here the "better resurrection" or "better life" (ἀναστάσεως) speaks of resurrection, while the term "resurrection" (κρείττονος ἀναστάσεως) probably implies temporary resuscitation (see Moffitt, "Blood, Life, and Atonement," 215–16).

4. Ibid., 216.

5. Ibid., 216–17.

6. Ibid., 217–18. The key term in 7:15 is ἀνίσταται. Moffitt argues this particular point at length in "'If Another Priest Arises': Jesus' Resurrection and the High Priestly Christology of Hebrews," in *A Cloud of Witnesses: The Theology of Hebrews in Its Ancient Contexts* (ed. Richard Bauckham et al; London: T&T Clark, 2008).

7. Moffitt, *Atonement and the Logic of Resurrection*, 4–10 (see 4–5 fn. 2 for full bibliography of those holding to what Moffitt terms the "passed over" view); see F. F. Bruce, *The Epistle to the Hebrews* (New International Commentary on the New Testament; Grand Rapids: Eerdmans, 1990), 32–3; William Lane, *Hebrews 1-8* (Word Biblical Commentary 47a; Dallas: Word Books, 1991), 16.

8. For description and criticism of the "agnostic," "spiritual ascension," and "no resurrection" views, see Moffitt, *Atonement and the Logic of Resurrection*, 10–40.

over direct reference to the resurrection as a discrete event in the life of Jesus, but implicitly or indirectly notes its importance for his exalted service in the holy of holies.

The presence of resurrection is one thing, but far more interesting is the significance of the resurrection as articulated by Moffitt. He argues that atonement occurs in one place: the throne room of God. Hebrews 7.16 is crucial: Jesus is not a priest until he has the power of an indestructible life. Therefore, Calvary is out as a venue for atoning service: there was no priest present there, Jesus not having been perfected yet with "indestructible [that is, resurrected] life." Recent work on the nature of the Yom Kippur sacrifice by Jewish and Christian interpreters of Leviticus is referenced as a crucial background for what Hebrews says about the atonement. Jacob Milgrom and others have argued that it is not the death of an animal but the life of the sacrificial offering that makes atonement. Further, the moment of atonement takes place in the holy of holies when the blood is presented, rather than outside when the animal was slaughtered. I take the rendering of Lev. 17.11 that is argued by Jay Sklar, affirmed by Milgrom and others, and depended upon by Moffitt, to be not only valid but necessary.[9] Atonement is made by blood, that is, "by means of the life" of the blood. Further, when Moffitt argues that this approach allows us to read Hebrews 8.4 and a whole slew of texts that speak of Jesus making his offering in the presence of God in heaven (6.19-20; 7.26; 8.2; 9.11; 9.23-25; 10.12) seriously and without manipulation as some spiritual rendering completely restricted to the event of Good Friday, I am in agreement.[10] And yet I'll confess to finding a serious mistake in the argument of Milgrom and, still further, in the presumption that Milgrom's reading of Leviticus would be the foundational framework of the author of Hebrews.

Leviticus 17.11 does identify atonement with the giving of life, symbolized by blood, "for the life of the flesh is in the blood, and I have given it for you on the altar to make atonement for your souls, for it is the blood that makes atonement by the life." Yet as Hebrews addresses the role of blood in atonement, it makes plain that "without the shedding of blood there is no forgiveness of sins" (9.22). Yes, the translation of this phrase might be rendered "the outpouring of blood" rather than the "shedding of blood," but the Levitical background refers not only to the "ritual manipulation" of blood previously shed but also to the ritual shedding of it in the first place (see Lev. 4; 8.15; 9.9).[11] Blood is not redemptive in the abstract; shed blood—resulting in death—is redemptive when presented

---

9. See especially Jay Sklar, *Sin, Impurity, Sacrifice, Atonement: The Priestly Conceptions* (HBM 2; Sheffield: Sheffield University Press, 2005), 168–73.

10. Cf. Jon Laansma, *The Letter to the Hebrews: A Commentary for Preaching, Teaching, and Bible Study* (Eugene, OR: Cascade, 2017), esp. 179–84.

11. Contra Moffitt, *Atonement and the Logic of Resurrection*, 291 fn. 157. The closest that Moffitt comes to linking these two ritual acts—the shedding and the presentation of blood—is to say that the latter cannot be "completely abstracted" from the other (269). Surely this understates the ritual nature of *both* acts.

in the very holy of holies.[12] These observations have to temper Moffitt's insistence that atonement occurs only in the holy of holies and that the death of Jesus is not atoning.[13] Hebrews certainly looks beyond the death to the presentation of blood on the heavenly *hilasterion*, but it in no way suggests that the death is not itself also a part of the full sweep of Christ's service. While we can agree with Moffitt that Christ is not properly a priest after the order of Melchizedek until his resurrection in eternal glory (so Heb. 7.16), this is not the same as saying that his priestly work cannot begin in any fashion before then.[14]

In summary, Moffitt has argued for a significant, discrete accent upon the resurrection in Hebrews. He has argued that Hebrews should be read against the backdrop of Jewish apocalypticism rather than Middle Platonism, and he sees the eschatological hope of humans to be an embodied state rather than a mystical flight from the material.[15] In both this book and a recent SBL paper, Moffitt has made mention of the distinct phases, noting the various terms: resurrection, ascension, session.[16] It seems to me that his proposal could be clarified. Hebrews presents a robust account of Christ's heavenly session or exalted agency. Hebrews more than any other New Testament text speaks of the priestly work of Jesus (10.21). He remains the "great shepherd of the sheep" (13.20). Indeed, God's work "in us" is pleasing to God and is "through Jesus Christ" (13.21), suggesting that he remains operative as our cultic mediator. To that end, Hebrews addresses the ascension of Jesus Christ as well. Jesus, having made atonement, has gone into the presence of God (1.3-4; 10.12). His ascended enjoyment of God's presence is a pledge of what shall be ours: he has gone to it now via ascent, before God brings it to us in glory via divine descent. Finally, Hebrews presents the foundation of these exalted actions in the resurrection of the Lord Jesus. The resurrection is only explicit in a couple of places (e.g., 13.20), albeit it serves a fundamental role in

---

12. Nobuyoshi Kiuchi, *Leviticus* (Apollos Old Testament Commentary 3; Downers Grove, IL: IVP Academic, 2007), 321.

13. See also Laansma, *The Epistle to the Hebrews*, 34 fn. 35.

14. See further nuances prompted by engagement of early modern Protestant engagement with Socinian readings of Hebrews in this vein, sketched by Benjamin J. Ribbens, "The Ascension and Atonement: The Significance of Post-Reformation, Reformed Responses to Socinians for Contemporary Atonement Debates in Hebrews," *Westminster Theological Journal* 80, no. 1 (Spring 2018), 1–23; as well as more detailed analysis in Michael H. Kibbe, "Is It Finished? When Did It Start? Hebrews, Priesthood, and Atonement in Biblical, Systematic, and Historical Perspective," *Journal of Theological Studies* 65, no. 1 (2014), 25–61.

15. See especially David Moffitt, "Serving in Heaven's Temple: Sacred Space, Yom Kippur, and Jesus' Superior Offering in Hebrews," (Presented to the Hebrews Study Group at the National Meeting of the Society of Biblical Literature 2012), 3–6; Moffitt, *Atonement and the Logic of Resurrection*, ch. 2.

16. Moffitt, *Atonement and the Logic of Resurrection*, 42–3; Moffitt, "Serving in Heaven's Temple," 2, 15.

making sense of so many other explicit teachings. Here Hebrews 7.16 is decisive: only one who is resurrected—note: not resuscitated, but glorified and raised anew to "indestructible life"—is fit to serve in this way as a priest forever.[17]

In light of the location of resurrection teaching in the theologic of exaltation, dare I suggest that his book might have better been titled *Atonement and the Logic of Exaltation in the Epistle to the Hebrews*? The exalted Christ serves as minister unto his people from the throne room on high. In grasping the precious purpose of his exalted presence, Moffitt has returned our attention to something prized by classical Reformed theology in its alertness not only to the earthly sojourn but also to the heavenly service of our Lord. The Heidelberg Catechism inquired not only after the meaning of this exaltation but its significance as well.

> Q. 49 What benefit do we receive from Christ's ascension into heaven?
> A. First, that he is our Advocate in the presence of his Father in heaven. Second, that we have our flesh in heaven as a sure pledge that he, as the Head, will also take us, his members, up to himself. Third, that he sends us his Spirit as a counterpledge by whose power we seek what is above, where Christ is, sitting at the right hand of God, and not things that are on earth.[18]

We do well now to attend to something of the breadth of that exalted beneficence, following the exegetical prompts of Moffitt and tracing out more fully the scope suggested by Heidelberg.

The Son "Who Is Speaking ... Warns From Heaven" (12.25):
The Word of the Exalted Son

Having seen the significance of the exalted work of the Son, we turn now to press still further and consider whether or not his heavenly session also bears significance upon the prophetic ministry of his Word. Does the Epistle to the Hebrews attest or suggest that the risen Son also fills his prophetic office from the heavenly throne room? Does the "great shepherd of the sheep" speak even now, so that his flock is equipped and knowledgeable unto his will (13.20-21)? The reflections of David Moffitt upon the exalted priestly work of the Messiah may and should be matched by awareness of his ongoing prophetic work. We will consider three elements: the scattered allusions to the speech of the Son throughout the Epistle, the significance of Heb. 12.25 for affirming his ongoing speech, and then the implications for the practice of theology. The evidence for an ongoing prophetic ministry seems to be no less explicit and a good bit more widely suggested than is the case made by Moffitt regarding his priestly action.

---

17. Moffitt, *Atonement and the Logic of Resurrection*, 202–3.
18. "The Heidelberg Catechism (1563)," in *Reformed Confessions of the Sixteenth Century* (ed. Arthur Cochrane; Louisville: Westminster John Knox, 2003), 313.

Christ's Speech throughout the Epistle

The epistle begins with speech: "speech to our fathers by the prophets ... long ago, at many times and in many ways" (1.1), and speech "in these last days ... by his Son" (1.2). When identifying the Son through whom this latter-day speech has come, the author goes on to call him "the radiance of the glory of God and the exact imprint of his nature" (1.3). The Son's character is not only an "imprint" (*charaktēr*) of the Father, suggesting his divinity, but also a communicative manifestation of that divine, for he is not only glory but also the "radiance" (*apaugasma*) of that transcendent glory.[19] The Son does not become or assume the form of radiant communication; he *is* that resplendent manifestation.

And this exordium does not leave it at just that; the prior attestation of the Son's role in creation now extends into his work of preservation. With respect to creation, we have already read that the Son is the one "through whom also he created the world" (1.2). With respect to preservation, the Son is no less active: "He upholds the universe by the word of his power" (1.3). The two claims are tied together, for 11.3 will eventually remind us that "the universe was created by the Word of God." Luke Timothy Johnson comments that "The same 'power' (*dynamis*) has been at work from the beginning and continues now in the 'last of these days,' namely the power of God (see Heb. 2.4; 6.5; 7.16; 11.11)."[20]

The next chapter turns to focus more upon the sufferings of this Son in his incarnate form, and even here his speech continues to be affirmed with a new intonation. "He is not ashamed to call them brothers," so the Son's speech takes the form of identification with "his brothers in every respect" (2.11, 17). The author turns to Psalm 22, however, and says, "I will tell of your name to my brothers; in the midst of the congregation I will sing your praise" (2.12, quoting Ps. 22.22). That he will "tell" (*apangelō* replacing *diēgēsomai* from the LXX) takes up the language of the Psalmist not only turning to intra-Trinitarian discourse but in witness unto the "congregation." Such witness occurred while on earth; there is no reason, however, to presume that this testimony was concluded therein.

The third chapter identifies the Son with a distinctive title: "apostle and high priest of our confession" (3.1). While "high priest" comes in for detailed and extended elaboration throughout chs. 5-10, the term "apostle" (*apostolos*) also warrants our attention. His sending for the sake of testimony not only relates to past activity but also to ongoing agency: to the earlier affirmation that he "*was* faithful to him who appointed him" (3.2), we see added later that "Christ *is* faithful over God's house as a Son" (3.6). Again, a scriptural quotation expresses the form of this activity. Here the author turns to Psalm 95, which begins with the gripping words, "Today, if you hear

---

19. "Glory" language will be extended in 2.7,9,10, where it is tied to the exaltation of the Son and is shared inclusively with his brothers. Language of "honor" and "exaltation" occurs also in 5.4-5 and of his fullness he shares as "the source of eternal salvation to all who obey him" (5.9). In this context, priestly language conveys the notion not only of distinction from others but also of ministration unto others.

20. Johnson, *Hebrews*, 70.

his voice, do not harden your hearts" (3.7, citing Ps. 95.7). Notice that the words are said by the Holy Spirit (3.7, "as the Holy Spirit says"), though it goes on likely to attest another's speech ("his" in 3.7b probably referring to the Son and not to the Spirit who speaks).[21] We see this differentiation drawn out more explicitly when Ps. 95.7 reappears several verses later. "We have come to share in Christ, if indeed we hold our original confidence firm to the end. As it is said, 'Today, if you hear his voice ... '" (3.14-15, quoting Ps. 95.7). Here the identification of "his voice" with the Christ in whom one places one's confidence is all the more explicit. It seems to be the case that the apostolic mission of the Son continues even now over his house.

Hebrews will go on to speak of the mediatory work (*mesitēs*) of the Son in various contexts (8.6; 9.15; 12.24).[22] It fixes upon the priestly role of the Son, as noted earlier in our reflections on the work of Moffitt, and thus focuses on words rendered by the Son unto our Father in intercession (e.g., 7.25). These three passages, however, suggest that Hebrews presents an account of the Son speaking unto his household as well, wherein he fills the office of a prophet as well as a royal priest (7.1). One later passage extends this exalted speech more fully, and so we turn now to consider Hebrews 12.25 at slightly greater length before finally asking how this affirmation of Christ as an exalted prophet shapes the doctrine of Scripture found within Hebrews.

Hebrews 12.25

Zion and Sinai come in for comparison in Hebrews 12, and communication proves to be fundamental to each in its own way. "So terrifying was the sight" (12.21), and the author depicts various facets of the overwhelming vista: "blazing fire" and "darkness and gloom and a tempest" on the one side, and "innumerable angels in festal gathering" and "the assembly of the firstborn who are enrolled in heaven" on the other side (12.18, 22-23). Yet amidst all that whirling dervish and redolent brilliance, the author comes back to the vocal: "And a voice whose words made the hearers beg that no further messages be spoken to them" (12.19) on the one hand, and "Jesus" and "the sprinkled blood that speaks a better word than the blood of Abel" (12.24) on the other hand. Like Sinai, with its characterization of a promised sight of God from the rear and around the cleft of a rock, so here vision of God takes the form of hearing from God (see Exod. 34.6-7).[23]

---

21. Thomas Aquinas, *Commentary on the Epistle to the Hebrews* (trans. Chrysostom Baer; South Bend, IN: St. Augustine's, 2006), 83 (ch. 3, lect. 2).

22. See Daniel J. Treier, "'Mediator of a New Covenant': Atonement and Christology in Hebrews," in *So Great a Salvation: A Dialogue on the Atonement in Hebrews* (ed. Jon C. Laansma et al; LNTS 516; London: T&T Clark, 2019), 105–19.

23. For reflections on the epistemology of Sinai, see especially Gregory Nyssa, *Life of Moses* (trans. Abraham Malherbe and Everett Ferguson; Classics of Western Spirituality; New York: Paulist, 1978), esp. 91–3; see also Nathan Eubank, "Ineffably Effable: The Pinnacle of Mystical Ascent in Gregory of Nyssa's *De vita Moysis*," *International Journal of Systematic Theology* 16, no. 1 (2014), 25–41.

A moral summons draws out the reality of this speech explicitly: "See that you do not refuse him who is speaking" (12.25). The God who reigns may be identified as the speaking one here (*tòn laloũnta*); his character takes the form of communicative presence. The language of warning (*tòn chrematízonta*) expands and clarifies on this claim regarding divine speech. The exalted Son—this Jesus whose blood was sprinkled in the heavenlies (9.14; 10.22)[24]—warns and speaks and in so doing shakes not only the earth but also the heavens. This warning arises "from heaven" (*àp' oùranwn*). Divine agency and initiative come to the fore with the language of heaven employed here: not so much a geographic or spatial term in this context as an agential and operative appellation. Hebrews takes up the categories of Platonic philosophy and puts them to covenantal and active use, turning what might be perceived as solely metaphysical demarcations and throwing them in both a temporal and an ethical framework (albeit with no less ontological a lens).[25]

Edward Adams and James Thompson have thereby noted that this is "the main eschatological passage of the epistle."[26] Indeed, Adams suggests that while this voice comes from heaven, its effects are felt tangibly upon this earth. To this end, Adams points to the physical and meteorological impress of "shaking" in the Sinai event (12.18-21, 26a read that occurrence as involving what he deems a "global earthquake").[27] Irrespective of one's judgment regarding the best interpretation of the "shaking" language, whether metaphorical or directly meteorological, the vocabulary and conceptuality surely speaks to divine agency and its vivid effect (whether catastrophic materially or in other registers).

Again, mediation and identification are not juxtaposed or at least not mutually exclusive. Just as God spoke through and to prophets (1.1-2), so now Christ speaks (12.25) even when others speak in his name.

> There is a general rule in the words, namely, that we are diligently to attend unto, and not to refuse any that speak unto us in the name and authority of Christ. And so it may be applied unto all the faithful preachers of the gospel, however

---

24. The Christological focus manifests itself in reading 12.25 against the backdrop of Jesus' speech in 12.24.

25. Further analysis of the relation of Platonic language in Hebrews exceeds the bounds of this chapter. See the sketch of the issues so well portrayed by Luke Timothy Johnson, *Hebrews: A Commentary* (NTL; Louisville: Westminster John Knox, 2006), 18–21.

26. Edward Adams, *The Stars Will Fall From Heaven: "Cosmic Catastrophe" in the New Testament and Its World* (LNTS; London: T&T Clark, 2007), 185; see also James W. Thompson, *The Beginnings of Christian Philosophy: The Epistle to the Hebrews* (CBQMS 13; Washington, DC: Catholic Biblical Association of America, 1982), 42–3.

27. Adams, *Stars Will Fall From Heaven*, 189; *contra* Anton Vögtle, *Das Neue Testament und Die Zukunft des Kosmos* (KBNT; Düsseldorff: Patmos, 1970), 88.

they may be despised in this world. But it is here the person of Christ himself that is immediately intended.[28]

Hebrews 12.25 prompts our communicative imagination to be alert to the exalted Son's warning amidst and through the words of his emissaries. This apostle proves faithful over his household oftentimes (3.1, 6)—perhaps we must say ordinarily—through the delegated agency of his own apostles.[29] We turn finally then to ask how this exalted Christology and its distinctively prophetic aspect flavors the way in which Hebrews speaks of the Word of God in written form.

Word of God: Hebrews 4.12-13 and 13.8 and the Doctrine of Scripture

The Epistle to the Hebrews has much to commend regarding the doctrine of Scripture, and recent studies have offered analysis of its contribution to a Christian theology of Holy Scripture, both its being and the appropriate ethic of its recipients. The leading studies—as in the recent essays of Treier and Schenk or the earlier monographs of Graham Hughes and F. Synge—analyze what may be called the "doctrine of Scripture practiced in Hebrews."[30] Much can be gleaned inductively from watching an apostolic emissary refract the witness of earlier prophetic

---

28. John Owen, *Exposition of Hebrews 11:1-13:25* (Edinburgh: Banner of Truth Trust, 1991), 354.

29. See D. Johanne Polyandro, "Disputation 42: On the Calling of Those Who Minister to the Church, and on Their Duties," in *Synopsis Purioris Theologiae*, Volume 2: *Disputations 24-42* (ed. Henk van den Belt; trans. Riemer Faber; Studies in Medieval and Reformation Traditions 204; Leiden: Brill, 2016), 620-1 (thesis 1).

30. The language comes from Treier's subtitle. See Daniel J. Treier, "Speech Acts, Hearing Hearts, and Other Senses: The Doctrine of Scripture Practiced in Hebrews," in *The Epistle to the Hebrews and Christian Theology* (ed. Richard Bauckham et al; Grand Rapids: Eerdmans, 2009), 337-50; cf. Ken Schenck, "God Has Spoken: Hebrews' Theology of the Scriptures," in *The Epistle to the Hebrews and Christian Theology* (ed. Richard Bauckham et al; Grand Rapids: Eerdmans, 2009), 321-36; Luke Timothy Johnson, "The Scriptural World of Hebrews," *Interpretation* 57 (2003), 237-50; T. Lewicki, "*Weist nicht ab den Sprechenden!*": *Wort Gottes und Paraklese im Hebräerbrief* (Padorborner Theologische Studien 41; Paderborn: Schöningh, 2004); Graham Hughes, *Hebrews and Hermeneutics: The Epistle to the Hebrews as a New Testament Example of Biblical Interpretation* (SNTSMS 36; Cambridge: Cambridge University Press, 1979); see also the comments on what might be termed prosopological exegesis found in Karen Jobes's essay, "Putting Words In His Mouth: The Son Speaks in Hebrews" in *So Great a Salvation*. Many additional studies could be culled from the literature that address portions of the text as readings of prior scripture (e.g. the catena of texts cited in 1.5-13 or the narrative allusions in ch.11), much of which was summarized well in George H. Guthrie, "Hebrews' Use of the Old Testament: Recent Trends in Research," *Currents in Biblical Research* 1 (2003), 271-94. The literature focusing on specific case studies has grown exponentially since 2003. Only the rare study manages to

testimony. We do well to ask another question, however, regarding what light the attestation of the exalted Son as an active prophet might shed upon the doctrine of Scripture taught by Hebrews? May we work deductively as well to glean further insight into its implications for a Christian theology of Holy Scripture and of theological knowledge?

Oftentimes discussion of hermeneutics and of bibliology move too much in the categories of peripheral disciplines or later (and perhaps misleadingly anachronistic) eras.[31] While such comparative and conversational approaches may open up new angles by which we might see more within the witness of Scripture itself, we do well nonetheless to attend to claims internal to and overt within the text itself. A recent example of much benefit in this regard can be found in the way that Uche Anizor uses the biblical-theological category of "royal priesthood" to describe the ideal reader of Scripture in its own terms.[32] Readerly virtue there finds exposition in specifically doctrinal terms. In the space that remains, I wish to explore a similar approach regarding our account of scripture's voice that seeks to honor the claims of that scripture itself. In so doing, we will remain focused upon the Christological claims of Hebrews, especially as we find them in 4.12 and then in 13.8.

"For the word of God is living and active, sharper than any two-edged sword, piercing to the division of soul and of spirit, of joints and of marrow, and discerning the thoughts and intentions of the heart" (4.12). The oft-benighted sixteenth-century reformer Huldrych Zwingli riffs on this language in testifying to what he deems the clarity and the certainty of the Word. To Hebrews' "living and active," Zwingli resounds with the pairings of "sure and strong," "alive and strong," and "alive and sure."[33] In expounding the certainty or power of the Word in 1522, Zwingli attests not its literary or syntactical simplicity but its theological nature.

---

move beyond its immediate focus to range more widely regarding the canonical, covenantal, and theological shape of Hebrews more broadly; such an example can be found in David M. Allen, *Deuteronomy and Exhortation in Hebrews: A Study in Narrative Re-Presentation* (WUNT 2:238; Tübingen: Mohr Siebeck, 2008).

31. Such analyses find their way even into case studies focused on portions of Hebrews, such as Dale Leschert, *Hermeneutical Foundations of Hebrews: A Study in the Validity of the Epistle's Interpretation of Some Core Citations from the Psalms* (Lewiston, NY: Edwin Mellon, 1994); to a lesser extent, one can observe similar valuation arising from anachronistic principles in A. T. Hanson, *The Living Utterances of God: The New Testament Exegesis of the Old* (London: Darton, Longman, & Todd, 1983). A case study approach that avoids modern anachronism by gleaning from the history of interpretation (specifically Augustine and Calvin) can be found in Gregory W. Lee, *Today When You Hear His Voice: Scripture, Covenants, and the People of God* (Grand Rapids: Eerdmans, 2017).

32. Uche Anizor, *Kings and Priests: Scripture's Theological Account of Its Readers* (Eugene, OR: Pickwick, 2014).

33. Huldrych Zwingli, "The Clarity and Certainty of the Word of God," in *Zwingli and Bullinger* (ed. G. W. Bromiley; Library of Christian Classics; Louisville: Westminster John Knox, 2006), 68, 70, 72.

The Word packs a punch because it is a glove, not itself a fist; the scriptural Word has significant impact because the force of the mighty hand and outstretched arm of the Almighty stands behind its collision course with sinners.[34] We must tend to several elaborations found herein.

God's Son lives and acts with the life and agency of one raised into glorified existence in God's own presence. His being now is not merely his own but he lives for us and we exist in him. Hebrews employs the language of Platonism here also in its deployment of covenantal agency and identity. We have talked now at some length about this exalted existence of God's own Son and also about his verbal agency, which prompts us to say that not only does Jesus live and acts but his own Word is "living and active" as well (Heb. 4.12). We do well now to consider the purpose and the object of that active speech. Unto whom does it speak? And to what ends?

God's Word pierces. Zwingli finds the Word of God to pack a powerful punch in as much as it serves as a tool in the Spirit's agency. As Daniël Timmermann says, "Just like Luther's principle of the general priesthood, Zwingli's emphasis on the inner illumination of believers primarily bears a soteriological connotation."[35] Hebrews uses a term here—*merismos*—which speaks to division of that which is most fundamental and internal to the person. The divided pair—*pneuma* and *psychē*—are not natural opposites (cf. 1 Thess. 5.23), and that is precisely the point. The Spirit's Word not only sorts that which is overtly distinct and obviously contradictory but even divides that which is seemingly woven together in the fabric of our sinful form.

God's Word discerns. "As with 'soul and spirit, joints and marrow,' the discernment between thought and conception is the more impressive because the difference between them is so slight and unavailable to human perception."[36] The paragraph will crescendo with the cryptic line *pros hon hēmin ho logos* (4.13), often translated "To him is our account directed," and likely meaning something more relational and less formally tied to a household servant's accounting unto his or her master, as might be rendered "with whom we have to do" (RSV).[37]

In so doing, God's Word cuts "sharper than any two-edged sword." A theology of divine discipline lies beneath this imagery—judgment takes not only punitive but also paternally restorative and thus pedagogical intonations here. True enough, Hebrews speaks of that which shall be judged: "If it bears thorns and

---

34. See especially W. P. Stephens, *The Theology of Huldrych Zwingli* (Oxford: Clarendon, 1986), 51-2; Gottfried W. Locher, *Die Theologie Huldrych Zwingli sim Lichte seiner Christologie, Erster Teil: Die Gotteslehre* (Zürich: Zwingli Verlag, 1952), 93-5.

35. Daniël Zimmermann, *Heinrich Bullinger on Prophecy and the Prophetic Office (1523-1538)* (Reformed Historical Theology 33; Göttingen: Vandenhoeck & Ruprecht, 2015), 85.

36. Johnson, *Hebrews*, 135.

37. See E.-M. Becker, "'Gottes Wort' und 'Unser Wort': Bemerkungen zu Heb 4,12-13," *BZ* 44 (2000), 254-62.

thistles, it is worthless and near to being cursed, and its end is to be burned" (6.8). But the sword attests not only, and perhaps not even primarily, the division of wheat and tares, and sheep and goats, but more fundamentally the division within the people of God which can better be termed true and false. Hebrews 12.5-13 speaks to this fatherly discipline (drawing on Prov. 3.11,12) which marks legitimate sons (13.7).[38] The living and active Word of the great shepherd of the sheep disciplines and forms his own, extending grace by addressing them with life and confronting them with his own active presence. The category of "discipline" proves fundamental here to speak of the purposive character of Scripture in Christ's own hands, in as much as it speaks to the continual conversion or ongoing sanctification of his own company. His apostolic embassy serves to trumpet and to transform with his vocal pronouncement. And in so doing he does not allow us to wallow in our self-enclosed spiritual echo chambers; he pierces and discerns and, as needs be, cuts so as to bring us into the life and action which are his own. Hebrews presents an exalted Christology that heralds the prophetic work of the Son, and it ties this ever so closely to his living and active Word. Thus, bibliology and soteriology are bound up together, not conflated but coordinated Christologically for the sake of hearkening God's people onward in their journey while it is yet today.

Conclusion

We have seen in this chapter that Hebrews does draw out the exalted mediation of the Son, in so doing relying on, adjusting, and furthering the arguments of David Moffitt. Then we have pointed to an even more prevalent emphasis on the speech of this exalted Son, culminating in the attestation of 12.25. Finally we have seen that the exalted prophecy of the Son provides the lens through which we ought to view the teaching of Hebrews regarding the nature and power of the Word of God, and we have found the polemical ruminations of Huldrych Zwingli to be a useful prompt in drawing out the shape of this "living and active" speech of the Son. Before concluding, we do well to attend to one further Christological confession of this sermon.

"Jesus Christ is the same yesterday and today and forever" (13.8). Such words do not undercut the integrity of each era. They do not negate the events of any epoch by placing them in relief with the vivid activity of any other season. They certainly do not demean the present amidst the palpable gravity of the past or the pressing hope of the future. Rather, they attest the ongoing agency and being of the Son who was before all things, through whom all things perdure, and to whom all things aim (cf. Rom. 11.33). The "pastoral eschatology" offered in Hebrews manifests an alert eye to the goodness of the old and yet the greater glory of the

---

38. On the background to this discussion, see Matthew Thiessen, "Hebrews 12.5-13, the Wilderness Period, and Israel's Discipline," *New Testament Studies* 55, no. 3 (2009), 366-79.

new. There is truly and only "a better hope" (7.19).[39] Appreciating the significance of the exalted agency of the Son helps attune us to the present proclamation of his Word, whereby he ministers unto his own that which is "living and active" (4.12).

The invariable integrity of the Word throughout all generations relates rather directly to a seeming shift in textual observation here. Michael Kibbe has observed that Heb. 12.18-29 suggests a rather negative judgment regarding Israel at Sinai when compared to the prior judgment suggested by Deut. 5.28. In that Pentateuchal text, we read Moses saying: "And the LORD heard your words, when you spoke to me. And the LORD said to me, 'I have heard the words of this people, which they have spoken to you. They are right in all that they have spoken.'" Kibbe notes that Zion exceeds Sinai in as much as the mediator has enacted a greater ministry in two ways. First, we are summoned into the holy place of heaven to find rest, rather than summoning us in and out and in and out. Second, the mediator not only enters for others but also with others.[40] We have an unbreakable union and we all may enjoy a personal communion with God. Therefore, Hebrews again and again speaks of the "better" and the "great," not the merely well and good.

What Deuteronomy portrays as well and good is viewed by Hebrews as actually being a good state for that prior era but now as a negative step backward. This judgment about the unity and varied administrations of the divine economy stems from a further awareness regarding the new mediator and the greater glory that he has communicated. "Jesus Christ is the same yesterday and today and forever" (13.8). In and through him, we too enter into the heavenly places boldly. The steady service of the Son—who stands "the same" in the very presence of God—undergirds our confidence and boldness. In just this way does the "great shepherd of the sheep" exercise his pastoral oversight and equip his disciples for "that which is pleasing in [God's] sight" (13.20, 21).

---

39. See John Webster, "One Who Is Son: Theological Reflections on the Exordium to the Epistle to the Hebrews," in *The Epistle to the Hebrews and Christian Theology* (ed. Richard Bauckham et al; Grand Rapids: Eerdmans, 2009), 72.

40. Michael Kibbe, *Godly Fear or Ungodly Failure? Hebrews 12 and the Sinai Theophanies* (BZNW 216; Berlin: De Gruyter, 2016), esp. 183. See also Benjamin J. Ribbens, *Levitical Sacrifice and Heavenly Cult in Hebrews* (BZNW 222; Berlin: De Gruyter, 2016), esp. 109-226 (comparing Old and New Covenant sacrifices in terms of their perfection[s]).

Chapter 3

THE CREATURE OF THE WORD

On God in the Reformation

The tale of modern theology could be told, perhaps, as a story not only of restating but also resituating epistemology. We do well to reflect on both the restatement and the re-situation. Restatement comes in the form of beginning elsewhere, with the self or the sensation rather than the Scriptures.[1] Restatement also appears in the commendation of technical mastery and objective protocols rather than the intellectual and theological virtues. Restatement manifests itself also with the turn toward the politics of power and identity shaping the approach to knowing God as opposed to contextualizing one's place within the economy of sin and grace.

Restatement fits with re-situation, however, and should not really be analyzed apart from it. Sources, protocols, and spaces are considered anew, precisely because the epistemological question has been removed from its classical location. Whereas Irenaeus, Calvin, and many others alike would have considered epistemology within a Trinitarian account of divine agency and also of grace—that is, divine gift to human creatures—modern accounts of Christian epistemology have been tempted to function within a markedly more claustrophobic world. Charles Taylor has called it an "immanent frame," while Hans Boersma has deemed it a "disenchanted" tapestry.[2] Taken together, there's a constrictive and a cloudy view.

A number of voices have suggested that this modern disenchantment or secularization not only has followed the rise of Protestantism but has flowed from its very own roots. Brad Gregory has spoken of the "unintended Reformation" in this regard, wherein naturalization has sped up from Luther's project.[3] Christian Smith has argued that "pervasive interpretive pluralism" marks the experience of

---

1. See, e.g., Paul D. Janz, *God, the Mind's Desire: Reference, Reason, and Christian Thinking* (Cambridge Studies in Christian Doctrine; Cambridge: Cambridge University Press, 2004), esp. 179–85 (where he addresses Bonhoeffer's call to "this-worldliness" [*Diesseitigkeit*] in theological reason).

2. Charles Taylor, *A Secular Age* (Cambridge: Belknap, 2007); Hans Boersma, *Heavenly Participation: The Weaving of a Sacramental Tapestry* (Grand Rapids: Eerdmans, 2011).

3. Brad Gregory, *The Unintended Reformation: How a Religious Revolution Secularized Society* (Cambridge: Belknap, 2012).

those who cry "*Sola Scriptura!*" and undercuts any genuine ecclesial authority.[4] Hans Boersma suggests not that the Reformation began the godless framing of the world and human experience within it but that it failed to respond to that festering medieval problem and only exacerbated its growth.[5] For these and other reasons, many are marking this anniversary with calls for lament as opposed to celebration, for sorrow rather than happy remembrance.

Can we imagine being reformed in a way that is still catholic? Perhaps all the more catholic? Or does reform in this Protestant vein eat like a parasite upon the catholic substance of Christian faith and practice? A witness has taken the stand. Kevin J. Vanhoozer testifies in *Biblical Authority After Babel* that the project of Protestantism ought not be treated in such ways by its cultured despisers but deserves our assent and our gratitude.[6] More specifically, he commends the reality and necessity of what he deems "mere Protestant Christianity" over against these criticisms, and he does so by returning to the root principles of reformational theology: the famous five *solas*. To commend the project of "mere Protestant Christianity," the volume offers twenty theses for consideration. The author clearly relates each sola to the perennial challenges thrown at Protestantism:

> *Sola gratia* addresses the charge of secularization by locating biblical interpreters and interpretation in the all-encompassing economy of triune communicative activity. *Sola fide* and *sola scriptura* address the charge of skepticism by focusing on the principle and pattern respectively of what I will describe as the economy of theological authority. *Solus Christus* addresses the charge of schism by focusing on the royal priesthood of all believers, and that is the proper context for understanding the sola ecclesia. Finally, *soli Deo gloria* returns to the scene of the crime—Protestant division over the Lord's Supper—in order to address the challenge of hyperplurality and interpretative disagreement in the church.[7]

Those familiar with Reformation theology will recognize that Vanhoozer is putting old slogans to use in significantly new ways. It is helpful to catch that he is redeploying the *solas* to inform discussion of more recent debates regarding the legacy of Protestantism itself. Perhaps this redeployment can be seen most overtly in the way that he speaks of a "formal principle" and "material principle" of "mere Protestant Christianity." Whereas those terms normally apply to the doctrine of *sola Scriptura* and to justification by faith alone, respectively, he uses the terminology in a very different vein. "Retrieving the *solas* yields the material principle of mere Protestant Christianity: the triune economy of the gospel … The *solas* summarize what the Father is doing in Christ through the Spirit to form a holy nation, and

---

4. Christian Smith, *The Bible Made Impossible: Why Biblicism Is Not a Truly Evangelical Reading of Scripture* (Grand Rapids: Brazos, 2011).

5. Boersma, *Heavenly Participation*, 84–93.

6. Kevin J. Vanhoozer, *Biblical Authority after Babel: Retrieving the Solas in the Spirit of Mere Protestant Christianity* (Grand Rapids: Brazos, 2016).

7. Ibid., 61.

this summary—a rule of faith, hope, and love—functions as a hermeneutical tool with which to arbitrate the conflict of interpretations."[8] "[W]e also need to recover a hitherto-underappreciated element in the pattern of Protestant interpretative authority: the principle of the priesthood of all believers. I call this the formal principle of mere Protestant Christianity."[9] In so doing, Vanhoozer points toward the vivid description of biblical interpretation in a world enchanted with God's presence and activity (over against the void of secularization) and locates such scriptural reading and theological judgment within the communion of the saints (contrary to the purportedly individualistic legacy of Luther).

Each chapter moves through a sequence whereby Vanhoozer describes the *sola*, locates it amidst its own initial context, and then applies it to the questions of interpretive individualism and pluralism. We need to appreciate that the primary focus of the work is not excavatory but applicatory: Vanhoozer is primarily serving here to show the way in which these fives *solas* shed light upon questions of interpretative activity, either individually or corporately but always theologically. While he does reference and quote primary and secondary sources on each *sola* with skill, this book is neither aimed at nor best for doing that kind of historical backward glance. Where it is uniquely beneficial, however, is asking after the impact these "mere Protestant" tenets have upon our thoughts about theological and exegetical work.

In a sense, then, this is a book that could very easily be received with false expectations. If one is looking for an academic exposition of the reformational debates in their nuance, you had best look elsewhere. But this book actually does something far more notable, for my money, in that it asks how retrieval of those insights might help us confront much later questions that demand an equally courageous protest. Identifying secularism and individualism is hard enough, responding to them each with truly theological and evangelical resources doubly so. Vanhoozer's focus upon the triune economy of the gospel and the churchly character of the *solas* proves remarkably promising in this regard.

Perhaps an example proves helpful. The chapter on *sola fide* focuses upon the way in which this reformation-era principle attunes us to the way the "Spirit uses words to effect faith."[10] In other words, we must catch the link between pneumatology and philology. Modern subjectivism provides one lush trap we must avoid this side of the Reformation, whether in the forms of philosophical rationalism or later romanticism. And perhaps the most common rebuke of those subjectivisms has been the recent turn to community and tradition-based rationality (as in the work of Alasdair MacIntyre and Stanley Hauerwas).[11] Vanhoozer rightly shows that we

---

8. Ibid., 28, 29.
9. Ibid., 29.
10. Ibid., 79.
11. See especially Alasdair MacIntyre, *After Virtue: A Study in Moral Theory* (3rd ed.; Notre Dame: University of Notre Dame Press, 2007); Stanley Hauerwas, *After Christendom: How the Church Is to Behave if Freedom, Justice, and a Christian Nation Are Bad Ideas* (Nashville: Abingdon, 1991).

actually need a much more fundamental appreciation of the church as creature of the Word so as to appreciate the finitude and dependence of the church, the ongoing agency of the Word, the inscripturated form of the Word's work now by the Spirit, and the distinctiveness of the church over against other social forms.[12] Tradition-based sociology will not keep us from falling into individual subjectivism; we demand an appreciation of the society of Christ and the communion of the saints that is rooted ultimately in the unique action of God here and now.[13] We also need to tend appropriate virtues as the "epistemic fruits of faith" and ward off luring vices regarding theological labor, commending confidence and diligence rather than undue pride and bitter sloth.[14] Like many in the recent theological interpretation of Scripture conversation (especially Scott Swain, Todd Billings, and John Webster) as well as some late modern theologians in the Reformed world (such as Bavinck), Vanhoozer seeks to deploy fundamental evangelical principles not only to frame our understanding of salvation but also of theological exploration, not only for our eschatological destiny but also for our epistemic practice.[15] In light of the dominance of Enlightenment-era scientific method and the screed of critical theory and identity politics in shaping the pursuit of knowledge now, such a distinctly Christian and theological approach stands in great relief. Further, the book is useful not only for putting basic Protestant convictions to good epistemic work but also for drawing out some easily overlooked tenets of reformational faith and practice for more careful examination. As mentioned earlier, the Reformation demands our attention precisely because it had to do with God, before whom we are always summoned.

We do well to remember in addressing the polemics of the Reformation, then, that we dare not move away from the catholic doctrine of God.[16] Debates regarding justification and assurance, on the one hand, and authority and Scripture, on the other hand, are fundamentally discussions concerning the way in which the triune

---

12. Ibid., 102.
13. Ibid., 83, 94.
14. Ibid., 106.
15. See especially Scott R. Swain, *Trinity, Revelation, and Reading: A Theological Introduction to the Bible and Its Interpretation* (London: T&T Clark, 2012); Todd Billings, *The Word of God for the People of God: An Entryway to the Theological Interpretation of Scripture* (Grand Rapids: Eerdmans, 2010); and John Webster, *Holy Scripture: A Dogmatic Sketch* (Current Issues in Theology; Cambridge: Cambridge University Press, 2003); "The Domain of the Word" and "Resurrection and Scripture" in *The Domain of the Word: Scripture and Theological Reason* (London: T&T Clark, 2012), 3–49.
16. David Yeago has made a similar argument with respect to Luther's development in 1517–19 in his "The Catholic Luther," in *The Catholicity of the Reformation* (ed. Carl E. Braaten and Robert W. Jenson; Grand Rapids: Eerdmans, 1996), 13–34 (esp. 26); and later in idem, "The Bread of Life: Patristic Christology and Evangelical Soteriology in Martin Luther's Sermon on John 6," *St. Vladimir's Theological Quarterly* 39, no. 3 (2001), 257–79. I do not think Yeago's rightful construal of Luther's Protestant reform being a catholic turn, however, must lead to his skepticism regarding Luther's late autobiographical account of his shift in 1517.

God has acted, is acting, and has pledged to act in our midst. And Philip Schaff's *Principle of Protestantism* points to their entangled nature:

> The material element without the objective basis of the formal becomes swarming inwardism, and in the end sheer subjectivity. The formal element without the material, however, conducts to stiff, lifeless, and soulless externalism, the idolatry of the letter; and comes besides to no right understanding of the Scriptures, to which the key is found only in justifying faith as produced by the Spirit of God.[17]

Fixation solely on faith and justification can easily elide the concreteness of the Christian in whom they find their substance, turning Jesus into a cipher or symbol for a balm to the conscience or freedom from the pressing expectations of society. Similarly, Schaff says that staring at scriptural writings apart from the divine wind which blows through them and makes them life-giving will invariably turn stiff and soulless. The material and the formal principles of the Reformation must be viewed together, in as much as they are both aspects of triune action.

Lest we lapse into subjectivism or externalism, then, we must appreciate the link between *solus Christus* and *sola Scriptura* as a way of grasping a bit more fully how the life of God leads unto the reform of God's holy people. The connections can be traced still further, though, and we do well to see why. Another assessment, this one a century ago from the Dutch theologian Herman Bavinck, proves helpful.

> The root principle of this Calvinism is the confession of God's absolute sovereignty. Not one special attribute of God, for instance His love or justice, His holiness or equity, but God Himself as such in the unity of all His attributes and perfection of His entire Being is the point of departure for the thinking and acting of the Calvinist. From this root principle everything that is specifically Reformed may be derived and explained. It was this that led to the sharp distinction between what is God's and creature's, to belief in the sole authority of the Holy Scriptures, in the all-sufficiency of Christ and His word, in the omnipotence of the work of grace .... By this principle also the Calvinist was led to the use of that through-going consistent theological method, which distinguishes him from Romanist and other Protestant theologians .... For this reason the Calvinist in all things recurs upon God, and does not rest satisfied before he has traced back everything to the sovereign good-pleasure of God as its ultimate and deepest cause. He never loses himself in the appearance of things, but penetrates to their realities. Behind the phenomena he searches for the *noumena*, the things that are not seen, from which the things visible have been born. He does not take his stand in the midst of history, but out of time ascends into the heights of eternity. History is naught but the gradual unfolding of what to God is an eternal present. For his heart, his thinking, his life, the Calvinist cannot find rest in these terrestrial things, the sphere of what is becoming, changing, forever passing by.

---

17. Schaff, *The Principle of Protestantism*, 123.

From the process of salvation he therefore recurs upon the decree of salvation, from history to the idea. He does not remain in the outer court of the temple, but seeks to enter into the innermost sanctuary.[18]

The Reformed tradition emerges as a distinct strand of catholic Christianity not owing to myriad discrete decisions. Were it merely a political occurrence or the conglomeration of multiple judgments of contingent form, we would expect to see such distinct threads. But Bavinck sees a principled vision underneath the various judgments, and he insists that we have not only a full but an operative doctrine of God as we think about every other topic. Here Bavinck lists numerous tenets of faith and practice, ranging from what may seem to be merely Reformed inflections of ecumenical theology to what seems rather parochial. In each case, he reduces the tenet or habit to the more radical commitment of God's perfection and sovereignty, the divine self-sufficiency that marks him off as the only true and living Lord. Bavinck's sketch, then, agrees with the more limited analyses of Schaff and Vanhoozer, each of which reminds us that triune agency and divine fullness remain operative across the full sweep of our theological contemplation.

A Dogmatics of Word and Church

To flesh out the way in which the doctrine of God remains operative when we turn to matters of Scripture and church, we may be helped by attending to a classic confessional statement of the early Swiss Reformation, the Ten Theses of Berne (1528). The first thesis reads as such: "The holy, Christian Church, whose only Head is Christ, is born of the Word of God, abides in the same, and does not listen to the voice of a stranger."[19] My reflections will seek to unpack this confession in its four constituent moments before drawing together a few final remarks on the character of the church as the creature of the Word.[20]

---

18. Herman Bavinck, "The Future of Calvinism" (published 1894 in *The Presbyterian & Reformed Review*: http://scdc.library.ptsem.edu/mets/mets.aspx?src=BR1894517&div=1).

19. "The Ten Theses of Berne, 1528," in *Reformed Confessions in the Sixteenth Century* (ed. Arthur C. Cochrane; Louisville: Westminster John Knox, 2003), 48 (Thesis 1).

20. My own reflections on the link between the doctrine of God and the Scripture principle have been prompted by Christoph Schwöbel, "The Creature of the Word: Recovering the Ecclesiology of the Reformers," in *On Being the Church: Essays on the Christian Community* (ed. Colin Gunton; Edinburgh: T&T Clark, 1989), 110–55; David Yeago, "The Bible: The Spirit, the Church, and the Scriptures: Biblical Inspiration and Interpretation Revisited," in *Knowing the Triune God: The Work of the Spirit in the Practices of the Church* (ed. James Buckley and David Yeago; Grand Rapids: Eerdmans, 2001), 49–93; and two essays by John Webster: "Scripture, Church, and Canon," in *Holy Scripture: A Dogmatic Sketch* (Current Issues in Theology; Cambridge: Cambridge University Press, 2003), 42–67; and idem, "The Domain of the Word," in *The Domain of the Word: Scripture and Theological Reason* (London: T&T Clark, 2012), 3–31.

Christ Is Lord: The "only Head of the holy, Christian Church is Christ"

Any approach to church or to authority will only be as good as the theology beneath it. This first thesis reminds us that we begin always with the first commandment. In thinking of the church, we dare not have any other god before us. Temptation befalls us when we view ecclesiology as the realm solely of gratitude, a truth that can bedevil us if removed from its paired terms and if prompting us to relate the human assembly of God solely to divine action which occurred in the past. Christ's action can easily be narrowed to involve invocation, that is, having called this human assembly into being during his earthly sojourn. Jesus can be reduced here to the initiating cause of the church, though not the sustaining guide and governor of her path. What fills the void? Well, Protestants might have looked previously to powers of ecclesiastical or political sway. Luther and Zwingli surely saw popes and councils as the pertinent threats to Christ's own lordship. The early reformers saw a distinctly ecclesiastical idolatry as the pertinent challenge of the day.

Idolatry must be considered and its forms should be contemplated. We live in a day where that threat is no doubt compounded by other challengers. The pope or the ecclesiastical authority continues to hold sway in many realms and for many persons. We are naïve to think that this is a mere piece of antiquity in the premodern world. Yet other temptations exist also and perhaps more insidiously for us. We now struggle also to fill the void absented by the missing Christ, that is, the no longer present Lord Christ, with the sovereignty of the sociological marketer and the therapeutic guru, the branding expert or the political talking head. When Philip Rieff identified the challenge of "therapeutic man" decades ago, he surely was on to something which Charles Taylor and others have now further analyzed, namely, a developing sense of the self (and, by extension, of any society of selves) unrooted from a classic metaphysics or what Taylor has called a "moral ontology."[21] The idols of our age may move into the sanctuary but likely where it is renamed an auditorium or theater. The threats of our day may take residence on the leadership teams of our churches but typically when they are envisaged as managers and executives. The allurements of our context may affect our pedagogy but only when catechetical formation follows therapeutic guidance or consumer entertainment. And the seductions of our setting may well address the confessions of our communions but more likely than not when its concerns are dominated by sociopolitical principles of the times.

If we observe that the challenges of the sixteenth century involved an overly confident ecclesiastical power structure, then we must note that today the challenge will likely come from ministers who lack any sense of churchly

---

21. See Philip Rieff, *Freud: The Mind of the Moralist* (3rd ed.; Chicago: University of Chicago Press, 1979), 329–57 on "the emergence of psychological man"; idem, *The Triumph of the Therapeutic: Uses of Faith after Freud* (2nd ed.; Chicago: University of Chicago Press, 1987); and Charles Taylor, *The Sources of the Self: The Making of Modern Identity* (Cambridge: Harvard University Press, 1989).

confidence. That is not to say that they lack self-confidence, of course, but they will lack confidence in the viability of the church in her own resources. Hence the watchword will be "conversational" or "interdisciplinary" dependence on other resources. The rightful claim that "all truth is God's truth" will be mangled from its paired affirmation that all our thinking must be sanctified and that theology serves as queen of the sciences. But we do well to note that our challenge—the threat of the idolatrous being brought into our worship and ministry in the church—is not actually new. The first commandment itself was given to Israelites who had marinated in polytheistic Egypt and were soon to bake in the oven of Canaanite idolatry. Their temptation would be exemplified by that of Nadab and Abihu, of taking the religious practices of the pagan world and bringing them into their worship of YHWH (Lev. 10.1). The judgment of their rightful God was to remind them through Moses: "Among those who are near me, I will be sanctified" (Lev. 10.2); that is, the people of God must not forget that God is set apart from the gods of the peoples and therefore may not be worshipped in any which way that we might imagine or fashion for ourselves. This ancient and ever-present threat deserves our attention.

So we find that this first thesis returns to the most basic Christian confession: "Jesus is Lord" (Rom. 10.9). This statement stands at the head of all Reformed ecclesiology. We dare not misinterpret it, however, as if it were a statement of memorial or of honorific remembrance, much like a plaque in the foyer which acknowledges the beneficence of a significant ancestor or a founding pastor. Jesus is the author of faith, to be sure, but he is also its perfecter (Heb. 12.2). He not only plants the church as a sower does his crop but he also abides as the head of the body. In other words, we dare not miss the present and active aspect of his churchly lordship for he continues to be engaged as our mediator: our prophet, priest, and king.

This first thesis begins by employing the imagery of the head and the body (see also Eph. 1.22-23; 5.23-24; cf. Col. 1.18). The language connotes political authority. The head is not apart from the body, and so we must say that Christ is not alien to the church. His union with the church finds explanation in the still further specification that it is "Christ" who is the head and not simply the divine Son. Jesus Christ, the incarnate Son of God, serves even now as our risen and exalted Lord and, thus, also as our churchly head. Not merely as a human being but nonetheless truly as a human being do we attest that the divine, incarnate Son reigns forever and rules actively over and through and—yes, also—with his people. The head/body imagery ties Christ to us as the mediator who continues to live and move and have his being now as one of us.

Ian McFarland has identified three contributions of this imagery which we dare not miss:

> The biblical distinction between head and members is helpful precisely because it suggests both the inseparability of Christ and the church (inasmuch as the body is as incomplete without a head as the head is without a body) and their

distinction (inasmuch as the head is not to be confused either with any other member of the body in particular or with the body as a whole).[22]

It is fundamental to see both "inseparability" as well as "distinction." But McFarland says we must go one step further and specify the sort of distinction expounded here: the head/body imagery also connotes that distinction as specifically bearing the authority of one of us over the others. Christ alone bears this lordship and serves this role as director and guide of the body, just as the head alone gives instruction unto the hands and feet. Here we see that it is uniquely his perogative to serve in this capacity. God brokers no competitors, and Christ does not squander his sovereignty.

We do well, then, to remember that even a text such as the Epistle to the Hebrews continues to identify Jesus as "the great shepherd of the sheep" (Heb. 13.20; cf. "the shepherd and overseer of your souls," 1 Pet. 2.25). That epistle does call the congregation to "remember your leaders, those who spoke to you the word of God. Consider the outcome of their way of life and imitate their faith" (Heb. 13.7) and to "obey your leaders and submit to them, for they are keeping watch over your souls" (13.17). But the rightful role of human leaders does not undermine the categorical distinction of the pastoral place held still by Jesus. He is the one who fulfills the role of "great high priest" (Heb. 4.14) and is now the "great shepherd" of his flock.

Born of the Word: "The holy, Christian Church is born of the Word of God"

Beginnings matter. In this second statement, we see that the church has been born of God's Word, bespeaking its roots in God's own action. The church does not exist simply as a datum of reality and cannot simply be assumed. We see the apostle Peter struck by this reality: "Once you were not a people, but now you are God's people; once you had not received mercy, but now you have received mercy" (1 Pet. 2.10). Peter leans into this statement by evoking creational imagery of darkness, saying that God "called you out of darkness into his marvelous light" (1 Pet. 2.9). The *ekklesia* here has been called out not simply from varied demographics or existential backgrounds but from darkness, the chaos and void, itself. The church's existence is miracle, then, and wholly of God's doing.

Beginnings—especially the kind of miraculous initiation described here—have not only an initiating but also a sustaining effect upon a reality.[23] That the church is born of God does not merely explain the existence of the church but also the character of the church. The people of God are those who are gift, because they are given unto one another by another. We speak of a congregation in this regard, over against an aggregation, precisely because it is God's action bringing these men and women together.

---

22. Ian McFarland, "The Body of Christ: Rethinking a Classic Ecclesiological Model," *International Journal of Systematic Theology* 7, no. 3 (2005), 239.

23. See R. R. Reno, "Reading the Bible with the Church," *Calvin Theological Journal* 43, no. 1 (2008), 35–47.

We must confess that the church's holiness and her Christian character are also then gift, born of the Word of God. Saying such does not malign their integrity and reality, but characterizes the way in which they are enjoyed. First, the church is holy by grace, not by nature. Luther himself highlighted the way in which the Word of God was integrally connected to the holiness of God's people. In his 1539 treatise "On the Councils and the Church," he spoke of seven marks of the "holy, Christian church" and began: "First, the holy Christian people are recognized by their possession of the holy word of God." Indeed, "even if there were no other sign than this alone, it would still suffice to prove that a Christian, holy people must exist there, for God's word cannot be without God's people, and conversely, God's people cannot be without God's word."[24] He had suggested similar things as early as 1519 in debate at Leipzig. In this later text he extended its implications for how the Christian people are identified. Second, the church is Christian by grace, not by nature. Here the language of adoption is so crucial in as much as it is God's action of calling us sons and daughters that enfolds us into his family through Christ, with whom we are joint heirs.[25] Here the image of baptism reminds us that we cannot stamp ourselves "Christian"—we must be immersed in that identity by another.

The church's inception comes then from the invocation of her LORD. In attesting our nonexistence and our being birthed anew only by God's Word, we join with the apostle Paul in relating our spiritual character with our prior creational integrity: "For God, who said, 'Let light shine out of darkness,' has shone in our hearts to give the light of the knowledge of the glory of God in the face of Jesus Christ" (2 Cor. 4.6). Only in this way wherein the words of the life-giving one shed their life abroad do we see the love from which our reality flows.

Abides in the Word: "The holy, Christian Church abides in the same"

Beginnings matter not only with respect to protology and the inception point of something but also for the sake of preservation and the ongoing sustenance of the thing. Being created means being a creature, and being a creature means that an ongoing experience of dependence marks our life long after our existence has been derived from another. We live on borrowed breath or, as David Kelsey puts it, we have an eccentric existence.[26]

The thesis uses the verb "abides" to bespeak this dependent posture of ongoing existence. In so doing it surely alludes to Jesus' own instruction that we "abide" in him (Jn. 15.4-7). Here we read also that we "abide in his love" (verses 9-10) and that

---

24. Martin Luther, "On the Councils and the Church (1539)," in *Church and Ministry III: Liturgy and Hymns* (ed. Eric Gritsch; trans. Charles Jacobs; Luther's Works 41; Philadelphia: Fortress, 1966), 148, 150.

25. The language of being joint-heirs in Rom. 8.17 ("heirs of God and fellow heirs with Christ") conveys the character of our adoption as always mediated by union with the incarnate Son.

26. David Kelsey, *Eccentric Existence: A Theological Anthropology* (Louisville: Westminster John Knox, 2009).

his "joy may be in you" (verse 11). We often forget that a Christian, like a branch, is made to receive life, love, and joy from someone more elemental, someone to whom we are united. The Lord's Supper portrays this ongoing dependence, however, in that it is not only the beginning of Christian life (baptism) that requires a gift from the outside but also the ongoing character of that journey that demands constant replenishment (symbolized by his body and blood, food and drink for his people). Abiding, not autonomy, marks the maturity of the child of God.

More must be said of this text regarding why abiding involves his Word. In that context, of course, Jesus prepares his disciples for the seeming absence they will soon sense upon his ascension. He has just called them "Rise, let us go from here" (Jn. 14.31) as if to walk into the looming challenge which will bring a new chasm (13.33; 14.2-4, 15-30).[27] But then he lingers, as it were, and speaks of abiding, something of an ironic retort if ever there were one. The Jesus who has just scared them of a seeming departure now commissions them to abide in him. What a mystery! But he presses on still to describe this abiding: "you abide in me, and my words abide in you" (15.7; 1 Jn. 2.14).[28] Abiding in him occurs even as he is physically absent. In fact, "Already you are clean because of the word that I have spoken to you" (verse 3). The scriptural Word is the means of the ongoing presence of the incarnate Word just as it was the means of the miraculous purification. Put simply: we are Bible people because we are Jesus people. That may sound mechanical, I suppose, but it's personal and particular. If you were in love with a man or woman who moved far away, and they could not travel to you but could only communicate with you through letters, you would await those letters, read those letters (again and again), and cherish those letters. Those letters would be memorized. Such does not demand anything exalted about letters in and of themselves, but a posture of trust and delight placed specifically in *those* letters for that *personal* reason.

This talk of *presence* demands a bit more by way of expansion. "Every day the Church experiences the fruits and effects of Christ's sitting down at the Father's right hand; and the enemies of Christ, including even Satan himself, whether they like it or not, marvel at it, and tremble."[29] The words of the Leiden Synopsis here then provide reason for this confidence, relating the past action of Christ gathering his people to his ongoing work preserving them. "For Christ gathers his Church by his Word and Spirit, while they vainly resist; he preserves it against the tyranny of the whole world and the gates of hell, and he destroys the Antichrist by the spirit

---

27. For analysis of this seeming chasm and its effect on the Christian way, see Richard Hays, "Why Do You Stand Looking Up Toward Heaven? New Testament Eschatology at the Turn of the Millennium," *Modern Theology* 16, no. 1 (2000), 129.

28. cf. "if you keep my commandments, you will abide in my love" in Jn. 15.10 and then 1 Jn. 2.3-6.

29. *Synopsis Purioris Theologiae: Latin Text and English Translation*, Volume 2: *Disputations 24–42* (ed. Henk van den Belt; Studies in Medieval and Reformation Traditions 204; Leiden: Brill, 2016), 177.

of his mouth."[30] We live in a day and age whereby we view Christ as silent and God as polite enough to be absent.

The late John Webster once considered the imagery of the Book of Revelation, noting a perplexity perhaps different from the normal references of such astonishment.

> This vivid sense that the risen Jesus is speaker astonishes us or perplexes us. Where we are tempted to be embarrassed by its fervor, the apocalypse is not at all embarrassed to talk in very direct terms of the vocal presence of Jesus. Our perplexity, of course, is rooted in the fact that we find ourselves in a culture which functionally and theoretically has ceased to expect divine speech.[31]

But such an "immanent frame," to use the words of Charles Taylor, fits the frame of deism rather than the eschatological path sketched by Jesus in John 15 or surveyed in Revelation. So Webster went on:

> The conviction on which the apocalypse is based—that God in Christ is a speaker, and that if we are to interpret human history we have to listen to the voice of God—is to all intents and purposes not an operative one for us. We work on the assumption that God is silent. If true words are to be spoken, we ourselves have to say them.[32]

We must face the deistic hermeneutics of much modern biblical criticism and ecclesiological pragmatism.[33] The Epistle to the Hebrews makes this move in its Christological confession. Surely the insistence that "he upholds all things by his powerful word" (Heb. 1.3) applies to the church as well.[34] Thus the power

---

30. Ibid., 177.
31. John Webster, "The Hearing Church," in *The Grace of Truth*, 157–8 (on Rev. 3.13-14).
32. Ibid., 158.
33. Mark Bowald has helpfully traced the "Deistic" turn in modern biblical criticism owing to a metaphysics noninclusive of divine missions in his *Rendering the Word in Theological Hermeneutics: Mapping Divine and Human Agency* (Aldershot: Ashgate, 2007), 173; see Herman Bavinck, *Reformed Dogmatics*, Volume 1, (ed. John Bolt; *Prolegomena*; Grand Rapids, MI: Baker Academic, 2003), 384–5. A similar argument could be made regarding the deistic analysis of much modern ecclesiology (especially that influenced by so-called postliberalism).
34. The most fundamental matter shaping the ecclesiology of Hebrews is Christological: "Jesus Christ is the same yesterday, today, and forever" (Heb. 13.8); see Ceslas Spicq, *L'Epitre aux Hébreux II—Commentaire* (Paris: Gabalda, 1953), 2; George Hunsinger, "The Same Only Different: Karl Barth's Interpretation of Hebrews 13:8," in *Thy Word Is Truth: Barth on Scripture* (ed. George Hunsinger; Grand Rapids, MI: Eerdmans, 2012), 112–24. And this Jesus who is unchanging is a speaker: see Tomasz Lewicki, "*Weist nicht ab den Sprechenden!*": *Wort Gottes und Paraklese im Hebräerbrief* (Paderborner Theologische Studien; Paderborn: Schöningh, 2004), chap. 3; as well as B. F. Westcott, *The Epistle to the Hebrews: The Greek Text with Notes and Essays* (3rd ed.; London: Macmillan, 1903), 4.

of the present with its every implication for our existence and flourishing in correspondence with the nature of that existence demands an operative Christology. In this regard, the late Michael Ramsey was right to attest that "the Catholicism, therefore, that sprang from the Gospel of God is a faith wherein the visible and ordered Church fills an important place ... The Church, therefore, is defined not in terms of itself, but in terms of Christ, whose Gospel created it and whose life is its indwelling life."[35]

Might we hang our hat on a specific text that conveys how this ongoing agency of the Word of Christ relates to Christian ministry and churchly life? Turning to Ephesians 4 places us in the midst of a theological vision of the church, which conveys what we are in God through Christ: "one body and Spirit ... one Lord, one faith, one baptism, one God and Father of all, who is over all and through all and in all" (Eph. 4.4-6). Admittedly, the thick presence and action of God may not seem manifest in all these circumstances to the bare eye. Paul locates the action, though, in the throne room, pressing on to say that "grace was given to each one of us according to the measure of Christ's gift. Therefore, it says: 'When he ascended on high he led a host of captives, and he gave gifts to men'" (Eph. 4.7-8, quoting Ps. 68.18). The apostle attests that the risen Christ reigns triumphantly and acts in that exalted state so as to give grace to all (literally "each one," not some prized subset). And he attests this by morphing the language of the Psalm, which had spoken of the victorious king receiving gifts from the nations, to attest how the servant king uses his triumph as an occasion to continue giving and serving. The exalted Christ gives and graces.

What does the exalted Son and victorious Lord give to each one of the saints? Paul goes on, after a parenthetical riff, to say: "And he gave the apostles, the prophets, the evangelists, the shepherds and teachers to equip the saints for the work of ministry, for building up the body of Christ" (Eph. 4.11-12). The offices of the church are mentioned in their variety here, though it is worth noting that they find commonality in their shared ministry of another's Word. Each of them, from the apostle all the way to the teacher, trades in the work of commending the communication of the triune God and not of themselves. They each also serve to shape (or "equip") the saints as the trainer or tutor might prepare one physically or intellectually for a looming task. The saints must be readied here for the work of ministry, that is, the building up of Christ's own body. The church's wise discernment for the calling of love and service, then, finds its strength and

---

35. Michael Ramsey, *The Gospel and the Catholic Church* (Peabody, MA: Hendrickson, 2009), 56. However, Ramsey's development of the Christological character of the catholic church raises questions about rightly distinguishing divine and human agency (to which he is insufficiently attuned). Cf. John Webster, "The Church as Witnessing Community," *Scottish Bulletin of Evangelical Theology* 21, no. 1 (Spring 2003), 21–33; Michael Allen, "The Church and the churches: A Dogmatic Essay on Ecclesial Invisibility," *European Journal of Theology* 16, no. 2 (2007), 113–19; repr. in *The Knowledge of God: Essays on God, Christ, and Church*, ch. 11.

sustenance in the ministry of the Word by those ambassadors who point unto God's life-giving testimony. The Word works, then, in the communion of the saints in a unified yet differentiated fashion, whereby the body of Christ grows and goes about its maturing service.

As mentioned earlier, the Reformation demands our attention precisely because it had to do with God, before whom we are always summoned. Yet Kevin Vanhoozer helps us appreciate the way in which some of the assumptions of the Reformation can no longer simply be assumed. Drawing on the work of my colleague Michael Glodo, Vanhoozer suggests a sixth *sola* apart from which the others do not make sense: *sola ecclesia*.[36] "The church alone is the place where Christ rules over his kingdom and gives certain gifts for the building of his living temple."[37] Vanhoozer suggests elsewhere that we need to attend to the significance of epistemic "means of grace" in describing the theological journey.[38] Such did not need to be said with the same gusto in the 1510s or 1520s, not until the Radical Reformation, on the one hand, and modern individualism, on the other hand, would eat away parasitically at the churchly character of Christianity in their varied ways.

Yet the reformers rightly attest that the Church "abides in the same" word by which it was born, for here we find the living Lord to be active and engaged for our good and our growth. With Martin Bucer, we attest that

> our dear Lord Jesus is truly present in his church, ruling, leading, and feeding it himself. But he effects and carries out this his rule and the feeding of his lambs in such a way as to remain always in his heavenly nature, that is, in his divine and intangible state, because he has left this world. Therefore, it has pleased him to exercise his rule, protection and care of us who are still in this world with and through the ministry of his ministers and instruments.[39]

Bucer gathers a litany of relevant texts (Mt. 28.18-20; Lk. 24.45-47; Jn. 15.16; Jn. 20.21-23; Mt. 16.19; Mt. 10.20; 1 Cor. 3.5-7; 1 Cor. 4.1; 2 Cor. 3.2-6; 1 Thess. 1.45; 1 Thess. 2.13) and conveys that these scriptures attest the ministry exercised and empowered by the Lord Jesus. We do well to trace the gift-giving concern of Christ all the way through the churchly instrument by which he promises to deliver the goods.

Having No Other Gods: "The holy, Christian Church does not listen to the voice of a stranger"

These affirmations seek to commend Christ as he heralds his Word amidst his people, indeed, as he gathers and guards his people by that very act of heralding

---

36. Vanhoozer, *Biblical Authority after Babel*, 29 fn. 120. See also Michael J. Glodo, "*Sola Ecclesiae*: The Lost Reformation Doctrine?" *Reformation & Revival* 9, no. 4 (2000), 91-7.
37. Ibid., 29.
38. Ibid., 115, 175.
39. Martin Bucer, *Concerning the True Care of Souls* (trans. Peter Beale; Edinburgh: Banner of Truth Trust, 2009), 17.

his Word. Heralding the Word instills health because of the sufficiency of the Word. Clement of Alexandria proves helpful here: "He who possesses the Word, who is Almighty God, needs nothing and never lacks for any of the things he desires, for the Word is an infinite possession, and the source of all our wealth."[40] But we do not always remember this; indeed we frequently run after others for that which we desire. We need a Jeremiah, do we not, to come and fulfill the prophetic commission "to pluck up and to break down, to destroy and to overthrow, to build and to plant" (Jer. 1.10). The final claim of this first thesis of Berne, then, reminds us that we must be warned away from that which is false, and we must see how the Word will deconstruct the idolatrous temptations that may be near or far.

In our day and age the therapeutic ideal and the marketing machine will no doubt be amongst the most imposing such strange voices, each suggesting ways in which we might fit the theological hand in a consumerist glove. Sociologists have assessed these approaches and their results, whether in the guise of expressive individualism or of moral therapeutic deism.[41] However their form and results might be described, we do well to heed the warning of David Yeago that too often "the church figures only as the vehicle for something essentially disembodied and non-public: a set of beliefs and values, an abstract 'message,' an inward religious experience."[42] Such an approach to the church and culture invariably leaves the people of God clamoring for "relevance." We do well to note, however, that the Word of God evokes a culture, not merely a message, as Yeago goes on to say: "the church is a culture in its own right; the church has its own culture, which is not simply a function of the cultures of the nations among which it dwells."[43] While we cannot address the "encounter of cultures" which Yeago helps prosecute, thickening normal discussions of Christ and culture, we do well to realize that such assessment highlights the significance of attending to the full breadth of the Word of God ("the whole counsel of God," Acts 20.27) as a necessary protocol for being capable of identifying and shirking the strange voices that seek to accost the people of God or, perhaps more frequently, to elicit the church's affirmation. We do well to listen that the singularity of God stated most pointedly in the *shema* of Deut. 6.45 immediately turns to the holistic pedagogy and formative fullness of the life of the people of God (cf. Deut. 6.6-9), wherein the *ekklesia* of Israel does form a sanctifying counter-culture amongst

---

40. Clement of Alexandria, *Christ the Educator* (Fathers of the Church; Washington, DC: Catholic University of America Press, 1984), III.7.

41. On expressive individualism, see Charles Taylor, *The Ethics of Authenticity* (Cambridge: Harvard University Press, 1992); on moral therapeutic deism, see Christian Smith with Melinda Lundquist Denton, *Soul Searching: The Religious and Spiritual Lives of Emerging Adults* (New York: Oxford University Press, 2005).

42. David Yeago, "Messiah's People: The Culture of the Church in the Midst of the Nations," *Pro Ecclesia* 6, no. 1 (1997), 149.

43. Yeago, "Messiah's People," 150.

the nations.⁴⁴ Avoiding the stranger who lurks within will only occur as we attend to the catholicity of the Word itself.

Avoiding the stranger does not merely relate to how we view external threats but also the manner in which we view internal realities such as church tradition and ecclesiastical authorities. So we must consider ways in which tradition and authority serve as ministries of the Word over against approaches whereby they become idolatrous. Confessing that the church is a creature of the Word in no way empties the church of her historical, social reality, though it does grant us certain lenses and categories for being alert to her true nature in God's promise. We are not called to look elsewhere than the real church or to look only to its spiritual moments.⁴⁵ We are, however, summoned to look to the church with the eyes of faith. Calvin reminded us that we confess that we "believe one, holy, catholic, and apostolic church" rather than that we "believe in" such a church.⁴⁶ In so doing, he reminds us that the church is an instrument of God, not to be confused with God himself. Tradition is not inerrant or indefectible, then, and we do well to view tradition as a reality brought by grace but not yet glorified.

In recent Roman Catholic accounts of tradition, notably those provided by Lewis Ayres and Matthew Levering, tradition finds description in Christological and pneumatological forms. Ayres suggests that we must grasp the economy of God's speech as one "in which the mystery of God is spoken among us, through the interaction of Word and Spirit, word and answering word."⁴⁷ And Levering adds that "the way to understand the active place of the Church in divine revelation is to reflect upon the missions of the Son and Spirit."⁴⁸ This is very promising. Yet tradition—whether in the form of the history of biblical exegesis (in Ayres) or of

---

44. For reflections along these lines, see Raymond Blacketer, *The School of God: Pedagogy and Rhetoric in Calvin's Interpretation of Deuteronomy* (Studies in Early Modern Religious Reforms; Dordrecht: Springer, 2010), esp. 104–6.

45. See also Chapter 10 ("Reformed Retrieval").

46. John Calvin, *Institutes of the Christian Religion* (ed. John T. McNeill; Library of Christian Classics; Louisville: Westminster John Knox, 2004), 1013 (IV.i.2).

47. Lewis Ayres, "The Word Answering the Word: Opening the Space of Catholic Biblical Interpretation," in *Theological Theology: Essays in Honour of John Webster* (ed. R. David Nelson, Darren Sarisky, and Justin Stratis; London: T&T Clark, 2015), 49. For further reflections on Scripture and tradition and a posture of critically receptive theology as a way forward for modern Roman Catholic theology, see also Lewis Ayres, *Nicaea and Its Legacy: An Approach to Fourth Century Trinitarian Theology* (New York: Oxford University Press, 2004), 384–429.

48. Matthew Levering, *Engaging the Doctrine of Revelation: The Mediation of the Gospel through Church and Scripture* (Grand Rapids, MI: Baker Academic, 2014), 56. For further reflection upon the missions of Son and Spirit and a graced participation of human mediating figures within those missions, see also Matthew Levering, *Christ and the Catholic Priesthood: Ecclesial Hierarchy and the Pattern of the Trinity* (Chicago: Hillenbrand, 2010); idem, *Participatory Biblical Exegesis: A Theology of Biblical Interpretation* (Notre Dame, IN: University of Notre Dame Press, 2008), esp. 90–140.

liturgy (in Levering)—is described in ideal terms. So Ayres: "we may conceive of these later 'ecclesial' readings of the New Testament as truer, deeper readings of the literal sense."[49] And Levering: "The liturgy is the true home for the reading of Scripture ... it is in and through the liturgy that revelation is truly proclaimed, interpreted, and enacted for the life of the world."[50]

Reformed retrieval will demur from assuming the ideal or expounding the church only in terms of divine grace. Reformed ecclesiology, and its consideration of tradition as one key element in this broader topic, will also consider the church's tradition in an eschatological hue, graced out of darkness but not yet glorified into undimming light.[51] With Ayres, Reformed retrieval will focus upon church tradition in its various forms as lineaments of the history of the Word and, thus, of exegetical reasoning. It will do so because such an interrogation of the tradition offers more promising grounds for hearing the Word more faithfully. Other potential interrogations—regarding the political, social, missiological, or philosophical constructions of the church—may offer benefits but do not necessarily put us in conversation with the ultimate source of authority and the promised bearer of life, the prophetic witness of the Holy Scriptures. Even in its retrieval of the tradition, Reformed Christians will remember the axiomatic words of the first thesis of Berne: "The holy, Christian Church, whose only Head is Christ, is born of the Word of God, abides in the same, and does not listen to the voice of a stranger."

And yet it is also precisely here where we see that a Reformed ecclesiology will not take the form of cynicism or of modern progress's sneer toward the past. Admittedly, the agonistics of indwelling sin continue to plague us as well. We are no more glorified than the saints of days past or the councils of centuries old. Retrieval of our traditions and acknowledgment of authentic ecclesiastical

---

49. Ayres, "Word Answering the Word," 46; italics added.
50. Levering, *Engaging the Doctrine of Revelation*, 80.
51. Levering does suggest ways in which the doctrine of the indefectibility of the church might be maintained along with an awareness of errors on nonessential matters (*Engaging the Doctrine of Revelation*, 27). For further Reformed analysis of the indefectibility of the church, see Michael Allen, "'The Church's One Foundation': The Justification of the Ungodly Church," in *Justification and the Gospel: Understanding the Contexts and the Controversies* (Grand Rapids, MI: Baker Academic, 2013), 153–78. Affirming the sinful yet holy character of the church does not thereby implicate one in claims akin to those of Ephraim Radner, who argues for the pneumatic deprivation of the Western church (so, e.g., *A Brutal Unity: The Spiritual Politics of the Christian Church* [Waco, TX: Baylor University Press, 2012]). While Radner's argument may find fit with certain prophetic texts read figurally, it cannot attend to the breadth of the apostolic witness regarding the nature of the Christian community. Whereas Levering attends too exclusively to texts attending to divine mission in defining the church and her tradition, Radner responds by focusing single-mindedly upon texts of divine abandonment. The key is to see that God has come to the church, but that God continues to come to the church; she is in a state of grace, but not yet in the realm of glory.

authorities attest our remembrance of this common location and this shared vocation to know God more fully while on this journey unto the promised glory of Canaan's shore. Ultimately, however, we listen only to the voice of the Word of God, which is both norm and limit to our own testimony, and we do not listen to the voice of a stranger who might shape our faith or practice. And this insistence finds its force only from the known voice of our incarnate Lord: "the sheep follow him, for they know his voice. A stranger they will not follow, but they will flee from him, for they do not know the voice of strangers" (Jn. 10.4-5).

Conclusion: Remarks on Ecclesial Theology

We do well to think about what ethical implications mark this church whose creation and cultivation are invoked by God's own Word. By way of conclusion, then, let us attend to the hope and the posture of such a church as well as the health and manner of her theological practice.[52] First, we might ask, what sort of hope is there for the church? Our hope is in God through Christ. He is the one who has told us in the prologue to the Apocalypse: "Grace to you and peace from him who is and who was and who is to come" (Rev. 1.4). The God who has not changed and will not turn from us proves to be our bulwark and our guide. Any attention to human exemplars and teachers occurs only in the wake of that theological conviction. Observe that Hebrews 13 summons attention to imitation the faith of the "leaders" who "taught you the Word of God" (13.7) only because the object of their faith remains steadfast today: "Jesus Christ is the same yesterday, today, and forever" (13.8). The witness of the minister only carries authoritative weight in as much as the abiding object of that ecclesiastical testimony remains faithful. Jesus was, is, and shall be; therefore, his Word and the church's witness to that Word can be trusted.[53]

We might also ask, what kind of posture should such a churchly creature of the Word exhibit in her journey? The dependence of the church upon God's Word, spoken unto her from the outside, finds fruition in the stature of faith and the stance of trust. We attend to it. We are alert about it. And we pray unto him for illumination unto that end. Reliance upon the divine Word, then, betokens a posture that does anything but beef up the status quo of sinners. By attesting the whole counsel of God—his Word again and again—we see that our sinful self-fascinations find themselves exposed and judged afresh.[54]

---

52. For further reflections on the gospel promise for theological contemplation, see Chapter 1 ("In Your Light Do We See Light").

53. In this vein we profess to "believe the holy, catholic church" rather than "believing in the holy, catholic church" (see Calvin, *Institutes*, IV.i.2).

54. See especially John Webster, "Culture: The Shape of Theological Practice," *Stimulus* 6, no. 4 (Nov. 1998), 2–9; repr. in John Webster, *The Culture of Theology* (ed. Ivor J. Davidson and Alden C. McCray; Grand Rapids: Baker Academic, 2019), 43–62.

Second, we can and should also ask how that kind of health will help guide our theological culture toward a particular end. We can return to the Son's instruction regarding the way in which his Word abides in us, unto the goal of flourishing. Notice that he pushes beyond the obvious lineaments of the metaphor of the vine and its fruit at the end here. Far from simply speaking of survival of the branch, he depicts fruit (verse 8) or the keeping of his commandments (verse 10). What marks the fruitful, obedient person? Two things: (1) abiding in his love, that love shared originally with the Father, and (2) possessing his joy to the fullest, the very joy that carried him in his darkest hours (Heb. 12.2). While our frame is dependent and our posture is one of attentive listening to another, this proves to be the pathway to glory for that other is Glory Personified. As it is no knock on creation's glory that it was summoned into being by the voice of God on high (so Gen. 1.1), so it is no dismissal of the integrity or beauty of the church that she was born of and abides wholly upon God's Word. Indeed, therein lies her strange glory and thus is displayed the gospel from which she draws her life.

Chapter 4

DIVINE TRANSCENDENCE AND THE READING OF SCRIPTURE

Reading and Revealing—Impasse?

Recent discussion regarding the reading of Scripture has suffered from much confusion. Many evangelicals (and Protestants more generally) have pled for the primacy of divine action in revelation. For their own part, many catholic-minded theologians have explored the necessity of human activity, particularly in its ecclesial form. Both accounts have much for which to be commended and leave much to be desired. The bipolar nature of the debate, however, bespeaks the confused nature of doctrinal formulation in these days. Both sides have assumed that their emphasis competes with the concerns of the other side—such an assumption may seem politically savvy, though it fails to sit well with the traditional doctrine of divine transcendence. Given the nature of God's difference (or transcendence), affirmation of his agency need not imply distance from human activity.

A dogmatic argument of God's transcendence will be shown to necessitate discussion of both divine and human action. According to classical Christian doctrine, God's transcendence and otherness allow for and do not impede creaturely activity. God is divine. Humans are not. God is his own existence. Humans exist as God's own. For humans to be free to act is not to take causal authority away from God. Rather, God's fullness provides for and grants existence to creaturely causal agency. At least since the rise of nominalism in the high Middle Ages, Christian theology has begun to sense tension between the existence of divine and human action.[1]

---

1. The tie between a competitive view of divine and human action and the rise of nominalism cannot be defended in this chapter. In short, the nominalist consideration of God and humanity under the umbrella of a common concept of "being" allows for a competitive view of causality. Whether or not this competitive view and the tension that it creates between scriptural and doctrinal affirmations of both divine sovereignty and human responsibility can be tied to the rise of nominalism will not be discussed here. The tie of nominalism to the persons of Duns Scotus and William of Ockham cannot be discussed here either—controversial as this may be. For discussion on this issue of nominalism's influence and the role of Scotus, in particular, see the fascinating debate in *Modern Theology*

Competitiveness between divine and human activity is not necessary, traditional (in Christian doctrine), or gospel-centered.

A "thick description" of the reading of Scripture will be offered which takes account of both divine and human action.[2] To further this description, the recent work of Stephen Fowl and John Webster will be employed to explore the human and divine activities which, respectively, go into Christian reading of Scripture. Neither account stands alone, albeit for distinct reasons: divine revelation could occur apart from creaturely agency yet the triune God elects to work through such media, while human intellectual and spiritual activity quite literally cannot exist apart from God's agency. My argument will proceed in several steps: (1) a sketch of the apparent opposition between these two modes of theology: Christian pragmatism and dogmatic theology; (2) summary and critique of John Webster's account of the holiness of Scripture and Scriptural reading; (3) summary and critique of Stephen Fowl's account of Christian reading of Scripture for ecclesial formation; (4) dogmatic discussion of the doctrine of divine transcendence; (5) cautions related to the supposed need for a magisterium, the presence of indwelling sin, and the need to avoid an over-realized eschatology and pre-emptive assumption of interpretive closure; therefore, "thick description" is necessary to a Reformed-catholic theology. The necessity of "thick description" in depicting theological reality will be demonstrated dogmatically by engaging the doctrine of divine transcendence and found to be particularly fruitful in discussing the reading of Scripture. A Reformed-catholic account of Scriptural reading, tying Word to Spirit and also attending to the particular role of the ecclesial location of Scripture, will be shown to circumvent many of the wrong turns that have plagued recent reflection on Scripture and hermeneutics.[3]

The Apparent Opposition

Before examining the works of Webster and Fowl in some depth, a few initial remarks regarding their apparent disjunction will be helpful. By plotting Webster and Fowl within the current hermeneutical debate, the disjunction will be adequately highlighted.

---

21 (2005), 539–661; for an accessible introduction, see William Placher, *The Domestication of Transcendence: How Modern Thinking about God Went Wrong* (Louisville: Westminster John Knox, 1996).

2. Clifford Geertz, *The Interpretation of Culture: Selected Essays* (New York: Basic Books, 1973), 93–4.

3. Matthew Levering describes the plague as such: "[P]resumptive nominalist metaphysics has limited the ability of many modern biblical exegetes, and thus also of many modern theologians, to read Scripture in the ways required by the Scriptural revelation of divine providence as the order of divine gift" (Matthew Levering, "Participation and Exegesis: Response to Catherine Pickstock," *Modern Theology* 21 [2005], 597).

Current hermeneutical debate, at least within Christian circles, revolves around questions regarding the ontology of texts, the structure and genre of texts, and the possibilities for reading. Textual ontology relates to the role of authors in the life of the text beyond the initial speech-act: Do author's intentions or motives define meaning? Can such a thing as either an author's intention or an author's motive be discovered within a text?[4] Structures of texts receive much discussion, particularly by those who have answered these two questions with a "no." If meaning is not lodged primarily within some notion of authorial action, the particular structure of a text may be the key to adjudicating meanings of words and phrases.[5] Finally, if authorial action and textual structure do not result in crystal-clear meaning, readerly action must pick up the slack. Some continue to posit that readers can apprehend authorial action; however, many now argue that readers' interpretation, in some degree, changes the speech-act and helps create meaning (to some degree or another).[6] These three questions might be helpfully related to three movements within literary theory: Romanticist theory, New Criticism, and post-structuralism.[7]

Fowl advocates a hermeneutic which emphasizes the role of readerly activity in the interpretative process. Fowl explicitly argues for the possibility of apprehending some type of authorial intention in the text. But this is not *the* meaning of the text, though it may be quite helpful at times. Fowl is most interested in backing the debate up beyond the question of readerly possibilities to question the particular ends for which Christians interpret Scripture and the effects such reasons ought to have. Theory takes a backseat to questions of teleology. In short, Fowl advocates an *underdetermined* notion of interpretive pluralism as the best means by which Christians might flourish in interpreting the Scripture.

Webster comes at the debate from a different vantage point: that of dogmatic theology in the Reformed tradition. Previously known as an able interpreter of Barth and Jüngel, Webster has recently given much attention to the notion of *holiness*, particularly as it relates to Scripture. If we notice nothing else about Webster's project, we must notice the priority given to describing divine action in revelation, sanctification, and inspiration. Webster fears the equation of human action (even the human action of the *ecclesia*) with divine action, and he emphasizes the continual need to discuss reading as receptive of divine action (rather than being inventive).[8]

Webster and Fowl, then, are two strange bedfellows. The dogmatic theologian and the Christian pragmatist do not seem to have much in common. Both will

---

4. Vanhoozer, *Is There a Meaning in This Text?*, ch.2.
5. Ibid., ch.3.
6. Ibid., ch.4. See also Stanley J. Grenz and John R. Franke, *Beyond Foundationalism: Shaping Theology in a Postmodern Context* (Louisville: Westminster John Knox Press, 2001), esp. 72–5.
7. Vanhoozer, *Is There a Meaning in This Text?*, 25–9.
8. Webster, *Holiness*, 54–7.

be found to be correct (at least in some of their major assertions), however.⁹ To appreciate the particular payoff in a project of bringing these two into conversation, another dialogue must first be discussed: this one between Webster and another British theologian, David Ford.

David Ford published a highly innovative work, entitled *Self and Salvation: Being Transformed*.¹⁰ Webster offered an extended review which called into question Ford's entire conversational approach to theology.¹¹ Whereas Ford had engaged ideas and thinkers as disparate as Levinas, Ricouer, Jüngel, the Paulinist's letter to the Ephesians, the eucharist, Therese of Lisieux, and Dietrich Bonhoeffer in his monograph on human flourishing, Webster called for a more thoroughly dogmatic theology, centered on discussion of traditional *loci* such as election, justification, and so on. Ford, in response, noted the particular value of the type of *theological theology* for which Webster has been calling.¹² Ford noted the occasional need for both dogmatic and conversational modes of theology, even as he notes the necessity (but not sufficiency) of Webster's style of dogmatic theology.

The Christian doctrine of creation seems to necessitate that all sources of thought be taken seriously. The planting of the *imago Dei* within each and every human, both before and after the entrance of sin into the world, necessitates a thoughtful engagement with whatever form of divine attestation may be found in various discourses and sources (be they Christian or not). Such cross-disciplinary concern will grate on the modern institutional sensibilities of specialized professionals and the secular mindset which fears ideological mutation of objective data. A dogmatic account of creation will not allow for such restraint, although such an account will provide for a stringent caution against naively receiving the plunders of the Egyptians. Though the Christian *polis* must bring in guest lecturers from every part of the globe, consideration of such propaganda must be Word-centered and, therefore, distinctly Christian. This is not a pragmatic concern apart from its dogmatic foundation: the Spirit blows where he wills, but the Spirit is the Spirit of the Son and, therefore, attests to the Son's glory wherever it may blow (albeit more or less explicitly). Distinctly Christian engagement of disciplines and concerns

---

9. This broad agreement with Fowl and Webster should not be taken as comprehensive agreement. Both have certain weaknesses, some more pertinent than others, which will not be dealt with here unless necessary for my argument.

10. (Cambridge: Cambridge University Press, 1999).

11. Webster, "David F. Ford: *Self and Salvation*," *Scottish Journal of Theology* 54 (2001), 548-59. Ford has elsewhere noted the "conversational mood" of recent British theology to be its distinctive strength, by which theologians mediate their doctrinal concerns through topics of historical revision, feminism, economics, pluralism, etc. See "Theological Wisdom, British Style," *Christian Century* 117 (2000), 388-91.

12. John Webster, *Theological Theology: An Inaugural Lecture Delivered Before the University of Oxford on October 28, 1997* (Oxford: Clarendon, 1997); repr., *Confessing God: Essays in Christian Dogmatics II* (London: T&T Clark, 2005), ch.1.

distinguished from theological study (in modern times, though not classically) is mandated by the doctrine of creation.[13]

The "linguistic turn" has, if nothing else, demonstrated that theological use of language will necessarily demonstrate affinity with other sociocultural uses of language. Theology cannot testify to the gospel in culture apart from use of cultural terminology—classically, language from philosophical discourse. Webster's project, if it is seeking a dogmatic theology free of philosophy, must be doomed to failure.[14] At best, one can offer a plea for the primacy of distancing engagement with philosophy from the theological task or for emphasis upon traditional areas of dogmatic inquiry (as opposed to current philosophical debate). Such a concern might be prophetic in our day, when more and more theological monographs fail to engage traditional dogmatic concerns at all.[15] John Milbank and Catherine Pickstock have also pled for the overcoming or consummation of philosophy.[16] Such concerns tend to be tied to historical judgments regarding the effects of particular philosophical commitments to the freedom in which Christian theology can attest to the gospel and ought to be read in that context.

Webster's plea ought to be charitably read as a plea against the broad retreat of theologians into doing *mere* philosophy, sociology, hermeneutics, or seemingly anything other than distinctive Christian doctrine. Barth argued against the *analogia entis* and the captivity of theologians to philosophy in its neo-scholastic and Kantian permutations. Barth never sheds the engagements and use of philosophical terms, categories, and interests, however.[17] Milbank and Pickstock

---

13. See, e.g., the intent of "Radical Orthodoxy" to be "more mediating and less accommodating" in John Milbank, Catherine Pickstock, and Graham Ward (eds.), *Radical Orthodoxy: A New Theology* (Radical Orthodoxy; London: Routledge, 1999), 2. I have noted my own concerns elsewhere about Radical Orthodoxy as a dogmatic proposal, amidst an appreciation for their work in cultural exegesis; see my "Putting Suspenders on the World: Radical Orthodoxy as a Post-Secular Theological Proposal *or* What Can Evangelicals Learn from Postmodern Christian Platonists?" *Themelios* 31, no. 2 (Jan. 2006), 40–53.

14. See the polemics especially in Karl Barth, *Church Dogmatics*, Volume II.1: *The Doctrine of God* (ed. G. W. Bromiley and T. F. Torrance; transl. T. H. L. Parker et al; Edinburgh: T&T Clark, 1957).

15. For example, Jürgen Moltmann wrote an entire "systematic contribution to theology" on Christology without once mentioning the Council of Chalcedon (*The Way of Jesus Christ: Christology in Messianic Dimensions* [transl. Margaret Kohl; Minneapolis: Fortress, 1994]).

16. John Milbank, "Only Theology Overcomes Metaphysics," in *Word Made Strange: Language, Theology, Culture* (Oxford: Blackwell, 1997), ch. 2; Catherine Pickstock, *After Writing: On the Liturgical Consummation of Philosophy* (Challenges in Contemporary Theology; Oxford: Blackwell, 1999).

17. Bruce L. McCormack, *Karl Barth's Critically Realistic Dialectical Theology: Its Genesis and Development* (Oxford: Clarendon, 1997). McCormack notes the continual use of a somewhat chastened Idealism in Barth's developed theology.

have shown little restraint in their polemic regarding nominalism and its modern and neo-scholastic bastards.[18] No reader could ever claim that in so doing they leave philosophy behind. In fact, Milbank's epoch-making book, *Theology and Social Theory*, is notably subtitled *Beyond Secular Reason*, rather than behind social theory or sociology.[19] Milbank continues to be chock-full of sociological and political concern and has no desire to leave such disciplines behind *en toto*. Rather, Milbank attempts to get beyond a particular secular version of social theory by use of Augustinian metaphysics.[20]

Hyperbolic language, as found in Webster, Milbank, and Barth, ought to be read within its particular polemical context. Milbank wants to move theology beyond a "false humility," because "once theology surrenders its claim to be a meta-discourse, it cannot any longer articulate the word of the creator God, but is bound to turn into the oracular voice of some finite idol, such as historical scholarship, humanist psychology, or transcendental philosophy."[21] At the end of the day, however, such hyperbolic exhortation cannot stand alone. Christian theology must engage other disciplines. Such engagement must and should take various forms, categories, and moods.[22] Though Webster's concerns regarding the danger of losing truly *theological* moods of doing theology must be heeded, Ford persuasively depicts the need for multiple architectural designs in the theological city.[23]

Having stated these concerns tied to the doctrine of creation and the necessary multiplicity of theological forms, it will now be demonstrated that the theological designs erected by Webster and Fowl mutually complement one another and, when taken together, go a long way toward a theological depiction of the task

---

18. Milbank, Pickstock, and the "Radical Orthodoxy" movement tie the "false humility" of theology to its embrace of the univocity of being and nominalist metaphysics and tie this decline to the influence of Duns Scotus, in particular, argued most recently by Catherine Pickstock ("Duns Scotus: His Historical and Contemporary Significance," *Modern Theology* 21 [2005], 543–73). Etienne Gilson predated this claim in his *Jean Duns Scot: introduction à ses positions fondamentales* (Paris: Librairie Philosophique J. Vrin, 1952).

19. John Milbank, *Theology and Social Theory: Beyond Secular Reason* (Signposts in Theology; Oxford: Blackwell, 1990).

20. Ibid., chs.11–12.

21. Ibid., 1.

22. That such multiplicity is not mere submission to historical necessity may be evidenced by the existence of the fourfold gospel witness in Scripture (each of which engages various cultural terms and categories—imperial cult, Greco-Roman religion, etc.); see William Placher, *Narratives of a Vulnerable God: Christ, Theology, and Scripture* (Louisville: Westminster John Knox, 1994), ch.4.

23. David F. Ford, "Salvation and the Nature of Theology: A Response to John Webster's Review of *Self and Salvation: Being Transformed*," *Scottish Journal of Theology* 54 (2001), 560–75.

of reading Scripture.²⁴ Webster's dogmatic project provides theological space for description of human reading, and Fowl's depiction of readerly activity requires a theological account of divine action as related to the notion of vigilant or intrusive reading.

Webster and Divine Revelation

Webster has offered an account of the ontology of Scripture as a means of interaction with recent hermeneutical discussion in modern theology.²⁵ Both fundamentalism and liberalism have fallen prey to a common problem: lack of a theological ontology.²⁶ Current hermeneutical theory, likewise, suffers the fate of anemic discussion of ontology.²⁷ The danger of ontological discussion will be the tendency to slip into phenomenological depiction of readerly activity tied to a flawed metaphysics; therefore, a distinctly *theological* ontology will be necessary.²⁸ Such a concern leads Webster to deny all attempts which begin by constructing a general hermeneutic to, then, apply to the reading of Scripture.²⁹

Webster outlines four points that must be made in discussion of Christian reading of Scripture: (1) God is present and communicative in Himself as Word to us; (2) the Bible is primarily an instrument of divine action and, only secondarily, a text-act; (3) the primary modes of being human are having faith, hearing, and obeying (creatureliness precedes creativity); (4) such description must be description of the *church's* reading (as *creatura Verbi divini*).³⁰

Such a theological ontology requires that primacy be given to Trinitarian description.³¹ The uniquely *self-manifesting* revelation of God, an ingredient part of the Trinitarian life, commands attention.³² God's self-communication is free, sovereign, and spiritually purposeful. Webster notes that the term "Word of God" is a good deal preferable to "revelation," as it denotes the particular presence of

---

24. Much more would need to be said about the inspiration of prophets and apostles, the acknowledgment of the canon, and the perfections of Holy Scripture. I am limiting my discussion here to the *reading* of Holy Scripture construed as a theological act.

25. Most pertinent to Webster's hermeneutical discussion will be *Holy Scripture* (Cambridge: Cambridge University Press, 2003); idem, "Hermeneutics in Modern Theology: Some Doctrinal Reflections," in *Word and Church: Essays in Christian Dogmatics* (Edinburgh: T&T Clark, 2001), 47–86; idem, *Holiness*.

26. Webster, *Holy Scripture*, 21.
27. Webster, "Hermeneutics in Modern Theology," 49.
28. Ibid., 58.
29. Ibid., 58–9.
30. Ibid., 64.
31. Ibid., 65.
32. Webster, *Holy Scripture*, 13; idem, "Hermeneutics in Modern Theology," 66.

Jesus which commissions our reading in the Spirit.[33] The presence of Jesus, in fact, demonstrates the incarnational principle of *sacramentum*, the hallowing of creaturely reality for divine purposes, which Webster will apply to Scripture.[34]

The Bible must then be placed within the life of the Triune God. Webster reiterates, again and again, that in moving from depiction of the Triune God to that of the Bible, one has not left the doctrine of God behind. In fact, "Christian theology has a singular preoccupation: God and everything else *sub specie divinitatis*. All other Christian doctrines are applications or corollaries of the one doctrine, the doctrine of the Trinity."[35] The Bible is an instrument of divine action, best described by the categories of revelation, sanctification, and inspiration.[36] The sacramental depiction allows both the divine and human action of the Scripture to be discussed by taking particular note of the *indirect* nature of God's "real and effective" agency.[37] The Bible, then, is both dynamic and partially determined; therefore, meaning is never final.[38] God remains free to speak continually through the particularly human conventions of the text-act in fresh ways. By noting that the Bible's holiness is due to God's hallowing of it, objectification of the text-act is avoided.[39] More importantly, the instrumental nature of Scripture distances it from the *Logos*, avoiding immanentist and incarnational depictions of Scripture which fail to do justice to the unique nature of the *Logos ensarkos*.[40] Christology, particularly affirmation of the unique lordship of the God-man, retains precedence to bibliology, precisely because Christ is the Word of God in a personal sense which surpasses the identity of Scripture as "word of God."

The being of Holy Scripture is its reference to revelation, using textual visibility to witness to the *viva vox Dei*.[41] In short, Webster articulates (though not in so many words) that "the being of Holy Scripture is in becoming."[42] Throughout his discussion, Webster "relativizes the Bible, because to talk of the text as an instrument of divine action is primarily to say something about God, not about

---

33. Webster, "Hermeneutics in Modern Theology," 68–70. Stanley Hauerwas has suggested to me in correspondence that talk of revelation "constantly threatens to become an epistemological category, which it plainly is not." Webster avoids this by witnessing to divine antecedence.

34. Webster, *Holy Scripture*, 17–8, 21.

35. Ibid., 43.

36. Ibid., ch.1.

37. Webster, "Hermeneutics in Modern Theology," 74.

38. Ibid., 72.

39. Webster, *Holy Scripture*, 30–4.

40. Ibid., 23.

41. Ibid., 49–50.

42. Bruce McCormack, "The Being of Holy Scripture Is in Becoming: Karl Barth in Conversation with American Evangelical Criticism," in *Evangelicals and Scripture: Tradition, Authority, and Hermeneutics* (eds V. Bacote, L. Miguelez, and D. Ockholm; Downers Grove, IL: InterVarsity Press, 2004), 55–75.

the text."[43] Dogmatic theology can only address Scripture as being within the economy of salvation, an aspect of creaturely reality set apart by God for his particular purposes at particular times.[44] By relativizing the Bible to this wider context in particular (the divine economy), Webster claims to ground Scripture on a surer, stronger footing.

Webster chastens the hermeneutical discussion by referring to interaction with the Scriptural texts as "reading" rather than the more pro-active term "interpretation."[45] In fact, "reading Holy Scripture is 'faithful' reading: exegetical reason caught up in faith's abandonment of itself to the power of the divine Word to slay and to make alive."[46] Readers do not actualize the text, nor do they finish its text-act (at least not in an ultimate sense). Rather, readers demonstrate true humanity by means of faith, hearing, and obedience.[47] Webster continually brings in language of mortification and vivification to describe the effects of consensual reading, addressing a particular danger of radical reader-response criticism.[48] The particularly *intrusive* nature of mortification seems to rule out any theory which states that readers have an unchecked ability to construct textual meaning.[49]

Likewise, in limiting the creaturely ability to manipulate the text-act, Webster also limits the need for the elite to decipher the text-act. The clarity or perspicuity of the text is a divine quality bestowed upon the text so that it might be termed "self-interpreting."[50] As he puts it, "Scripture's clarity is neither an intrinsic element of the text as text nor simply a fruit of exegetical labor; it is that which the text becomes as it functions in the Spirit-governed encounter between the self-presenting Savior and the faithful reader."[51] While "reading Scripture cannot but involve the acts which are part of all reading: construing words, grasping their relationships, following a narrative or argument, and so on,"[52] much more is going on than human ingenuity. Graciously, the "Spirit has been and continues to be given to illuminate the reader, and so exegetical reason may trust the promise of Christ to lead us into the truth by the Spirit's presence and power."[53] The divine role in human reading is overwhelmingly emphasized in Webster's account of the receptive posture of faithful humans before Scripture.

Finally, Webster describes the particularly *ecclesial* nature of reading Scripture. The reading of Scripture requires certain "dispositions and skills which are deployed

---

43. Webster, "Hermeneutics in Modern Theology," 73.
44. Telford Work, *Living and Active: Scripture in the Economy of Salvation* (Sacra Doctrina; Grand Rapids: Eerdmans, 2002).
45. Webster, *Holy Scripture*, 86.
46. Ibid.
47. Webster, "Hermeneutics in Modern Theology," 82.
48. Ibid., 80–1.
49. Ibid., 84.
50. Webster, *Holy Scripture*, 93–5.
51. Ibid., 95.
52. Ibid., 91.
53. Ibid.

by the wise Christian reader" and can only be cultivated within the church.[54] Webster's contribution to discussion of the corporate nature of interpretation/reading lies in his warning that talk of the "corporate aspects of Christian reading ... not allow theological language about the church to dissolve into generic language about 'forms of life,' 'sociality,' even 'ecclesiality.'"[55] The church, the elect community of the intrusive grace of Christ, requires distinctly theological description at the communal level.[56] As with the individual, "the church, if it reads well, always reads against itself."[57] Ruled behavior will provide the type of skills and structures in which proper receptive reading might take place to chasten and exhort the community of God's electing work. The witness of the Spirit in the church ever points to the Word, requiring distinctly Christian explication.[58]

John Webster has articulated the place of Scripture within the economy of God's saving grace. At each step, he has articulated all actions *sub specie divinitatis*. Human action, while not denied or ignored, is accorded a secondary role in theological description of reality. Such an account provides theological space for description of human action in the activity of reading and will be quite incomplete apart from such depiction. Webster's account must precede that of Fowl, ontologically speaking, for divine action precedes (prevenes) and provides for (creates) creaturely activity. The doctrines of creation and election necessitate intellectually rigorous attention be directed at the particular human means by which God reveals himself; such leads us to the need for an account of human interpretation and its provision by the work of Fowl, considered secondarily and *sub specie divinitatis*.

Fowl and Faithful Reading

Stephen Fowl has written a book quite different from Webster's *Holy Scripture*. Four points provide a rather helpful path through his picture of theological interpretation of Scripture: (1) access to authorial intention is plausible, albeit in a chastened form; (2) human authorial intention is not *the* exclusive meaning of

---

54. Webster, "Hermeneutics in Modern Theology," 85.
55. Ibid.
56. Such is the danger of interacting with much postmodern theory: that Christians would be content to depict their existence (individually and/or corporately) in merely sociocultural terms with nonecclesial carryover. The warnings of George Lindbeck to allow the text to absorb the world, while one-sided, provide a helpful supplement to such secular jargon (*The Nature of Doctrine: Religion and Theology in a Postliberal Age* [Philadelphia: Westminster Press, 1984]). See George Hunsinger, "Postliberal Theology," in *The Cambridge Companion to Postmodern Theology* (ed. Kevin J. Vanhoozer; Cambridge Companions to Religion; Cambridge: Cambridge University Press, 2003), 42–57.
57. Webster, "Hermeneutics in Modern Theology," 86.
58. Webster, *Word and Church*, ch.7.

Scripture; (3) theological interpretation has as its goal the cultivation of virtue and excellence among the people of God; and (4) an *under*determined theory of interpretation will provide a more helpful manner for talk of meaning. In short, Fowl's account of readerly activity supplements Webster's account of activity and, in fact, requires something like the account of divine action provided by Webster to account for the vigilance and mortification present in Christian reading of Scripture.

First, Fowl has revived the importance of the author by positing that her intentions can, in fact, be evident in texts and apprehended by readers.[59] Intentions and motives must be distinguished, avoiding tying intentions to psychological factors involved in the writing of the text, which answer the question, "*Why* is the author doing this?" Rather, intentions answer the question, "*What* is the author doing here?"[60] Finitude and sinfulness limit the author's self-knowledge, thus making the quest for motives perilous for the author and even more so for the reader.[61] Intentions, in contrast to motives, are present in the grammatical, linguistic, and rhetorical features of the particular text and, therefore, can be apprehended by the conscientious interpreter.[62] Such intentions can be spoken of in a "coherent and constrained way."[63] Fowl, in short, has argued for the possibility that one might encounter the author's intentions in the reading of a text.

Second, Fowl places great emphasis upon the need for interpreters to note the plurality of interpretive interests and, therefore, resist claims to exclusivity with regard to meaning.[64] Fowl continues to affirm the plausibility of referring to the author's intention as a meaning of the text; however, it is simply *a* meaning and may not be the most useful meaning at any given time or place.[65] Any attempt to limit meaning to human authorial intention is question-begging, for the definition of meaning is exactly what everyone seems to disagree about.[66] Fowl perceives the lack of "a general, comprehensive theory of textual meaning that is neither arbitrary nor question-begging."[67] Not only is "any attempt to tie a single stable account of meaning to authorial intention" theoretically problematic, it also places Christians

---

59. Stephen, Fowl, "The Role of Authorial Intention in the Theological Interpretation of Scripture," in *Between Two Horizons: Spanning New Testament Studies and Systematic Theology* (eds Joel B. Green and Max Turner; Grand Rapids: Eerdmans, 2000), 73-7.
60. Fowl, "The Role of Authorial Intention," 74.
61. Ibid., 73.
62. Ibid., 75.
63. Ibid., 73.
64. Ibid., 77-82; see also Stephen Fowl, *Engaging Scripture* (Oxford: Blackwell, 1998), ch.2 (esp. 33-40).
65. Fowl, "The Role of Authorial Intention," 86. As I note in fn. 110, Fowl's movement beyond the human authorial intention may be nuanced by interaction with the practice of typological and/or figural reading by the post-Reformation Reformed orthodox theologians.
66. Fowl, "The Role of Authorial Intention," 79; idem, *Engaging Scripture*, 35.
67. Ibid.

in an "awkward relationship to the OT."[68] Fowl also notes that, even in the robust medieval fourfold interpretation of Scripture, the so-called *determinate* meaning (*sensus literalis*, or literal) was anything but single and static. He demonstrates that advocates of tying meaning exclusively to human authorial intention have to write off centuries of Christian interpretation as methodologically skewed and theologically misleading.[69] In summary, Fowl has argued that for theoretical, theological, and historical reasons, human authorial intention can and should only be one of several meanings of Scripture.

Third, Fowl has centered the hermeneutical conversation on the particular ends for which Christians are to interpret and embody Scripture.[70] Christians are to read Scripture so as to live faithfully before God and deepen communion with God and others in their present context; therefore, varying contexts will require various styles of reading.[71] "Theological interpretation of Scripture therefore needs, ultimately, to advance these ends for which Christians are called to interpret Scripture."[72] Following Alasdair MacIntyre, Fowl affirms the particularly canonical (or text-based) focus of communal argument which fosters creativity in faithfulness to the tradition.[73] The practical necessity of embodying Scripture for all Christians necessitates a theory of interpretation that renders the Bible accessible to all Christians, avoiding a magisterial elitism. Fowl, drawing on the trenchant historical work of Eugene Rogers, finds such a theory in Thomas's notion of the *sensus literalis*, a diverse "plain sense" of Scripture.[74] As discussed above, many texts in the OT do not minister to the people of God now apart from a creative

---

68. Ibid., 80. To note the difficulty of tying meaning solely to human authorial intention, see David Steinmetz, "The Superiority of Pre-Critical Exegesis," in *The Theological Interpretation of Scripture: Classic and Contemporary Readings* (ed. Stephen E. Fowl; Oxford: Blackwell, 1997), 28.

69. Fowl, "The Role of Authorial Intention," 82–5; see also Eugene Rogers, "How the Virtues of the Interpreter Presuppose and Perfect Hermeneutics: The Case of Thomas Aquinas," *Journal of Religion* 76 (1996), 65. Rogers notes that, while the *sensus literalis* is that which the author intends, Thomas understood God to be the primary author of Scripture. Such a divine view of Scripture's authorship led Thomas to emphasize the diversity of literal meanings.

70. In addition to "The Role of Authorial Intention" and *Engaging Scripture*, see also Stephen, Fowl and L. Gregory Jones, *Reading in Communion: Scripture & Ethics in Christian Life* (Grand Rapids: Eerdmans, 1991), esp. chs.1–3 and 7.

71. Fowl, "The Role of Authorial Intention," 86–7.

72. Ibid., 86.

73. Fowl, *Engaging Scripture*, 6–7. Note that Fowl emphasizes the functional authority of Scripture in the church. Such a non-ontological argument, of course, is not necessarily contradictory to an ontological description of Scripture's authority (as in Webster's argument for Scripture's *holiness*); see also Alasdair MacIntyre, *After Virtue: A Study in Moral Theory* (2nd ed.; Notre Dame: University of Notre Dame Press, 1984).

74. Fowl, *Engaging Scripture*, 38–9; Rogers, "Virtues," 65–74.

4. Divine Transcendence and Reading of Scripture 61

re-reading in light of later revelation.[75] The particular ends for which Christians read Scripture necessitate diverse methods of reading at particular times and places, leading Fowl to argue for a pragmatic theory of meaning which acknowledges a plurality of methods as useful.[76]

Finally, Fowl advances what he calls an *underdetermined* theory of interpretation which will posit some manner of determinancy without tying meaning solely to the human authorial intention.[77] Fowl attempts to navigate between two foils: (1) those who tie meaning solely to authorial intention, and (2) those who attempt to deconstruct any and every attempt to read a text. Fowl, while noting the benefits of acknowledging the unfinished work of interpretation, finds deconstructive theorists to be guilty on three accounts: (1) limiting interpretation to professional readers, who have the wherewithal to find determinate meaning and overthrow it;[78] (2) poor historical narration of the metaphysics of presence;[79] and (3) exalting text *qua* text to the point of denying the possibility of interaction with the other (author) apart from violence.[80] By noting the determinate nature of texts, with certain formal limits (i.e., grammar, rhetoric, etc.), Fowl argues that the meaning of Scripture will, for a Christian, fall within a certain field or matrix allowed by the *regula fidei*.[81] Christian accounts of the Triune God and his engagement with

---

75. Fowl mentions the French monk who must preach Psalm 137 in the fourteenth century, the famed example of Steinmetz in his essay on "The Superiority of Pre-Critical Exegesis," 28.

76. Here Fowl's argument is particularly weak in that he fails to offer broader salvation-historical parameters within which the OT may be reappropriated by the people of God after the ascension of Christ. His lack of interest in salvation-historical movements paves the way for his errant reading of Acts 10-15 regarding parallels to the full inclusion of practicing homosexuals into the church. For all his interest in the history of biblical interpretation, Fowl has failed to notice that interpreters as diverse as Origen, Augustine, Thomas, Calvin, and Barth all value the necessity of salvation-historical development for Christian reading of Scripture (obviously in different ways, as seen in comparing Origen to the others). Such is the hermeneutical problem best expressed by Fowl's dogmatic weakness: a tendency to sever the witness of the Spirit from the ministry of the Word; see Katherine Greene-mccreight, *Ad Litteram: How Augustine, Calvin, and Barth Read the "Plain Sense" of Genesis 1-3* (Issues in Systematic Theology 5; New York: Peter Lang, 1999), ch.1. For further response to his reading of Acts 10-15, see Michael Allen and Scott R. Swain, *Reformed Catholicity*, 74-8, 112-13.

77. Fowl, *Engaging Scripture*, 56ff.

78. Ibid., 47.

79. Fowl, *Engaging Scripture*, 48-52. Fowl makes particular note of the manner in which Catherine Pickstock demonstrates the ways in which to avoid finality in interpretation without overthrowing the entire Western metaphysical tradition. See Pickstock, *After Writing*.

80. Fowl, *Engaging Scripture*, 55-6.

81. Stephen, Fowl, "The Conceptual Structure of New Testament Theology," in *Biblical Theology: Retrospect and Prospect* (ed. Scott J. Hafemann; Downers Grove: InterVarsity Press, 2002), 232-5.

the world in the story of Israel and Christ provide limits to the range of meanings which may be drawn from the canonical Scripture. Where other meanings may be drawn out by Marxists or Muslims, such readings will not be Christian readings unless they conform to this *regula fidei*. Meaning must make sense of the words. Careful attention to the particular textual features cannot be avoided. But meaning may be quite diverse and, oftentimes, will enjoin supplementation of human authorial intent, precisely within these ecclesially noted (and we might add: biblically sketched) limits.[82]

Fowl has argued that Scripture ought to be interpreted for its *underdetermined* meaning—without adherence to one particular method, but with a constant eye to the *regula fidei* and the ends for which Christians are to interpret Scripture, particularly the cultivation of virtue and faithfulness. Webster's discussion of receptive reading and the communal task of virtuous listening resounds with clarity in Fowl's depiction of charitable conversation with fellow readers present and past within the church. The mutual inherence of both accounts is only rendered possible by a classical account of divine transcendence which provides for a noncompetitive account of divine and human action and allows radical immanence of the wholly other lord who speaks.

God Transcends Creation: Joseph, Compatibilism, and Noncompetitiveness

In this attempt to draw on the strengths of both Webster and Fowl, differentiation of modes of discourse must be sustained. These theologians are not doing the same thing; however, that does not mean that they cannot be describing the same thing in different ways or genres. The doctrine of divine transcendence, characterizing the categorical distinction between God and world, must be articulated to account for the diversity of human reports on the event of Scriptural reading.

At this point, it would be helpful to remember the climactic statement uttered by Joseph: "As for you, you planned evil against me, but God planned it for good" (Gen. 50.20). Use of the same verb, *hasab*, to denote the actions of both his brothers and God demonstrates that Joseph sees one action (or series of actions) from two perspectives. Human actions have been described in the preceding 13 chapters (and accurately so). Only now (with the sole exception of Joseph's statement in Gen. 45.5-9) are these very same events articulated as properly *theological* events,

---

82. Fowl, "The Role of Authorial Intention," 85. By adding the phrase "biblically sketched," I mean to affirm that Fowl's account affirms the pluriform nature of meaning (oftentimes) at the expense of singular canonical unity about the *res* of Holy Scripture. While noting the discontinuities in revelation at various stages of redemptive history, a deeper appreciation for the biblical-theological continuity of the covenant of grace would be instructive.

divine actions.[83] Such multiperspectival description of action occurs throughout the Scriptures,[84] demonstrating the simultaneous work of God and humans in the events of history. The hermeneutical point to be taken is this: both modes of discourse are appropriate and correct and, at the same time, partial apart from each other. A dogmatic argument such as this entails discussion of the divine attribute of transcendence, a characterization of the distinction between God and world. Philosophers have attested such a distinction in the articulation of various *compatibilist theories* regarding the relationship of divine and human action, which require that one encourage description of both divine and human action as it pertains to Scriptural reading. Without endorsing such philosophical accounts *as is*, the particular import of a doctrine of transcendence can be sketched by articulating the pay-off of compatibilism.

A *compatibilist theory* commonly entails that "determinism does not undermine freedom and responsibility."[85] Without entering into the quagmire of debate regarding degrees of determinism, definitions of liberty and responsibility, or the applicability of the term "determinism" to the Trinitarian interaction with human history, it must be said that something approximating the *compatibilist* commonality would necessitate the assignment of intellectual effort to description of both levels of action—divine determination or action and human action or responsibility. Applied to the current hermeneutical discussion, two currents of thought must be present: description of revelation (a divine action) and reading (a human activity). Both descriptions must be attempted and not played off against one another, chastening one another without calling one another's right to exist into question. There is no tension.

Perhaps the best way to characterize such a *compatibilist* theory of interpretation would be as an attempt to offer a "thick description" of human and divine action centered on the readerly interaction with the canonical texts of the Church.

---

83. The narrator, of course, knows that the dream recounted in Genesis 37 has been at work all along; however, the theological characterization of the actions of Joseph's brothers is only now presented in hindsight for pedagogical purposes (i.e., comfort). See Walter Brueggemann, *Genesis* (Interpretation; Atlanta: John Knox Press, 1982), 370–4; for similar judgments regarding the larger context of Genesis, see Murray H. Lichtenstein, "An Interpersonal Theology of the Hebrew Bible," in *Jews, Christians, and the Theology of the Hebrew Scriptures* (eds Alice O. Bellis and Joel S. Kaminsky; SBLSS 8; Atlanta: SBL, 2000), 61–82.

84. Victor P. Hamilton notes the later parallels to the multi-perspectivalism present in the Joseph-story in the stories of Daniel, Esther, Ruth, and (most explicitly) Judas (*Genesis* [NICOT; Grand Rapids: Eerdmans, 1995], 707). The most extreme example of multiperspectival rendering of an action is Peter's interpretation of the crucifixion in Acts 2.23—addressing both the divine action of delivering Christ to death, and the sinful action of the humans who brought about his murder. This was the greatest act of love and the greatest sin.

85. Ishtiygue Haji, "Compatibilist Views of Freedom and Responsibility," in *The Oxford Handbook of Free Will* (ed. Robert Kane; Oxford: Oxford University Press, 2002), 202.

Dogmatic reflection on the gospel requires one to center such an account on the traditional doctrine of divine transcendence. God is wholly other than creation, so the tradition has argued. God's activity, therefore, cannot be competing with human activity. Rather, God's activity actually enables humans to live, move, and have our very being. Applied to scriptural reading, such an account must take note of the manner in which God uses human texts to reveal Himself to others, without neglecting the human activity of reading to hear God's speech.

The doctrine of divine transcendence, undercut for too long by the univocity of being, has found recent prominence in the writings of Kathryn Tanner.[86] Tanner has emphasized the gift-giving which is at the heart of the gospel: the Triune God granting life and freedom to creation.[87] Classic accounts of transcendence are mined from the texts of Thomas Aquinas and John Calvin, who are found to hold to the noncompetitiveness of divine and human action in the most thoroughgoing manner.[88] A "god of the gaps" would find no place in such an account, for Tanner and the classical tradition suggest that creational activity accounts for all events. Obviously, epistemic limitations will limit humans from ascertaining such causality in varying degrees with regard to different events. But the causality of created beings remains total—extending to all occurrences.[89] Renaissance humanists were right to attempt to account for the immanent causes of natural events. The classical account provides for the broadest account of creational agency and freedom on the market: God gives life and agency to created beings.

But the secular naturalists went wrong in assuming that their accounts, insofar as they link natural causes to observable effects, negate the simultaneous agency of the Triune God. A Christian account of divine transcendence will remind us that God is completely other, veiled beyond our sight and fluid beyond our categories of conceptuality. God cannot be accounted for by Newton or Einstein, for he is utterly different from composite, created beings. God is spirit and utterly free to move and be. God's fullness is the very fount of creaturely freedom, for "the fuller the giver the greater the bounty to others."[90] God's freedom and completely actualized existence allow God to bless others with God's overflow of actuality. The breadth of divine sovereignty and actualization allows for human agency, rather than creating any perceived tension between two agents.

---

86. Kathryn Tanner, *God and Creation in Christian Theology: Tyranny or Empowerment?* (Oxford: Blackwell, 1988); idem, *Politics of God* (Minneapolis: Fortress, 1992); idem, *Jesus, Humanity, and the Trinity: A Brief Systematic Theology* (Minneapolis: Fortress, 2001); idem, *Economy of Grace* (Minneapolis: Fortress, 2005).

87. Tanner, *Jesus, Humanity, and the Trinity*, 1–2.

88. Ibid., 3; see also Tanner, *God and Creation in Christian Theology*, 105–19.

89. Miracles, traditionally called supernatural events, are the exceptions to the rule. But the traditional account of divine transcendence treats miracles as a subcategory of broader divine engagement of the world. Whether such a distinction is merely epistemic or also ontological remains a topic for debate.

90. Tanner, *Jesus, Humanity, and the Trinity*, 3.

The incarnation, when the Son of God took upon himself human form, represents the most intense example of this relationship between Creator and created. Two levels of agency, in contrast to all *monothelite* and *monophysite* tendencies, are within one person, this Jesus of Nazareth. Christ's divine agency, as judge and eternal Son, in no way undermines the genuine human agency of the obedient Nazarene. "Most generally, Jesus is the one in whom God's relationship with us attains perfection. In Jesus, unity with God takes a perfect form; here humanity has become God's own."[91] Perceived tension between the humanity and divinity of Christ fails to note the categorical distinction between these two levels of existence, Creator and created. Precisely because they are so distinct can they be so close: transcendence provides for immanence.[92]

A dogmatic account of divine transcendence which provides for radical immanence is a necessary prerequisite to any account of human action. Without such an account one will drift toward Pelagianism, with its faulty ontology and inadequate doxology, or into Stoic fatalism, with its inadequate account of the doctrines of creation and election. In short, a noncompetitive understanding of divine and human action proves essential to provide for an extensive theological account of any event within salvation-history.

John Webster has recently articulated this dogmatic distinction between divine and human existence in terms of God's immensity:

> in theological usage, transcendence, like infinity, is non-comparative: its content cannot be reached either by the magnification of creaturely properties (so that immensity is mere vastness) or by their negation (so that immensity is simply lack of spatial limitation). God's immensity is his qualitative distinction from creaturely reality, and can only be grasped on the basis of its enactment in the ways and works of God ... immensity is thus not quantitative disparity but a "differential of quality."[93]

Webster has yet to articulate the effects such an account should have upon the actual task of dogmatics: the freedom of God to create necessitates coextensive accounts of covenantal agency at both the human and divine levels.[94] Such a dogmatic account, with broad rhetorical similarity to philosophical accounts of compatibilism, must be in place for theological discussion of the reading of Scripture.

Christian interpretation of the OT requires mention at this point, for it is such textual interaction that has necessitated much of this debate. "Thick description" of such reading will not fail to include historical-critical study of what God did

---

91. Ibid., 9.
92. For further exposition, see Michael Allen, "Christ," in *The Knowledge of God: Essays on God, Christ, and Church* (London: T&T Clark, 2022), ch. 7.
93. Webster, *Confessing God*, 94.
94. See his forthcoming 2007 Kantzer Lectures for greater specificity in this regard: *Perfection and Presence: God with Us according to the Christian Confession* (Grand Rapids: Eerdmans, forthcoming).

through the original writers and compilers (as Jewish text *qua* Jewish text); however, it will also and essentially pay attention to the present appropriation of these texts as locales for God's speech to the church today (as Christian text *qua* Christian text). God does not speak to us the same way he spoke to Hosea and Joel. Yet God does not speak to us apart from how God spoke to Hosea and Joel.[95] As history has developed, moved forward, the people of God have the benefit of a history of listening. Present-day believers may hear the words God spoke to our ancestors, an inheritance to be ignored only at our peril. However, God continues to speak and requires constant attention. Scriptural reading in each context finds fresh meaning in the text, demonstrating God's faithfulness to speak to generation after generation in its own time and place. The origin of Scripture itself requires complex description, as divine and human action. However, the divine use of created reality to reveal himself continues even now and, therefore, contemporary readerly activity requires multiperspectival description as well.

In these varied instances of reading with their diverse range of meanings granted, humans are reading. At the same time, God is revealing: granting existence, providing proper cranial functioning, removing the fog of sinful limitation in some measure, and providing at least a hint of the *visio Dei*. Both God and creature are busy about their work. The task of theological reflection upon such an event cannot shortchange either agent's activity. All these elements will fit into what might be called a "thick description" of God's revelation in Scripture.

Doctrines of Sin, Eschatology, and Ecclesiology: Reformed and Catholic Emphases

Who knows which type of reading may be more or less helpful at various times and places? Whatever style of reading is adopted, the dogmatic account of divine transcendence and its radical provision for noncompetitive divine-human relations provided here allows sufficient theological foundation for sustained reflection on both levels of agency (and, therefore, allows the conjoining of Fowl and Webster's accounts of the reading of Scripture).

Something like figural or typological reading of Scripture is certainly necessitated to account for the plurality of ways in which God has made use of Scripture to perpetuate the flourishing of the church.[96] The purpose of

---

95. John Milbank, *The Suspended Middle: Henri de Lubac and the Debate Concerning the Supernatural* (Grand Rapids: Eerdmans, 2005), 58.

96. Steinmetz, "The Superiority of Pre-Critical Exegesis," 37; see also Daniel J. Treier, "The Superiority of Pre-Critical Exegesis? *Sic et Non*," *Trinity Journal* 24 (2003), 77–103. The "figural reading of Scripture" is a more Christ-centered hermeneutical theory than the four-fold medieval approach (see Westminster Confession of Faith I.9), though full comparison of figural, allegorical, and four-fold readings of Scripture would take this essay way beyond my limits here; see David Dawson, *Christian Figural Reading and the Fashioning of Identity* (Berkeley, CA: University of California Press, 2002).

4. Divine Transcendence and Reading of Scripture 67

Scripture is human flourishing,[97] according to the famed statement in 2 Tim. 3.17: Scripture is inspired for usefulness in the church, "so that all God's people may be thoroughly equipped for every good work." The immediate objection to such an *underdetermined* theory of interpretation accuses it of "baptizing social readings" and endangering the church by opening the door to false, self-deceptive teaching.[98] Such a concern is most appropriate, given the immediate turn from the above-quoted statement regarding the purpose of Scripture to the warnings about false teachers in 2 Tim. 4.3ff.: "the time will come when people will not put up with sound doctrine." The ultimate cure for such a danger is not adoption of a particular methodology (neither historical-criticism nor reader-response), nor is it the work of some magisterium (neither the New Testament PhD nor the Roman Pontiff). Rather, the only cure for such danger will be the direct vision of God. That is, danger will only be dispelled by eschatological fulfillment and cannot be foreclosed by adoption of any method. Modern promises of closure and peace have been shown false and require deconstruction by dogmatic accounts of sin and eschatology.

The tendency of Christians to find comfort in the rules of method or magisterium resides in an over-realized eschatology which fails to understand the lingering effects of sin and finitude. If deconstructionists have demonstrated nothing else, they have pointed out the lunacy of claiming interpretive closure.[99] The Christian life, in all components, will undoubtedly be dangerous—by avoiding the segmentation of Scripture reading from the rest of Christian existence, one can gain a healthy appreciation for the place of danger in such reading. A dogmatic account of the tie between Word and Spirit aids in such a caution. The Spirit has been left for our comfort and enlightenment. But the Spirit testifies to the Word and comforts us *in the Word's absence and until the Word's return*. The very ministry of the Spirit throughout creation must always be tied to the doctrine of ascension (the distance between the Word and the creation) and eschatology (the promised return of the Word for closure). Shy of the *parousia*, reading of Scripture (and all human activity) will be flawed. The comforting ministry of the Spirit will never move the church beyond coping with its lamented distance from Christ (prior to his return). A Reformed emphasis upon the indwelling effects of sin must ever chasten our attempts to account for the practices of the church, in particular the reading of Scripture.

Such danger must be countered by the communal emphasis upon ruled reading and regeneration of readers. Both Fowl and Webster have articulated the need for virtue as a prerequisite to proper reading of Scripture. Reading requires patience, care, and compassion in attending to the oftentimes tedious and taxing nature of

---

97. Ellen Charry utilizes the language of "human flourishing" (*By the Renewing of Your Minds: The Pastoral Function of Christian Doctrine* [Oxford: Oxford University Press, 1997]).

98. Willie J. Jennings, "Baptizing a Social Reading: Theology, Hermeneutics, and Postmodernity," in *Disciplining Hermeneutics: Interpretation in Christian Perspective* (ed. Roger Lundin; Grand Rapids: Eerdmans, 1997), 117–27.

99. Fowl, *Engaging Scripture*, 52–4.

texts. Such virtue, of course, is not a form of nicety or uncritical affirmation but a particular focus upon seeing Christ as the glue holding all together. Webster, in particular, has highlighted the danger that discussion of human activity might fail to take particular note of the distinctiveness of Christian virtue and community.[100] Needed is not mere virtue but divinely wrought righteousness; not mere community, but the church in the economy of grace. This is one example of the chastening of discussion of human action by description of divine action; the election of the church and individuals by God requires *distinctive* description of those individuals (and their reading) as supplementation to the terms provided by a more creationally based sociology. Enough with Christian use of the term "community"—we need the church and language to suit it.[101]

Adequate virtue will not be acquired by all, resulting in the need for communal rules to note when and where someone's reading has gone wrong. Such rules will not deny that person's interpretation the claim to have found a "meaning"; rather, they will note that it is not a "Christian meaning." Fowl makes much of the way in which the *regula fidei* was developed to do just this in debates with early heretics.[102] The "rule of faith" does not specify a particular reading method or strategy. The "rule of faith" does not seek to define the term "meaning." Rather, the "rule of faith" articulates a particular meta-narrative within which all Christian interpretation must find its home.[103] All objections which find the interpretive program of Fowl to promote unchastened pluralism are answered (in part, at least) by the use of the "rule of faith" within the life of the Christian community. Things certainly become more complicated when one asks the truly difficult questions, such as those regarding the application of the "rule of faith" in judgment upon certain interpretations of Scripture. However, the difficulty must be seen to lie, not in the pluriformity of interpretations, but in the determining whether any of them are, in fact, contrary to the "rule of faith." The Reformed emphasis upon indwelling sin and its necessary thwarting of all pre-glorified human activity must be held in union with a catholic emphasis upon the Spirit's presence within the whole body of Christ, which chastens the readings of individual Christians or congregations.[104]

At this point, earlier comments regarding the tendency to turn toward a magisterium might have seemed hasty; however, the eschatological nature of

---

100. Webster, "Hermeneutics in Modern Theology," 85–6.
101. John Webster, "Christ, Church, and Reconciliation," in *Word and Church*, 211–30.
102. Fowl, "Conceptual Structure of New Testament Theology," 232–5.
103. Paul M. Blowers, "The *Regula Fidei* and the Narrative Character of Early Christian Faith," *Pro Ecclesia* 6 (1997), 199–228.
104. It is the Spirit's presence which maintains what the Word taught in his life and, particularly, in the time between his resurrection and ascension. For the ministry of the forty days and the development of the *regula fidei*, see Jaroslav Pelikan, *Acts: A Theological Commentary* (Brazos Theological Commentary on the Bible; Grand Rapids: Brazos, 2005), excursus on the post-resurrection teaching ministry of Christ in Acts 1.2–3.

interpretive agreement and accuracy must not be forgotten. While some notion of a magisterium does seem to be a healthy manner of applying the "rule of faith," it cannot be assumed to provide eschatological presence or immediacy. Nicholas Healy has commended the need to move away from idealized conceptions of the church *in via*.[105] In short, bureaucratic vision (even of the holiest sort) must not be allowed to replace the need for beatific vision. We cannot theorize beyond our sinfulness and brokenness. While communal discussion seems essential to survival (much less flourishing), magisterial infallibility falsely enslaves the church to modern considerations and inevitably leads to an escalation of the Spirit's work beyond mere comfort and testimony. Thus, any magisterial authority—be it a creed or confession, a presbytery or an elder—functions only in a ministerial or instrumental (and, thus, irreducibly contingent) role in the life-giving works of the self-revealing God.

Others might object that any credence given to Fowl's program carries with it the adoption of a nonrealist position.[106] Such an objection, if true, would be devastating. At this point, however, objections which might apply to certain pragmatists (e.g., Stanley Fish, Jeffrey Stout, and Richard Rorty) do not apply to those who supplement their epistemic pragmatism with ontological realism (as demonstrated here by the supplementation of Fowl's work with that of Webster, a move which Fowl may or may not himself support). While human actions require pragmatic description, their interaction with divine action allows epistemic pragmatism to coexist with a strong account of ontological realism.[107]

Such an equation of pragmatism with non-realism has also led to the objection that *underdetermined* theories of interpretation cannot account for the transforming nature of Scripture.[108] Such repentant reading is, in fact, humanly impossible apart from the divine gift of freedom. But God does elect and remain faithful to his chosen people: opening eyes, replacing hearts of stone with hearts of flesh, placing the law within them. Divine effulgence provides for creaturely obedience. The particularly *intrusive* nature of Scripture flows from the lordly appropriation of human texts for divine purposes and regeneration of human readers for holy reading.[109]

---

105. Nicholas J. Healy, *Church, World, and the Christian Life: Practical-Prophetic Ecclesiology* (Cambridge Studies in Christian Doctrine; Cambridge: Cambridge University Press, 2000).

106. Anthony Thiselton, *New Horizons in Hermeneutics* (Grand Rapids: Zondervan, 1992), 549–50.

107. For a similar response to similar objections aimed at the postliberal project of George Lindbeck, see Bruce Marshall, "Aquinas as Postliberal Theologian," *The Thomist* 53 (1989), 353–402; see also Andrew Moore, *Realism and the Christian Faith: God, Grammar, and Meaning* (Cambridge: Cambridge University Press, 2003).

108. Thiselton, *New Horizons in Hermeneutics*, 549.

109. Webster's discussion of regeneration as a primary category for discussing Scripture, in his *Holy Scripture*, 89ff, where he shows that proper reading requires rebirth.

The examples of sinful appropriation of Scripture to underwrite or justify sinful practices which can be so easily culled from history are tragic; yet they have no theoretical impact on a dogmatic account of Scripture provided that it maintains a Christian doctrine of sin and eschatology. Sinful readers will read sinfully, and, lamentably, the sinful readings of such readers will continue until the consummation of God's reconciling work in Christ. Tidiness is not an option, nor must it be sought apart from its divinely appointed medium: the presence of Christ. Again, the Spirit's work in method and magisterium (used ad hoc by the church) cannot replace the promise of consummating divine action of the Word. The Spirit acts, providing freedom for our action. But such human agency will not attain final perfection apart from the reentry of the Word himself into the creaturely realm.

"Thick Description" of Scriptural Reading

The reading of Scripture is a complex activity, with two subjects (divine and human) acting in regard to one object (canonical text) all at once, which requires a "thick description." To that end, the dogmatic project of John Webster has been explored to offer description of divine action in revelation and has been supplemented by the pragmatic, *underdetermined* theory of interpretation of Stephen Fowl as a depiction of human readerly activity. While neither theologian might approve of such a union, the benefits of such conjoining have been seen to include matters epistemic, ontological, ethical, and ecclesial.[110] Above all, the eschatological nature of human understanding reminds us that, in this time of spiritual and (even) interpretive suffering, the church ought to gather together often for exhortation lest any fall away from the truth. However, such perseverance might be managed;

---

110. For historical examples of such a multiperspectival account of the reading of Holy Scripture, inclusive of both divine and human action in a noncompetitive relation, see Richard A. Muller's sketch of the Reformed orthodox doctrine of Scripture, in his *Post-Reformation Reformed Dogmatics: The Rise and Development of Reformed Orthodoxy, ca. 1520 to ca. 1725*, Volume 2: *Holy Scripture: The Cognitive Foundation of Theology* (Grand Rapids: Baker Academic, 2003), esp. ch. 7. The orthodox theologians of the post-Reformation era have much to teach us formally, as well as materially, about the manner in which to hold together affirmations about divine self-manifestation through Holy Scripture and rigorous theoretical and practical reflections about exegesis and doctrinal elucidation. Furthermore, Reformed orthodox reflections about the nature of typological and/or figural reading are particularly helpful, in as much as they specify and hone the earlier reformers' critical appropriation of medieval and patristic exegetical practices. In this regard, Fowl's proposals might be nuanced by assessment from a distinctly Reformed approach to construing the history of redemption and its concomitant parameters for figural and/or allegorical reading of certain texts.

the temptation to fight uncertainty and sinfulness with method or magisterium must be chastened by calls to patience, strength, and courage, ultimately unto prayer.

A Reformed-catholic account of human agency will not be surprised by the tragic fallenness of human activity between the entrance of sin into the world and the return of Christ as well as the necessity of ecclesial reading for the purpose of forming faithful Christians in such a lamentable location East of Eden. A dogmatic account of divine transcendence and noncompetitive relations between human and divine agency, articulated in the co-inherent work of Word and Spirit, provides the conceptual framework for such a Reformed-catholic theology and witnesses to the gospel freedom provided by our free, other, and graciously near Triune Lord.

Chapter 5

SYSTEMATIC THEOLOGY AND BIBLICAL THEOLOGY

Introduction

Debates about the definitions of and relationship between systematic theology and biblical theology have become commonplace. Institutional and intellectual programs have taken sides and stood over against each other. Even within the relatively small world of confessional Reformed theology, the matter has garnered a good bit of attention and controversy. Matters have only grown more complex with the rise, more recently, of theological interpretation of Scripture or theological exegesis, which may or may not overlap with both systematics and biblical theology. This chapter seeks to reflect on perhaps the most influential proposals thus far and then to suggest a way forward. To that end, proposals by Geerhardus Vos, John Murray, and Richard Gaffin will be examined at length in Part One.[1] In each case, their argument will be traced patiently, with observations and questions raised in a preliminary manner. Deeper analysis and a counterproposal appear in Part Two.

Part One

Geerhardus Vos, "The Idea of Biblical Theology as a Science and a Theological Discipline"

On May 8, 1894, Geerhardus Vos delivered an inaugural lecture devoted to describing, defending, and delineating the appropriate path forward for the

---

1. Geerhardus Vos, "The Idea of Biblical Theology as a Science and as a Theological Discipline," in *Redemptive History and Biblical Interpretation: The Shorter Writings of Geerhardus Vos* (ed. Richard B. Gaffin Jr; Phillipsburg, NJ: P & R, 2001); John Murray, "Systematic Theology," *Westminster Theological Journal* 25, no. 2 (1963), 133–42 and "Systematic Theology: Second Article," *Westminster Theological Journal* 26, no. 1 (1963), 33–46; repr. as "Systematic Theology," in *Collected Writings of John Murray*, Volume 4: *Studies in Theology; Reviews* (ed. Iain Murray; Edinburgh: Banner of Truth Trust, 198?), 1–21; Richard B. Gaffin Jr., "Systematic Theology and Biblical Theology," *Westminster Theological Journal* 38, no. 3 (1976), 281–99.

academic discipline of biblical theology, fitting given his installation as the professor of biblical theology at Princeton Theological Seminary. The establishment of a new chair in that faculty as well as divergent—even dangerous—perceptions of the discipline prompted him to wax methodological rather than turning to one of the many material discourses which he offered on so many other occasions. First, Vos began by delineating the object of study. Affirming the Creator-creature distinction, he said that this had methodological implications. A "separate and specific object" demands a "separate science"; in this case "God, as distinct from the creature, is the only legitimate object of Theology."[2] That separation of this from other objects shapes the space within which the discipline of theology occurs. "In Theology the object, far from being passive, by the act of creation first posits the subject over against itself, and then as the living God proceeds to impart to this subject that to which of itself it would have no access."[3] In other words, God is not an inert object but a self-revealing object and, ultimately, the first subject of theology. God knows God (here Vos quotes from 1 Cor. 2.11), and God makes that knowledge communicable so that creatures may share or participate in it as well.

Because Vos describes the object of theology as himself subject, this is not only a science but also a sphere of grace. He goes on to offer a description of the work of Spirit and Word in bringing forth "the reflection in the regenerate consciousness of an objective world of divine acts and words."[4] Notice the direct object of that reflection or knowledge, namely, the sphere and history of God's deeds and disclosures. "Strictly speaking, therefore, we should say that not God in and for Himself, but God in so far as He has revealed Himself, is the object of Theology."[5] Vos does not turn to the distinction of *theologia* and *oikonomia* or immanent Trinity and economic Trinity, but he does clearly differentiate between the task of knowing God in and of himself and knowing God in as much as self-reveals.

Now, this particular disjunction is somewhat crass: the first element describes an ontological identity ("God in and for himself"), whereas the second element depicts an epistemological approach ("God in so far as He has revealed Himself"). Thus, it is unlikely that Vos is making an ontological point so much as an epistemological concern. Theology is a positive science that does not choose or create but whose "attitude from the outset must be a dependent and receptive one," following and "mirror[ing]" the divine self-disclosure in Holy Scripture. He then says: "This being so, it follows immediately that the beginning of our Theology consists in the appropriation of that supernatural process by which God has made Himself the object of our knowledge."[6] The phrase "that supernatural process"

---

2. Vos, "The Idea of Biblical Theology," 4.
3. Ibid., 5.
4. Ibid.
5. Ibid. In so doing he parallels comments on the formal object of theology in Francis Turretin, *Institutes of Elenctic Theology*, 1.5.4.
6. Vos, "The Idea of Biblical Theology," 5.

proves determinative to what shall come, in as much as Vos will soon call for following not merely content but also form in divine self-revelation.

A further manner of delineating and defining comes when he turns to matters of theological encyclopedia: How does biblical theology relate to other subdisciplines such as exegesis or dogmatics/systematic theology? Exegetical theology develops as a subdiscipline of Theology, wherein "a group of studies have gradually been separated from the rest and begun to form a smaller organism among themselves," this "inasmuch as the receptive attitude of the theological consciousness toward the source of revelation was the common idea underlying and controlling them."[7] This "group of studies" comprises various enterprises, such as the formation of the Scriptures, all of which fix their sights upon God as he has disclosed himself in Holy Scripture (as opposed to revelation more broadly). Within this cluster of exegetical studies, "Biblical Theology is that part of Exegetical Theology which deals with the revelation of God."[8] It looks not at the prehistory or the reception, but rather at the self-revelatory action of the text itself.

Biblical theology is text-focused, then, over against other categories of Theology and even relative to other subgroups of Exegetical Theology. A related concern manifests itself quickly, for biblical theology "discusses both the form and contents of revelation from the point of view of the revealing activity of God Himself"; indeed, "[i]n Biblical Theology both the form and contents of revelation are considered as parts and products of a divine work." Revelation does not come like a message encoded in an accidental instrument, from which it might be extricated; the textual and verbal character of revelation is ingredient to that revelation and, thus, to biblical theology as a discipline.

In particular, biblical theology must be distinguished from and related to systematic theology carefully. How does Vos coordinate these two enterprises?

"In Biblical Theology both the form and contents of revelation are considered as parts and products of a divine work ... Biblical Theology applies no other method of grouping and arranging these contents than is given in the divine economy of revelation itself."[9]

"In Systematic Theology these same contents of revelation appear, but not under the aspect of the stages of a divine work; rather as the material for a human work of classifying and systematizing according to logical principles."[10]

Notice that systematic theology fixes upon the same contents, though it treats them as "matter" apart from any mention of attention to "form" (the Platonic pairing—better, disjunction—is quite possibly intentional). Indeed, systematics or dogmatics classifies, nay systematizes "according to logical principles." So biblical

---

7. Ibid.
8. Vos, "The Idea of Biblical Theology," 6.
9. Ibid., 7.
10. Ibid.

theology deals with the content of Scripture in its own form, whereas systematic theology takes that content and organizes it in some extraneous form. Though Vos leaves underdeveloped any sketch of where those categories come from (whether ecclesiastical practice or tradition or the wider intellectual and cultural milieu), he plainly avoids affirming that systematics attends to the Bible's own form and overtly substitutes in a generic term that is plainly "other" in its origin ("logical principles").

So the argument thus far is that theology—which always turns to think receptively about God's divine self-disclosure—should develop a subdiscipline called biblical theology. This new discipline helps inasmuch as all theology needs to attend to the manner and mode of God's revelation, specifically to the texts of Holy Scripture. While other subdisciplines such as dogmatics will take that biblical teaching and seek to make it serviceable in contemporary categories or ecclesiastical categories or philosophical-apologetic categories, it is appropriate that an exegetical science works hard to trace the form by which that biblical content is delivered. Thus far, biblical theology is fitting.

Second, Vos argues that the material shape of Holy Scripture renders a discipline such as biblical theology to be not merely an appropriate but even a necessary enterprise. "Here, as in other cases, the organism of a science can be conceived and described only by anticipating its results," in this case, implications for method from "what the study of Biblical Theology itself has taught us."[11] He will identify three characteristics of Holy Scripture which shed light on biblical theology, perhaps inclining us to speak of its necessity and not merely its permissibility.

"The first feature characteristic of supernatural revelation is its historical progress .... The self-revelation of God is a work covering ages, proceeding in a sequence of revealing words and acts, appearing in a long perspective of time."[12] He will flip between speaking of deeds and addressing words, pointing out that God does both (and often does both in doing either). Yet the variety of verbs performed by God—whether accomplishing, applying, or announcing his redemption of sinners—plays out across a history, and Vos is consistent and repetitive in highlighting this extended way of redemption. If Augustine was startled by the claim that God would take a full week to create (thinking instantaneous action far more befitting the divine being as it performs the work of nature), then we might say that Vos is equally struck by the patient character of God's act of grace.

"As soon as we realize that revelation is at almost every point interwoven with and conditioned by the redeeming activity of God in its wider sense, and together with the latter connected with the natural development of the present world, its historic character becomes perfectly intelligible and ceases to cause surprise."[13] The first ground, then, for the historic shape of revelation is its interconnected tie with redemptive activity: "We now must add that in not a few cases revelation is

11. Ibid.
12. Ibid.
13. Ibid., 8.

identified with history. Besides making use of words, God has also employed acts to reveal great principles of truth."[14] "A second ground for the historic character of revelation may be found in its eminently practical aspect," which Vos argues by employing a fairly unsophisticated Hebrew/Greek dichotomy that purports to identify biblical revelation with a Hebraic emphasis upon practical knowledge over against Greek theory (overlooking the rich notion of paideia in Greek literature and missing the fusion of these cultures that took place long before the incarnation).[15]

The second feature characteristic of supernatural revelation is that "divine truth has been progressively revealed" in such a way that all revelation, wherever it may lay on that historic timeline, bears "an organic character."[16] Vos will linger over and massage this notion of the "organic character" of divine self-revelation throughout time. While it is "progressive," "this increase nowhere shows the features of external accretion, but throughout appears as an internal expansion, an organic unfolding from within." He offers contrasting images: over against "elements of truth" which are "being mechanically added" to each other "in lifeless succession," he affirms that each is "seen to grow out of each other," so that later elements were "prepared for by what preceded" and in turn "preparatory for what follows."[17]

Vos attests a literary and revelational claim here, namely, that divine self-revelation does not in discrete and disparate chunks added one atop another but that it flowers over in the form of ongoing organic growth. He locates the revelational image of organic growth, however, in his soteriological posture.

> The same principle may also be established more objectively, if we consider the specific manner in which God realizes the renewal of this sinful kosmos in accordance with his original purpose. The renewal is not brought about by mechanically changing one part after the other. God's method is much rather that of creating within the organism of the present world the center of the world of redemption, and then organically building up the new order of things around this center.[18]

Because "this supernatural process of transformation proceeds on organic principles," an axiomatic rule follows for thinking about Holy Scripture and divine self-disclosure: "revelation itself must exhibit a similar organic process."[19] That *must* deserves analysis: Is it inductive or deductive? Contextual reading suggests strongly the former approach, namely, that Vos is not bringing in an extraneous assumption about revelation but instead observing that divine self-disclosure, like divine transformation of the *kosmos*, works patiently in a manner that is

---

14. Ibid., 9.
15. Ibid., 10.
16. Ibid.
17. Vos, "The Idea of Biblical Theology," 11.
18. Ibid., 11–12.
19. Ibid., 12.

nonetheless persistent and coherent (so that the growth of the kingdom of God's impact does not lurch to and fro but expands organically, its inception being fundamentally of the essence of what it will later be in full flowering).[20]

The third and final feature characteristic of supernatural revelation involves the "striking multiformity of teaching employed for the same purpose."[21] What does he mean by speaking of "multiformity"? He points to various genres in the OT and the NT as well as "numerous minor variations, closely associated with the peculiarities of individual character" even "within the limits of those great divisions."[22] Due both to its historically compressed chronology, relatively speaking, and the wide range of authors, Vos shows that the NT evidences much greater variegation in this regard (i.e., four gospels disclosing the divine character as revealed in the same timeframe). That the heavily epistolary character of the NT might serve as counterevidence for this judgment of relative proportion, Vos does not pause and examine the evidence. His broader point stands: divine self-disclosure in Holy Scripture does take varied forms and come from diverse hands, thus the choir can only be heard as composed of peculiar, individual voices.

Where has Vos come then in this second section? What have these three characteristics of supernatural revelation accomplished methodologically? He offers another attempt at definition. "Biblical Theology, rightly defined, is nothing

---

20. Vos nowhere cites the relevant literature at this point but organic growth has become a common descriptor among Reformed theologians in the latter portion of the nineteenth century. Responding to Hegelian approaches to history as well as to ancient use of organicist imagery, Philip Schaff and Herman Bavinck have each made much of organic growth. On Schaff, see George H. Shriver Jr., "Philip Schaff's Concept of Organic Historiography Interpreted in Relation to the Realization of an 'Evangelical Catholicism' within the Christian Community" (Ph.D. Dissertation, Duke University, 1960); John Charles Meyer, "Philip Schaff's Concept of Organic Historiography as Related to the Development of Doctrine: A Catholic Appraisal" (Ph.D. Dissertation, Catholic University of America, 1968); and Elizabeth A. Clark, *Founding the Fathers: Early Church History and Protestant Professors in Nineteenth-Century America* (Philadelphia: University of Pennsylvania Press, 2011), 191–6. The closest examples to a wide comparative study are W. Maurer, "Das Prinzip des Organischen Kirchengeschictsshreibung des 19. Jahrhunderts," *Kerygma und Dogma* (1962), 256–92; and especially James Eglinton, *Trinity and Organism: Towards a New Reading of Herman Bavinck's Organic Motif* (T&T Clark Studies in Systematic Theology; London: T&T Clark, 2012), 55–6 and 72–8. As Eglinton shows, the difficulty in tracing the organic motif is twofold: first, assuming univocal use of the term as a "singular, generic phenomenon," and, second, taking an "Enlightenment-centric reading of organicist history" that considers Hegel to the exclusion of Aristotle (57). Even in complicating the philosophical history, there is a danger of assuming that the organic motif is drawn from natural reason, whereas Eglinton seeks to show that, for Bavinck at least, Trinitarian theology *ad intra* governs and mandates the organic shape of life *ad extra* (80, 81–130).

21. Vos, "The Idea of Biblical Theology," 13.

22. Ibid.

else than *the exhibition of the organic process of supernatural revelation in its historic continuity and multiformity.*"[23] Now he has material grounds for accenting this particular intellectual focus: because the Bible is historically extended, progressively and organically developed, and multiform in its expression, alertness to its form aids Christian efforts to grasp its content.

Third, biblical theology may be new to Princeton Seminary, at least as a faculty chair, but it is not a new discipline. She has a track record, and it is not particularly promising. "From the end of the preceding century, when our science first appears as distinct from Dogmatic Theology, until now, she has stood under the spell of un-Biblical principles."[24] He depicts the enterprise as being undertaken in the guise of "Rationalism," whereby "the historical principle merely served to eliminate or neutralize the revelation principle."[25] Now Vos depicts rationalism as a threat to all theological disciplines but a particularly enticing and treacherous one for biblical theology above all, "because its principle of historic progress in revelation seems to present certain analogies with the evolutionary scheme."[26] Inasmuch as biblical theology has followed rationalism and evolutionary analogies to its detriment, it has led to a denial of the validity of earlier forms (which are conveniently viewed as "more primitive" and in no wise organically related to later forms) or to a turn from metaphysics to religion, namely, from studying God as he discloses himself toward studying Israelite and early Christian religious belief about God. Theology becomes religious studies, and this cannot be your father's God or religion.

Over against rationalism and its evolutionary influence, Vos offers four points of reorientation, worthy of "special emphasis in the construction of our science on a truly Scriptural and theological basis": First, "biblical theology must insist upon claiming for its object not the thoughts and reflections and speculations of man, but the oracles of God."[27] Second, "the historical character of the truth is not in any way antithetical to, but throughout subordinated to, its revealed character."[28] Third, "Biblical Theology should plant itself squarely upon the truthfulness of the Scriptures as a whole."[29] Fourth, "in designating our science as Biblical Theology, we should not fail to enter a protest against the wrong inferences that may be easily drawn from the use of the name."[30] Here he expresses worry that this will be viewed in evolutionary or chronological terms ("theology of the Bible" preceding "theology of Origen," an example he gives), against which he offers a categorical

---

23. Ibid., 15 (italics original).
24. Ibid. For the famous lecture by J. P. Gabler, see John Sandys-Wunsch and Laurence Eldredge, "J. P. Gabler and the Distinction Between Biblical and Dogmatic Theology: Translation, Commentary and Discussion of His Originality," *Scottish Journal of Theology* 33 (1980), 133–58.
25. Vos, "The Idea of Biblical Theology," 15.
26. Ibid., 16.
27. Ibid., 19.
28. Ibid.
29. Ibid., 20.
30. Ibid.

distinction: biblical theology deals with God's self-revelation, and it is not human reflection on that disclosure (which is only possible truly after the Bible has been fully delivered, though the "first signs of the beginning of this process are discernible" in the NT).

Fourth, Vos concludes the lecture by observing enrichments of the student offered by studying biblical theology. He returns to key concepts: appreciating the organic character of truth and revelation, serving as an "effective antidote to the destructive critical views now prevailing,"[31] and its accenting with vividness and reality the truths of the faith. Interestingly he does not turn there to its variegation as a rhetorical benefit, but he fixes upon its historic character as a sign of its concrete reality and thus practical utility.[32]

The final benefit, however, merits our attention. "Biblical Theology is of the greatest importance and value for the study of Systematic Theology."[33] How so? Before he offers a visual comparison ("Systematic Theology endeavors to construct a circle, Biblical Theology seeks to reproduce a line"), he offers an analytic statement:

> Dogmatic Theology is, when rightly cultivated, as truly a Biblical and as truly an inductive science as its younger sister. And the latter needs a constructive principle for arranging her facts as well as the former. The only difference is, that in the one case this constructive principle is systematic and logical, whereas in the other case it is purely historical.[34]

Vos first grants that systematics is biblical and indeed inductive. Second, he admits that biblical theology demands an organizing principle (his use of the adjective "constructive" is even more *poietic* and active in intellectual description). Thus far they are of the same family. But younger sister differs from older brother in that one finds that principle to be "purely historical" and the other "systematic and logical." Note first that he defines biblical theology as organized in a "purely historical" manner, though he does not use a similarly exclusive adjective when speaking of the "systematic and logical" principles used in dogmatics. Indeed, he has neither excluded nor acknowledged the fact that the vast majority of governing principles in systematic theology are overtly intra-canonical categories. A second response is to ask: Does this description of biblical theology fit the description of Vos himself? When he offers material arguments for its necessity, he first affirms its historic character but then goes on to speak of its organic and multiform nature; in other words, historical principles simply will not suffice even the role of biblical theology that he himself has articulated.

---

31. Ibid., 22.
32. He does not bring up the Hebrew/Greek dichotomy again here, but it would be a rhetorical fit with this point (albeit historically and philosophically muddled, on which see comments above).
33. Vos, "The Idea of Biblical Theology," 23.
34. Ibid.

In any case, Vos concludes by saying that biblical theology will serve systematic theology well: "proclaim[ing] the fact ... that true religion cannot dispense with a solid basis of objective knowledge of the truth"; "demonstrate[ing] that the fundamental doctrines of our faith do not rest ... on an arbitrary exposition of some isolated proof-texts"; and "contribut[ing] to keep Systematic Theology in living contact with that soil of divine realities from which it must draw all its strength and power to develop beyond what it has already attained."[35] Notably the first two of these services as related to observations about unique historical weaknesses, whether the claim that "a solid basis of objective knowledge of the truth" is "too often forgotten and denied in our days" or that "many would fain believe" that dogmatics rests on nothing more than lame proof texts.

John Murray, "Systematic Theology"

The second essay that seeks to address the relationship of biblical theology and systematic theology, in direct dependence at points upon Vos, was published by John Murray, longtime Professor of Systematic Theology at Westminster Theological Seminary. Murray was the first of Westminster professors to self-consciously pattern their systematic approach upon the disciplinary coordination proposed by the earlier Princetonian. Whereas Vos began by defining biblical theology and in so doing relating it to systematic theology, Murray will begin by charting a sketch of systematics and then, halfway thru, relating it to biblical theology. We will seek to follow his argument, noting consistency and inconsistency relative to Vos. Because much is assumed, our sketch can be more compressed (as will be the case also with Gaffin).

First, Murray addresses the nature of systematic theology as an academic discipline: "The task of systematic theology is to set forth in an orderly and coherent manner the truth respecting God and his relations to men and the world," truth which is "derived from the data of revelation" in both general revelation and special revelation (specifically Holy Scripture).[36]

"The principal source of revelation is Holy Scripture."[37] Murray realizes that many would argue that this is biblicistic and insufficiently Christocentric. He works, therefore, to coordinate trust in the Word and trusting his Holy Word: "Scripture is not to be identified with him in this unique identity that is his. But it is apparent that we need more than the revelation which Christ is, and we can have no knowledge of, nor encounter with, the revelation that he is except through Scripture."[38]

Systematic theology is "most noble," for "[a]ll other departments of theological discipline contribute their findings to systematic theology and it brings all

---

35. Ibid., 24.
36. Murray, "Systematic Theology," 1.
37. Ibid., 2.
38. Ibid., 3.

the wealth of knowledge derived from these disciplines to bear upon the more inclusive systemization which it undertakes."[39] This occurs over time within the church, "always a duty, sometimes a necessity, which the fact of revelation places upon the church of God." Why is it necessary? "[T]he Word of God requires the most exacting attention so that we as individuals and as members in the solidaric unity of the church may be able to correlate the manifold data of revelation in our understanding and the more effectively apply this knowledge to all phases of our thinking and conduct."[40]

If revelation in God's Holy Word impels or summons this kind of rational work, what gives it strength to do so? Here Murray turns to what he calls "the doctrine of the presence and activity of the Holy Spirit .... It is this ceaseless activity of the Holy Spirit that explains the development throughout the centuries of what we call Christian doctrine."[41] Murray does speak of the embedded character of particular theologians within history, which actually makes possible their work in expanding or progressing the mind of the church, though their labor is no solo act and participates in the power of this enlivening Spirit.

As with Vos's concern to describe history in organic terms, Murray then considers ways in which the extended history of Christian doctrine should be viewed. "This progression does not mean that the advance has been uniformly continuous." He laments periods of "theological decadence." A pacific and measured tone marks his candor, however, for "the unfaithfulness of the church in any one period or place does not suspend, far less does it make void, the constant progression which systematic theology is accorded by the oversight of the church's Lord and the enlightenment of the Spirit."[42] Periods do vary, with times of decadence being matched by "periods of epochal contribution and advance," not least because theology, being "realistic," counters "oppose[s] error" and "is thus directed against sin."[43]

Murray argues that "we may not suppose that theological construction ever reaches definitive finality."[44] He describes the way in which John Calvin sought to clarify Nicene teaching on the eternality of the Son by affirming him as *autotheos*, purportedly over against some fourth-century understandings of language that he is "very God of very God." He argues that Calvin here is an example of continued vigilance, illustrative of the principle that "[w]hen any generation is content to rely upon its theological heritage and refuses to explore for itself the riches of divine revelation, then declension is already under way and heterodoxy will be the lot of the succeeding generation."[45]

---

39. Ibid., 4.
40. Ibid., 5.
41. Ibid., 6.
42. Ibid.
43. Ibid., 7.
44. Ibid.
45. Ibid., 8.

Murray concludes the first part of his essay by describing the duty of theology to its own time and place. He notes—surely thinking of modernists here—that many calls to attend to the present seek to adapt the gospel rather than apply the gospel. "Far more important is the reminder that each generation must be adapted to the gospel. It is true, however, that the presentation of the gospel must be pointed to the needs of each generation."[46]

Second, Murray turns in the second half of his essay to address ways in which "[b]iblical theology is indispensable to systematic theology."[47] This is no random turn, for he has already spoken of how theology is meant to be consistently progressing. One might ask: what lenses or approaches help the church approach the Word afresh so as to grow in her understanding of that divine self-revelation?

In offering initial definitions Murray takes after Vos. Both disciplines deal with "the data of special revelation," biblical theology "from the standpoint of its history" and systematic theology "as a finished product."[48] Thus the crucial distinction regards their method, not their matter, with biblical theology being "historical" and systematic theology being "logical." Nothing fresh appears at this juncture.

Murray invests far more time to make sense of biblical theology in its own terms, cognizant of the contested nature of the disciplinary need for definition. He specifically observes that there are "radical divergences" between the approach of Vos and that of other representatives.[49] He spends a disproportionate amount of time examining the more rationalistic approaches wherein layers behind the text garner greater attention, various texts or corpuses within the canon begin to be viewed as incoherent, and divine self-revelation tends to be identified specifically with the deeds or acts of God in history (of which biblical writings are a human witness, though not identified as such). Ultimately this concatenation of tendencies leads to the denial of biblical foundations in origin stories, purportedly relocating patriarchal elements (i.e., the institution of the covenant in Genesis 15 and 17) to a later epoch and editorial hand.

A better way has been charted. "When biblical theology is conceived of as dealing with 'the process of the self-revelation of God deposited in the Bible,' it must be understood that this specialized study of the Bible, so far from being inimical to the interests of systematic theology, is indispensable to the systematic theology that is faithful to the Bible."[50] In that statement he not only proffers a better way but in so doing claims its "indispensable" role in shaping another discipline, namely, systematic theology. Why? "Systematic theologies have too often betrayed a cold formalism that has been prejudicial to their proper aim and

---

46. Ibid., 9.
47. Ibid., 16.
48. Ibid., 9.
49. Ibid., 11.
50. Ibid., 15.

have not for that reason and to that extent promoted encounter with the living Word of the living God."

Murray's statement about the need and malady of systematic theology deserves further analysis. He realizes this himself, offering two clarifications. "First, there are certain phases of the truth with which systematic theology must deal and certain polemics which it must conduct that call for the type of treatment which to many people seems cold and formal."[51] Dry though they may sometimes be, there are places where polemic or confession demands patient, seemingly cold analysis in a systematic mode. "Second, the charge, insofar as it is warranted, is not the fault of systematic theology, but of the theologian or of the milieu of which his product is the reflection."[52] This is the case for logical analysis is no error; indeed it is seemingly unavoidable given that "we cannot say everything all at once" and thus must reflect in an orderly way on when to say something and how to say it. In this regard Murray compares the systematic impulse to that of an orderly preacher who must seek to proclaim the "whole counsel of God" (Acts 20.27).

Yet Murray does claim that systematics needs biblical theology, even in the face of these two qualifications. He begins by tying dogmatics to exegesis, for "[s]ystematics becomes lifeless and fails in its mandate just to the extent to which it has become detached from exegesis."[53] He moves in a further step, then, to say that biblical theology is important also, for "biblical theology is regulative of exegesis" because "these revelatory data occur within a particular period of revelation."[54] Interestingly Murray fixes solely upon Vos's first argument for the material necessity of biblical theology, namely, the historical nature of divine self-disclosure in the Bible. He does not pay attention to the multiformity of genre or of authorial inflections of the gospel, and he does not belabor the matter of understanding this historic character in organic terms.

He concludes: "only when systematic theology is rooted in biblical theology does it exemplify its true function and achieve its purpose."[55] First, he suggests that "the tendency to abstraction which ever lurks for systematic theology is hereby counteracted."[56] Like Vos, historical seems to mean for Murray's systematician what is concrete and thus practical, real, pertinent. Second, rooting systematics in biblical theology allows each text across the whole canon to contribute without shoehorning any text into saying something that does not befit its epoch; here Murray introduces briefly the notion of "organic" unity across the testaments.[57]

John Murray addressed the discipline of systematic theology in terms of its goals, sources, and its resources or principles. In doing so, he also tended to Word and Spirit. The Spirit is the animating source of the church's progress in the

51. Ibid., 16.
52. Ibid.
53. Ibid., 17.
54. Ibid., 19.
55. Ibid., 20.
56. Ibid.
57. Ibid., 20–1.

truth throughout time, even amidst fits and starts. He addressed the Word as the ultimate source: though general revelation contributes, the special revelation of prophets and apostles in Holy Scripture serves as the ultimate arbiter of Christian doctrine. Thus, exegesis of the Word is essential to systematics. Why? "Exegesis keeps systematics not only in direct contact with the Word but it ever imparts to systematics the power which is derived from that Word. The Word is living and powerful."[58] The utility of biblical theology serves as an instrument to aid that exegetical rooting, giving it historical/epochal texture and avoiding shoehorning or homogenizing its cross-canonical character.

Richard Gaffin, "Systematic Theology and Biblical Theology" and "Biblical Theology and the Westminster Standards"

Richard Gaffin, penned an essay titled, "Systematic Theology and Biblical Theology," which was more overt and obvious than that of Vos or Murray in that his title explicitly took up the relationship of the two disciplines. Years later, he was appointed to the Charles Krahe Chair, at which time he gave another inaugural lecture address disciplinary definition. This second lecture, titled "Biblical Theology and the Westminster Standards," turns to the question of the relationships of biblical theology to ecclesiastical symbolics/confessions (in his case, the Westminster Standards and their function within American Presbyterianism).

Gaffin concludes "Systematic Theology and Biblical Theology" rather bluntly:

> All this prompts the not entirely modest proposal, in view of objections that can be raised against the term 'systematic theology,' to discontinue its use and instead to use 'biblical theology' to designate the comprehensive statement of what Scripture teaches (dogmatics), always insuring that its topical divisions remain sufficiently broad and flexible to accommodate the results of the redemptive-historically regulated exegesis on which it is based.[59]

He has called for the replacement of systematics with biblical theology. We do well to ask how he purports to have arrived at that destination.

He lays groundwork for his argument by noting something of the history of terms. "Understood generally as the effort to provide a compendium or comprehensive summary of what the Bible teaches, systematic theology, or dogmatics, is almost as old as the church itself ... In contrast, biblical theology, conceived of in some sense as a distinct discipline, is comparatively new and has had a rather problematic history."[60] He then recounts the now common history of biblical theology, differentiating early pietist use of the phrase from its disciplinary function in the work of Gabler and his heirs. He also signals the internal incoherence or fracturing of that project:

---

58. Ibid., 17.
59. Gaffin, "Systematic Theology and Biblical Theology," 298.
60. Ibid., 281–2.

The virtual divorce of biblical theology from dogmatics has proven especially fatal, precipitating a crisis of historicism in biblical studies that is periodically glossed over but remains unsolved. The end result of this biblical theology—almost a "critical" commonplace today—is that there is none, that doctrinally and conceptually the Bible is a disunity, embracing a plurality of diverging and even competing theologies.[61]

If biblical theology was a reaction to a crisis within orthodox systematics, then it sought better "to do justice to the historical character of the Bible." Yet in seeking to honor the text's historical nature, it fell into historicism and lost the text qua text in favor of the text qua sources and segments (what Michael Legaspi has since called "the death of Scripture and the rise of biblical studies"[62]). Gaffin then notes that "it is of interest to inquire how biblical theology as a particular theological discipline came to have a positive place within the Reformed tradition," and here he turns to Geerhardus Vos.[63] But Gaffin follows Vos in trying to locate his role within an already existent Princetonian commitment to biblical theology. Charles Hodge noted the existence of this discipline, albeit briefly and rather ambiguously; A. A. Hodge made little of it, but described it briefly with greater definitional clarity; B. B. Warfield was the first to argue that systematics depended upon the results of biblical theology, though he lacked even the definitional precision of the less interested A. A. Hodge.[64] Finally, Gaffin turns to Bavinck and Kuyper before concluding: "within the Reformed tradition Vos has no predecessors for his conception of biblical theology. In this respect his work can be called creative and injects a fresh impulse into Reformed theology. In balance, however, the fact of his appointment, the more formal discussion of Warfield, and the material concern of Bavinck and Kuyper indicate at least incipient appreciation for the direction in which he was going as well as a recognition of its importance."[65]

The only attempts to coordinate systematics and biblical theology within the Reformed tradition, according to Gaffin, are those germinal comments in Vos and the essay by Murray. Gaffin observes that both men make two sorts of claims: first, they seek to treat the disciplines as parallel endeavors operating "side by side"; second, they both "are intent on bringing out the definite connection between the two disciplines, in particular the importance of biblical theology for systematics."[66] Gaffin asks what benefits they have shown biblical theology to have

---

61. Ibid., 283.
62. Michael C. Legaspi, *The Death of Scripture and the Rise of Biblical Studies* (Oxford Studies in Historical Theology; Oxford: Oxford University Press, 2011).
63. Gaffin, "Systematic Theology and Biblical Theology," 284.
64. See this history recounted in Gaffin, "Systematic Theology and Biblical Theology," 285–6. Gaffin offers further argument for precursors to Vos in his "Biblical Theology and the Westminster Standards," *Westminster Theological Journal* 65 (2003), 166 (165–79).
65. Gaffin, "Systematic Theology and Biblical Theology," 287.
66. Ibid., 290.

offered to theology generally and to systematics more particularly. He provides three answers.

First, "Biblical theology focuses on revelation as an historical activity and so challenges systematic theology to do justice to the historical character of revealed truth."[67] This is not totally new, of course, and Gaffin notes that the church took this call seriously at various points (e.g., he highlights the anti-Marcionite and anti-gnostic writings of early theologians such as Irenaeus as instances of consistent attention to the historical shape of divine self-revelation). "Rather it is largely a matter of correcting and balancing certain trends of the more recent post-Reformation past."[68] Gaffin, perhaps more than Vos or Murray, highlights the interventionist nature of biblical theology. Indeed, this is probably why he never employs the word "Rationalist" to depict mainstream biblical theology post Gabler (as do Vos and Murray in their historical accounts), namely, that Gaffin is attempting to highlight the way in which biblical theology was meant to address a problem in how theology did (not) deal with history. While neither Gaffin nor the earlier accounts of Vos and Murray give tangible examples of the lack of concern for history or the abstract nature of post-Reformation orthodox dogmatics (beyond the mention of adopting "Aristotelian" or "Cartesian" thought), he directly attributes the rise of the discipline (both in its mainstream and then its Reformed variants) to this need for crisis response.

Second, "Biblical theology is indispensable to systematic theology, because biblical theology is regulative of exegesis."[69] Particular passages are unified by their place in this one redemptive history. "The context that ultimately controls the understanding of a given text is not a literary framework or pattern of relationships but the historical structure of the revelation process itself."[70] Lest the reader take this to be a statement of priority—as if redemptive-history is merely of greater significance than other contextual questions like literary framework—Gaffin continues: "At issue is not one exegetical option among others ... Exegesis itself is misunderstood if biblical theology is seen as no more than a step (even the most important) in the exegetical process." And he claims the mantle of deep principles from the magisterial Reformation at just this point: "It does not appear to be going too far to say that in 'biblical theology,' that is, effective recognition of the redemptive-historical character of biblical revelation, the principle of context, of the analogy of Scripture, the principle that Scripture interprets Scripture, so central in the Reformation tradition of biblical interpretation, finds its most pointedly biblical realization and application."[71]

---

67. Ibid., 292.
68. Ibid., 292.
69. Ibid., 293.
70. Ibid., 294.
71. Ibid., 294.

Third,

it brings to light a factor of continuity, especially with the New Testament, that serves to keep the subsequent theological activity of the church firmly and organically rooted in the Scriptures, determined by them not only in its conclusions but also in the questions with which it begins. Reformed theology ought to challenge itself with the constant awareness that its prolegomena are given by the Bible itself.[72]

Biblical theology helps show not merely conclusions but methods of argument, scripture arguing by means of scripture (e.g., apostolic use of Old Testament scripture). The Bible ought to govern not merely our results but also our processes, therefore biblical theology serves as a helpful prompt for systematics.

His emphasis upon unity probably deserves special mention here, for Gaffin truly does argue that biblical theology helps manifest an organic connection of what may seem, at first blush, to be disparate elements of apostolic scripture. He asserts this point here, but he tries to illustrate it elsewhere. In a later essay, "Biblical Theology and the Westminster Standards," he sought among other things to challenge a worry that biblical theology narrows one's concerns, particularly by fixing upon redemptive history to the loss of a rich Reformed account of the *ordo salutis* or application of redemption. He argued that this was especially significant given that the entrance of the New Perspective(s) on Paul to New Testament studies had prompted some to take a juxtaposed approach to Pauline theology: *either* it was about the new ecclesial reality ushered in by the entrance of "faith" in redemptive history *or* it was still about that Reformational message of salvation by grace through faith.[73] Gaffin helpfully shows that this was a false dichotomy, and that both biblical theology and the Westminster Standards have concern for redemptive-history and for the *ordo salutis* (which is not to say that they are compatible with what was the "new perspective(s) on Paul," which were relevant at the time of his essay in 2003 but are now rather dated).[74] I mention this essay and its discussion of that particular case study simply to show that he really does make good on the claim that biblical theology seeks to get at a "multiform" reality in the Scriptures and is not reductive.

So, in light of these three reflections, Gaffin arrived at what he deemed his "ultimate resolution," namely, that we "discontinue" speech of systematics and instead "use 'biblical theology' to designate the comprehensive statement of what Scripture teaches (dogmatics)."[75] He proposed an interim ethic as well, namely, that "it will be the task of the latter [biblical theology] to minister to the former [systematic theology] the rich perspectives of revelation seen in the context of its

---

72. Ibid., 296.
73. Ibid., 169.
74. Gaffin, "Biblical Theology and the Westminster Standards," 175 (see 169–75).
75. Gaffin, "Systematic Theology and Biblical Theology," 298.

history and it will be the work of systematics to incorporate these perspectives into its constructions and formulations. Note here that gone is any sense, as found in Vos or Murray, that systematics is innately as biblical as biblical theology; gone also is a sense that systematics is as intrinsically committed to the epistemological or noetic principle of divine self-disclosure (revelation). Rather, biblical theology serves as the generative source or midwife who brokers that interaction.[76]

Gaffin offers an example here, demonstrating the need for biblical theology to inform systematic theology. "If there is one conclusion that a redemptive-historically sensitive interpretation of Scripture has reached, it is that eschatology is to be defined not only with reference to the intermediate state of individuals following death and to the second coming of Christ but inclusive of his first coming and the present existence of the church in the world."[77] Appreciating what is possessed by the Christian now depends upon seeing the kingdom of God come, union with Christ achieved, and gift of the life-giving Spirit of God granted. Gaffin argues that eschatology, then, cannot wait to be addressed as a final topic in theology but demands to be brought forward and to shape how others—Christology, pneumatology, soteriology, ecclesiology, for example—are to be addressed.

Concluding Analysis

Having come to the end of our historical survey, we can identify some common concerns in this trajectory: keeping exegesis at the core of the theological task, biblical theology as a historical and redemptive-epochal schematic for reading particular passages, and a sense that somewhere, somehow systematic theology has lost its exegetical swag in the modern era. Biblical theology has played a therapeutic function, then, in addressing a disciplinary problem. Indeed, Vos is very clear that redress of a modern problem prompts the entire endeavor. Some further emphasis can also be identified: a focus on biblical theology as manifesting the unity of the canon, concern that history be construed herein as organic, and a strong bent toward historical categories as being more inductive tools for theological development.[78] Some trends emerge: over time, Vos's multi-pronged approach to biblical theology is narrowed as Murray and especially Gaffin show

---

76. For a restatement of his argument and a few illustrative examples of biblical theology serving as midwife, see Gaffin, "The Vitality of Reformed Dogmatics," in *The Vitality of Reformed Theology: Proceedings of the International Theological Congress, June 20–24th 1994, Noordwijkerhout, The Netherlands* (ed. J. M. Batteau, J. W. Maris, and K. Veling; Kampen: Uitgeverij Kok, 1994), 16–50. Offering further detail about this midwifing process is the more recent argument by Vern Poythress, "Two Kinds of Biblical Theology," *Westminster Theological Journal* 70, no. 1 (2008), 129–42.

77. Gaffin, "Systematic Theology and Biblical Theology," 298–9.

78. See also the integrative project of Michael S. Horton, *Covenant and Eschatology: The Divine Drama* (Louisville: Westminster John Knox, 2003), esp. 220–64.

less concern for literary "multiformity" and eventually reduce biblical theology to a disciplinary alertness to redemptive-history, even as the need for biblical theology grows from a helpful tool in Vos eventually to a disciplinary replacement for systematics in Gaffin.

In sum, just when the description of biblical theology is less subtle was it also heralded more radically, that is, when it was reduced to historical analysis was just when it was claimed to be a satisfactory replacement for dogmatics. In so doing, there is also a growing danger that biblical theology can pull away from a textual or exegetical focus in as much as it singularly turns to historical or narrative analysis (which does not fit every genre or text in the same manner); analyses of timelines and trajectories and intertextuality and epochs can aid an interpreter in leaning in to listen more attentively or it can distracting as to further remove them from attending to the text itself, which is the living and active Word of God. For a discipline which Reformed theologians engaged to combat a perceived (though rather undefined) crisis, biblical theology itself has both provided remarkable contributions and also provoked notable crises. We will analyze this state of affairs and offer a constructive counterproposal in a subsequent essay, seeking to describe how both exegesis and dogmatics can and must function as disciplines of the Word of God and how biblical theology may serve as a helpful and temporary interpretative therapy should those disciplines fall out of biblical alignment.

Part Two

In many times and various ways some significant Reformed theologians have claimed that biblical theology must be coordinated with or contribute to the task of systematic theology. In these last days, they have even suggested that biblical theology should fill the place of systematic theology. What shall we to these things? Part One described the way in which Geerhardus Vos, John Murray, and Richard Gaffin have addressed the role of biblical theology in relation to systematic theology. Admittedly our examination has fixed upon a particular stream of thought, to which others might and should be added.[79] We have nonetheless seen a

---

79. Relevant literature on the definition and protocols of biblical theology is legion. Significant entries to the literature surely include: Brevard Childs, *Biblical Theology in Crisis* (Philadelphia: Westminster, 1970); James D. Smart, *The Past, the Present, and the Future of Biblical Theology* (Philadelphia: Westminster, 1979); Ben C. Ollenburger, "Biblical Theology: Situating the Discipline," in *Understanding the Word* (ed. J. T. Butler, E. Conrad, and B. Ollenburger; Sheffield: JSOT, 1985), 37–62; Graeme Goldsworthy, "'Thus Says the Lord': The Dogmatic Basis of Biblical Theology," in *God Who Is Rich in Mercy: Essays Presented to Dr. D. B. Knox* (ed. Peter T. O'Brien and David G. Peterson; Grand Rapids: Baker, 1986), 25–40; Hartmut Gese, "Hermeneutische Grundsätze der Exegese biblischer Texte," in *Alttestamentliche Studien* (Tübingen: Mohr Siebeck, 1991), 249–65; Brevard Childs, *Biblical Theology of the Old and New Testaments: Theological Reflection on the Christian Bible* (Minneapolis: Fortress, 1992); Peter Stuhlmacher, *Biblische Theologie des Neuen Testaments,*

number of common elements as well as trajectories of change. As promised, a few deeper analyses and counterproposals will be forwarded here. I will seek to show why biblical theology has served as a needed and valuable therapy or infusion to address a modern disciplinary malady, though I will also argue that it brings with it temptations toward imbalance and overreaction. Therefore, a vision for a potential disciplinary end game or exit strategy will be sketched, whereby biblical theology may have so accomplished its reorienting ends that it no longer need or should serve as a discrete, protest discipline. In doing so, comparisons with theological interpretation of Scripture (TIS) will be offered, reflecting upon that more recent movement in similar fashion.

Biblical Theology in Crisis

Biblical theology arose in response to a perceived crisis. As Gaffin said: "The question that needs to be asked is to what extent in the period following the Reformation orthodox Protestant dogmatics, by allying itself first with Aristotelian and then with Cartesian patterns of thought, fell into the vitiating tension between revelation and history it was trying to oppose."[80]

---

2 vols (Göttingen: Vandenhoeck & Ruprecht, 1992–1999); Rolf Rendtorff, *Canon and Theology: Overtures to an Old Testament Theology* (Minneapolis: Fortress, 1993); Francis Watson, *Text and Truth: Redefining Biblical Theology* (Grand Rapids: Eerdmans, 1997); James Barr, *The Concept of Biblical Theology: An Old Testament Perspective* (Minneapolis: Fortress, 1999); Scott J. Hafemann (ed.), *Biblical Theology: Retrospect and Prospect* (Downers Grove, IL: IVP Academic, 2002); Charles H. Scobie, *The Ways of Our God: An Approach to Biblical Theology* (Grand Rapids: Eerdmans, 2002); and Craig Bartholomew et al (eds.), *Out of Egypt: Biblical Theology and Biblical Interpretation* (Scripture and Hermeneutics Series; Grand Rapids: Zondervan Academic, 2011). These are only some of the most significant entryways to the discussion, to which we might add relevant texts regarding canon, intertextuality, figural reading, and typology. While the Studies in Biblical Theology series published landmark volumes mid-century and the Overtures to Biblical Theology series offered major volumes in the 1970s through the 1990s (both predominantly by mainline Protestant scholars), the most significant ventures in recent years have been the *New Dictionary of Biblical Theology* (ed. T. Desmond Alexander and Brian S. Rosner; Downers Grove, IL: IVP, 2000) and the New Studies in Biblical Theology series edited by D. A. Carson for IVP Academic Press (both mainly produced by evangelicals). There are also a whole range of texts aimed at introducing biblical theology to laypersons and to novice students; these, however, tend not to shape the ongoing disciplinary debate. Typologies of varying validity have emerged in recent years: Gerhard Hasel, "The Nature of Biblical Theology: Recent Trends and Issues," *Andrews University Studies* 32 (1994), 203–15; Vern Poythress, "Kinds of Biblical Theology," *Westminster Theological Journal* 70, no. 1 (2008), 129–42; Darian Lockett and Mickey Klink, *Understanding Biblical Theology: A Comparison of Theory and Practice* (Grand Rapids: Zondervan Academic, 2012).

80. Gaffin, "Systematic Theology and Biblical Theology," 293.

One of the most difficult elements in knowing if and when the situation might be righted, the crisis ended, is that the tangible problems are rarely if ever stated. What does it mean that history was not honored in post-Reformation theology? What are symptoms of this malady? And which post-Reformation theology is being described here? Given the presence of an increasingly diverse intellectual conversation within both the Protestant and Roman Catholic academies, as well as with those traversing the boundaries of the church and the realm of skepticism, we ought to expect variety. Gaffin does not say. Neither Murray before him. Nor Vos at the beginning of the thread. Much greater clarity might be expected of Vos and his followers, especially given the pride of place held by covenant theology within their own circles. If covenant (federal) theology had confessional standing in Reformed churches and functioned as a mainstay of post-Reformation Reformed Orthodox theology (e.g., Cocceius, Witsius, Owen, each in different ecclesiastical or generational contexts), then we might expect further clarity to ask what more was sought. If theology which traced redemptive history was found in that covenant theology, then was the problem not so much a matter of the absence of an approach to history but more so the presence of something else (in the guise of systematics)? Was that covenant theology somehow not integrated into their dogmatics? What ill needed addressing? Or was the problem actually much later (say, with post-Kantian rationalism or with late nineteenth-century dispensationalist approach to biblical theology)?

Biblical Theology in the Mainstream

Crisis measures have long-term palliative effect—in intellectual as well as physiological terms—when they shape not merely particular persons but also networks or neighborhoods. Thus, the theological therapy of Reformed biblical theology has rightly taken institutional effect. Quite apart from the lack of clarify regarding the descriptive task of what was wrong prior to this advent of Reformed biblical theology, much effort has gone into methodological, material, and institutional advancement of the enterprise prescriptively.

Ventures such as InterVarsity Press's New Studies in Biblical Theology series, edited by D. A. Carson, perhaps have done more than anything else to provide forums for scholars to practice the rhythms of analysis ingredient in a nuanced Vosian vision, not merely tracing themes across the canon but also tending to the particular texture of a given text or corpus. Notably, this series has hearkened back to the Vosian vision, rather than its later forms in Murray and Gaffin, in that both historical context and authorial multiformity are taken into account.[81] NSBT volumes trace given themes through the testaments, watching concepts develop intertextually. They also look to a given author, corpus, or genre, seeking

---

81. Methodological arguments in this direction can be found in D. A. Carson, "Systematic Theology and Biblical Theology," in *New Dictionary of Biblical Theology* (Downers Grove, IL: IVP Academic, 2000), 94–5.

to account for its particular contribution to Holy Scripture (which speaks one gospel in multiform ways).

That resources of such institutional scope exist means that this enterprise will have lingering and more significant impact. The care shown by NSBT volumes, by and large, to listen to the text's way of speaking as well as what it speaks of, will make an impact especially because it has been expounded in such range and variety. Other series, courses, lecture programs and conferences, journals, and monographs have developed to further biblical theology within the Reformed context.

Biblical Theology Ending by Way of Its Success

If biblical theology arose as a crisis measure, however, then we ought not be surprised if it does not make for the best long-term care. Just as psychological debates regarding the best therapeutic approaches to abnormalities or mental health illnesses or traumas can grow fiery to such an extent that only after decades does a branch of psychology arise to address the matter of health and wellbeing (what is now called positive psychology), so it is easy to assume that trauma or crisis marks the everyday in other disciplines. Attention to Christian history will show that the communion of saints has enjoyed even lengthy seasons whereby doctrine was severed neither from a historical concern nor from an exegetical method; one has only to read Irenaeus or Cyril or Augustine on the one hand or Luther, Calvin, and Bucer on the other hand to see this illustrated in spades.

Again, the lack of descriptive clarity makes it hard to ascertain when biblical theological emphases will have actually succeeded. This question becomes pertinent not merely as one thinks about some time in the future but as one also looks at a range of texts and approaches in our diverse church today: Where do we (not) see an appropriate attention to the manner of scriptural instruction such that both form and content about being tended to in the theological task? Do exegetes attend to particular passages or verses with an eye to their intertextual links forward and backward? Do commentaries locate given texts within their wider redemptive-historical epochs and comment or note ways in which epochal change modifies their given concerns? Are dogmaticians paying attention not merely to isolated propositions but also to the literary framework within which they appear? Indeed, are dogmaticians showing transparency to canonical categories in helping to frame their theological topics? Is it evident, increasingly so, that dogmatics is meant to help prepare one for more fruitful exegesis of Holy Scripture? When dogmaticians do interject topics unrelated to the redemptive-historical sequence into their loci, do they explain why the Scripture demand consideration of the topic and just what mandates its address at this point and in these connections to matters before and after? When dogmatics employs nonbiblical terms, does it show biblical reasons for the need to seek terminological clarity (likely in connecting multiple idioms from across the canon or in showing variance in a given idiom within Scripture)? Such diagnostic questions help us assess when exegesis and dogmatics may have learned their lessons sufficiently.

Theological Interpretation of Scripture? A Parallel Crisis Intervention

If biblical theology merits this kind of analysis, then we would be negligent not to mention a similar phenomenon in the last three decades: theological interpretation of Scripture or theological exegesis. Like biblical theology, TIS has been a contested notion; while some have spoken of it as a movement, it rather marks an overlapping set of concerns about the task of biblical interpretation in the modern West.[82] Again context matters, for TIS has also offered response to a perceived crisis: hermeneutical naturalism in its varied forms (whether applied to reader, text, or their interaction).[83]

Darren Sarisky has recently offered a sketch of that hermeneutical naturalism. Regarding the reading subject, interpretive acts can be reduced to technique (the proper application of given hermeneutical principles) or to sociopolitical location (the identification of determinative cultural factors). As pertains to the text, the Bible has been viewed in whole and part increasingly as a set of ancient religious testimonies or witnesses, culled together from a range of backdrops. The literal sense has been identified with human authorial intention or human authorial sense, and the given scriptures are construed as wholly resolved into their socio-cultural and religious backgrounds. Finally, reader and text meet in an interpretive event which can be described completely in term of human epistemology, no recourse being had to the exalted Christ's prophetic office, the Spirit's illumination, or the life-giving power of the Father's Word.

By and large, then, TIS has been far more specific about what ails modern biblical interpretation than was Reformed biblical theology in its Vossian forms. Naturalism has been diagnosed and described in specific forms, sometimes

---

82. The literature is voluminous. Key texts surely include Stephen Fowl, *Engaging Scripture: A Model for Theological Interpretation* (Oxford: Blackwell, 1998); Kevin Vanhoozer, *First Theology: God, Scripture, Hermeneutics* (Downers Grove, IL: IVP Academic, 2002). A range of textbooks have been written, and the most useful survey remains Daniel J. Treier, *Introducing Theological Interpretation of Scripture: Recovering a Christian Practice* (Grand Rapids: Baker Academic, 2008). A dictionary serves as a major reference point: Kevin Vanhoozer (gen. ed.), *Dictionary for Theological Interpretation of the Bible* (Grand Rapids: Baker Academic, 2005). *Ex Auditu* and *Journal of Theological Interpretation* and its adjoining Supplement Series (by Eisenbrauns) play a key role in furthering the conversation as does Baker Academic's Studies in Theological Interpretation series and IVP Academic's Studies in Christian Doctrine and Scripture series. The Brazos Theological Commentary on the Bible has probably done more than anything else to raise the profile of TIS, while Belief: A Theological Commentary on the Bible (WJK) and the T&T Clark International Theological Commentary are seeking to develop the commentary genre still further (albeit in distinct ways).

83. See now the assessment of Darren Sarisky, *Reading the Bible Theologically* (Current Issues in Theology; Cambridge: Cambridge University Press, 2019); see also Mark Bowald, *Rendering the Word in Theological Hermeneutics: Mapping Divine and Human Action* (London: Routledge, 2007); Craig Carter, *Interpreting Scripture with the Great Tradition: Recovering the Genius of Premodern Exegesis* (Grand Rapids: Baker Academic, 2018).

debated of course but not suffering from underdetermination. TIS has varied a good bit more in its purported prescriptions, whether over philosophical proposals, hermeneutical principles, ecclesiological mandates, or dogmatic divergences (which can but do not always match denominational divides).[84] TIS differs with regard to its posture toward historical criticism and also to biblical theology.[85] TIS, at least in its measured moments, has nonetheless been helpful in reconstruing the task of reading scripture as both wholistic (involving virtue and relations as well as technique) and as spiritual (not reducible to human agency but itself located within the divine economy). TIS has also helped in drawing attention to the canonical and scriptural implications of a Christian doctrine of Scripture for the exegesis of the Bible. Ecclesiological and philosophical gains are debatable, though arguments can be made for genuine contributions here too.

All those benefits being acknowledged, eventually TIS should be a moot point and a needless project, at least in terms of discrete disciplinary practice. Again, it was initially invoked as a crisis measure, so this is not an alien restraint upon the project but a taking seriously of its own roots. Right now it is helpful to have graduate and postgraduate programs that focus on theological exegesis (both the University of St. Andrews and Wheaton College have offered such programs in the past two decades), as well as a range of publishing outlets (monograph series, journal, commentary series, dictionary). The significant methodological debate, which has not abated in over 20 years now, and the growing litany of examples of TIS in practice both serve well to address what it might mean to read theologically and how it connects to other elements of theological work or apply in various literary contexts. At some point, the revolution will have become a major stream within the status quo, and those of us who have participated in TIS in various ways can simply return again (at least in some contexts) to speaking of exegesis. While hermeneutical naturalism will surely still have a significant place in the Society of Biblical Literature and like endeavors, TIS may well become mainstream enough that it no longer needs to posture itself as a protest movement and can instead rest satisfied knowing that its theological and hermeneutical foci have leavened major tributaries in the guild and in the church.

Biblical Theology and the Quest for Wholeness

Further, we ought not overlook the need to assess whether emergency measures cause other complications. Unfortunately, such self-assessment has not always been welcomed. In describing some critics of even Reformed biblical theology, Gaffin chides: "At any rate anyone who thinks he detects the specter of a relativizing

---

84. Daniel J. Treier, "What is Theological Interpretation? An Ecclesiological Reduction," *International Journal of Systematic Theology* 12, no. 2 (2010), 144–61; Bradley Raymond East, "The Church's Book: Theology of Scripture in Ecclesial Context in the Work of John Howard Yoder, Robert Jenson, and John Webster" (Ph.D. Dissertation, Yale University, 2017).

85. See the typology and proposal in Daniel J. Treier, "Biblical Theology and/or Theological Interpretation of Scripture? Defining the Relationship," *Scottish Journal of Theology* 61, no. 1 (2008), 16–31.

historicism in biblical theology rightly conceived of simply reveals the flaws in his own theological foundations." He has just pointed out the real threat of historicism, so this is a rather startling comment.

Historicism takes varied forms. Historicism can take the sort of materialist approach whereby anything beyond matter is denied (i.e., the soul is denied). But historicism can also take the form of suggesting that those beings who participate in the realm beyond matter are nonetheless shaped by history. We do well to consider how biblical theology can go awry, both in its own project and especially in how it is taken to impact systematic theology.[86] Gaffin's own example manifests the danger in operating with critical care measures alone. He rightly points to the extensive use of eschatological language across the New Testament. Point of fact, he could extend (as does Vos) eschatology not merely across the apostolic writings but into the prophetic writings themselves. So he is surely right to note that eschatology involves more than that which we await and takes in, by contrast, all that which God has been doing to bring creation to its fitting fulfillment. In this regard, eschatology really does predate soteriology and even fall, in as much as Gen. 1.28-30 come prior to Genesis 3. So far, so good.

And yet Vos, Gaffin, and Ridderbos were not the only ones pointing to the eschatological conception of all apostolic or biblical teaching. Eschatology was being discovered afresh across the theological world. Albert Schweitzer, Martin Kähler, and Ernst Käsemann each wrote influentially on the way in which the New Testament witnesses were inflected with extensive eschatological language and imagery. And systematicians have been listening well beyond the walls of Westminster and the Reformed world. Richard Gaffin plead for biblical theology to fill the place to that time held by systematics in his 1976 essay. By that time, Wolfhart Pannenberg, Jürgen Moltmann, Carl Braaten, and Robert Jenson had made careers writing on the eschatological shape of all Christian teaching. In their approaches, not only was eschatology formative for Christology, ecclesiology, and politics but also for theology proper. Revisions to so-called classical theism have marked each of their projects in overlapping yet distinct ways.[87] They claim that God's own being and identity becomes; eschatology here is not only prior

---

86. For another recent example, see Grant Macaskill's helpful observation that debates about apocalyptic or salvation-historical readings of Pauline theology suffer from a failure to probe the relationship of historical events to the life of God in himself and the work of God's own providential agency ("History, providence, and the apocalyptic Paul," *Scottish Journal of Theology* 70, no. 3 (2017), 410 [409–26]).

87. For analysis of the most thoroughgoing project in this regard, see Scott R. Swain, *The God of the Gospel: Robert W. Jenson's Trinitarian Theology* (Downers Grove, IL: IVP Academic, 2013). See also Matthew Levering, *Scripture and Metaphysics: Aquinas and the Renewal of Trinitarian Theology* (Oxford: Blackwell, 2003); Francesca Aran Murphy, *God Is Not a Story: Realism Revisited* (Oxford: Oxford University Press, 2007); and Kevin J. Vanhoozer, *Remythologizing Theology: Divine Action, Passion, and Authorship* (Cambridge: Cambridge University Press, 2010).

to soteriology, but eschatology is definitive of and constitutes theology proper. Historicism, even in this "evangelical" form, is a real temptation for theology shaped definitively and exclusively by the biblical narrative. It can have serious doctrinal effects when severed from metaphysical analysis.

Biblical theology, especially when reduced as in Murray and Gaffin to redemptive historical reading, also has a tendency to flatten the terrain of biblical teaching and to malnourish the exegetical task. It is one thing to say that every text is impacted by its redemptive-historical aspect, that is, by its location historically in some epoch of the divine economy.[88] Indeed, many texts make their claims by means of overt reference to the movement of the economy, whether through intertextual development or other literary means. Aspectivally, all texts are historically located; partitively, only some texts are historical. Story can be just as reductive, and narrative can easily become a shoehorn for exegesis of the better part of Scripture. Here we can and should say two things: First, Vossian definitions are superior to those of Murray or Gaffin just at this point, namely, the nonreductive character of Vos's vision of biblical theology.[89] For Vos, literary multiformity is just as important as historical location. Why? Because both moves shape how we read the text in its own terms. Second, we should go beyond Vos, however, to reconsider whether or not biblical theology ought to play an ongoing role in our theological curriculum as such or whether it may well render itself moot owing to its own success. Biblical theology in a single-minded focus on redemptive history can narrow the canonical form of Holy Scripture and, in so doing, not only miss key elements to which systematic theology might alert us but also mangle exegesis of passages and books (even genres such as wisdom literature) that do not fit that narrative mold.[90]

---

88. See, e.g., discussion of narrative in Paul's epistles, as discussed in Bruce Longenecker (ed.), *Narrative Dynamics in Paul: A Critical Assessment* (Louisville: Westminster John Knox, 2002).

89. Interestingly, the later narrowing to redemptive-history in Reformed biblical theology as opposed to the broader Vossian definition may be one reason explaining the evangelical fascination with the new perspective(s) on Paul as a polemical target, on the one hand, and relative disinterest in engaging polemically with apocalyptic readings of Paul (i.e., J. Louis Martyn and his students). Surely other factors play into the disproportionate concern, relative to the two approaches' influence in the field of Pauline studies, but the fact that NPP issues map more decisively onto a redemptive-historical grid and sit more lightly to literary and genre-based approaches contributes to the reception history. On the other hand, the apocalyptic approaches to Paul trade more in literary analysis as opposed to narrative analysis and have drawn remarkably thin reaction from figures in the Reformed biblical theology conversation.

90. For an argument that both salvation-historical and apocalyptic approaches to Paul do so by failing to miss connections between Christology and creation, see Edwin van Driel, "Climax of the Covenant vs Apocalyptic Invasion: A Theological Analysis of a Contemporary Debate in Pauline Exegesis," *International Journal of Systematic Theology* 17, no. 1 (2015), 6–25; see also John M. G. Barclay, *Paul and the Gift* (Grand Rapids: Eerdmans, 2015), 411–14.

Maturity and the Theological Disciplines

What is ultimately necessary in terms of disciplinary definition and coordination? Proverbs promises that the one who tends to the Word will receive two things:

> My son, if you receive my words and treasure up my commandments with you, making your ear attentive to wisdom and inclining your heart to understanding; yes, if you call out for insight and raise your voice for understanding, if you seek it like silver and search for it as for hidden treasures, then you will understand the fear of the Lord and find the knowledge of God.
>
> (2.1-5)

The fear of the Lord and knowledge of God are necessary; to that end, we hearken to the Word. To receive that Word well—to search it out as for hidden treasure—we pay attention to the one and the many, to the Lord who is ever its center and also to its varied, textured breadth and cosmic scope. In other words, we think exegetically or receptively about the Word as a whole (what we call dogmatics) and about each constituent passage or part (what we call exegesis).

The exegetical task endeavors to listen well to the Word of God, in so doing attending to the specific shape and texture of its literary form. A host of intellectual virtues and spiritual fruit equip one to read with docility and humility, and a spate of verbal facilities play into doing so thoughtfully. While I have dealt with some of the ascetic facets of the theological and exegetical task elsewhere, here we consider its literary and canonical facets. How shall we read of the assumption of royal office by Saul first and David second; in what ways do the texts depict each? Here reading one text takes the form of catching its connections—historically and literarily—with adjacent episodes in a given text (say, 1-2 Samuel) or in wider redemptive-history. In so doing, emphases of so-called biblical theology will mark thorough and alert reading: how does a given passage fit within a flow of divine instruction (building on or modifying earlier statements in some respects?) and how does it sit alongside texts by other authors or in diverse literary forms (what are distinctive vocabulary? literary structures and features? parallels?). Good exegesis has and should be marked by those traits accented by biblical theology and theological interpretation of Scripture (at their best). Books, conferences, and classes may continue to focus on either discipline in an ad hoc way—perhaps to great significance—yet so long as exegesis occurs, the disciplines qua disciplines are extraneous. To the extent that exegesis fails to attend to the form of the text and the epochal history which it relates to, biblical theology may well be needed as an interpretive infusion. On occasions where the place of the reader, the text, or the interpretive act are dislocated from the divine economy and pursued via hermeneutical naturalism, theological interpretation of Scripture may be sought as an emergency room procedure. But the task that matters ultimately is exegesis, because here the biblical text—the living and active Word of God which alone cuts and divides soul and spirit, joint and marrow (Heb. 4.12-13)—is engaged in its concrete and particular specificity. Here faith shapes intellectual action by turning in docility and patience to be addressed by the promise and the summons of this divine Word. The biblical text—not some redemptive-historical schema—is the divinely appointed means of communion and instruction for his covenant people.

What of systematic or dogmatic reasoning? Again, we seek to listen to God's Word, though now we tend to its totality rather than to a given point or passage. Here conceptual connections are traced not merely on a linear plot but across various topics. How shall we relate the exercise of a human kingly office with the claim that God is king over all? Here we come to metaphysical judgments that shape the storied flow of scripture but themselves are not reduced to it. Dogmatics shapes the way in which we read any portion of Holy Scripture by attending to the breadth of the Word, tracing its proportions, catching its emphases, and seeking to grasp its connections or coherence. Thankfully some biblical theologians have from time to time claimed that their discipline stood against the fragmenting or atomistic shape of modern historical criticism.[91] To the extent that biblical theology has and does show evidence of canonical unity, that is to be celebrated for it alerts us to a truth. Attention to unity, however, is a hallmark of Christian systematic theology, which never satisfies itself to study Matthew's language for conversion or Micah's definition of justice but always seeks the "whole counsel of God" (Acts 20.27).

John Webster argues that dogmatics order itself from and toward exegesis.

> Dogmatics is the schematic and analytical presentation of the matter of the gospel. It is 'systematic,' not in the sense that it offers a rigidly formalised set of deductions from a master concept, but in the low-level sense of gathering together what is dispersed through the temporal economy to which the prophets and apostles direct reason's gaze. What dogmatic reason may not do is pretend to a firmer grasp of the object of theological reason than can be achieved by following the text.[92]

He speaks then of the "rhetorical sufficiency" of Scripture, which means that all theology ideally takes the form of commentary (whether with a narrow lens or wide angle lens). Good dogmatics traces out biblical teaching, at times employing formal terms (not least when scripture itself speaks with diverse terminology on a matter or when heresy demands refinement through the use of extra-biblical language for clarity's sake) though seeking to be as transparent not merely to biblical content but also biblical rhetoric as possible.

---

91. See, e.g., the subtitle and repeated references in the essays in Scott J. Hafemann and Paul House (eds.), *Central Themes in Biblical Theology: Mapping Unity in Diversity* (Grand Rapids: Baker Academic, 2007).

92. John Webster, "Biblical Reasoning," in *The Domain of the Word: Scripture and Theological Reason* (London: T&T Clark, 2012), 131; see also idem, "Scripture, Theology, and the Theological School," in *Holy Scripture: A Dogmatic Sketch* (Current Issues in Theology; Cambridge: Cambridge University Press, 2004), 130–2; idem, *Holiness* (Grand Rapids: Eerdmans, 2003), 3–4.

Similarly, organization flows from and alerts readers to the schematics of the canon; not for nothing do classical systematic theologies (whether single- or multivolume) tend to move through the scope and sequence of events in the divine economy and insert other biblical topics amongst that narrative sequence as necessary to help make sense of the character and their relations (e.g., prolegomenal matters or the doctrine of God at the forefront to help lay the ground for all subsequent discussion, anthropology perhaps at the tail end of material on creation to help rightly identify a character of consequence throughout the whole economy). Given that many portions of the canon do not fit neatly into a redemptive-historical epoch (i.e., Proverbs), it is necessary to find other ways to connect them, in their cohesion and also their distinctiveness, to the rest of Holy Scripture. While logic is exercised in shaping these categories (as repeatedly noted by Vos and his heirs), it is misleading to suggest that the Bible shapes the categories of biblical theology as if this is not true of systematic theology (*contra* Vos and his heirs). Logic and Scripture shape the organizational rubrics of both disciplines. Biblical theology debates endlessly central themes or centers of the whole Bible, a given testament, genre, or corpus, or even a particular biblical author or book. Biblical theology also organizes itself around redemptive history. Systematics— not the revisionist style of the recent Workgroup on Constructive Theology but the classical approach that spanned all denominational traditions—employs that redemptive-historical or creedal sequence, inserting other topics for clarity's sake at what are deemed helpful places (not least by identifying God as its head, so as to differentiate him from all other beings, owing to the Bible's own fundamental polemic against idolatry). Dogmatics will say more than the redemptive historical sequence but it is no less attuned to that sequence for doing so, and only by saying more can it attune us to attend to that sequence with reverential cognizance for what sort of sequence it actually is, namely, a divine economy.

As above, it is always appropriate for exegetes to question if the organization of theology is truly transparent or helpful in drawing attention back to the whole text of Scripture in its emphases and proportions; for example, Patrick Miller has rightly challenged the way in which the first article of the creed (and engagement of Israel's life and history with God, in particular) has not always had the place it warrants given its significance not merely in the Old Testament but also in the apostolic writings.[93] Without endorsing his particular exegesis or suggestions in all its details, I take his proposal as a good faith effort to ensure that doctrinal and confessional categories are sufficiently broad as to alert us to both the specificity and the span of biblical teaching. If dogmatics is not operating in a manner that is shaped by both form and content, the historical flow and the multiform genres of biblical teaching, then biblical theology may be needed to help infuse elements of the canonical diet and to remedy that malnutrition. When dogmatics may fail to prioritize biblical and canonical reasoning and the primary use of biblical

---

93. Patrick D. Miller Jr., "Rethinking the First Article of the Creed," *Theology Today* 61, no. 4 (2005), 499–508.

terminology as being epistemologically significant (given the divine nature of this text over above all others), then theological interpretation of Scripture and retrieval of the great tradition of historic biblical exegesis may be needed as a steroid to help reenergize our canonical confidence as theologians. Yet the task that matters here is thinking whole and together, reflecting systematically or dogmatically, upon the whole Word of God.

In the end, then, perhaps we have much to learn from the witness of those saints who have gone before us. Calvin wrote his *Institutes of the Christian Religion*, to be sure, but he also invested significant time in what are now his commentaries. This division of labor amongst genres—not persons, not schools, not churches, but particular texts and genres—was rooted in earlier texts. Bonaventure would write a *Breviloquim* and then would give commentary on the Gospel according to John or Ecclesiastes. Thomas worked on four *summae* of varying sorts, yet his daily work was to lecture as master of the sacred page, leaving us commentaries on a range of books from both testaments. This is why some of us who are involved in writing systematic theology have also devoted ourselves to penning biblical commentaries, and why the cultures of dogmatic and exegetical reasoning need to kept in the closest connection. And, far more definitive for our purposes, Paul himself proclaimed the "whole counsel of God" while also teaching page by page through the *torah*. Both tasks are crucial, and neither task can be done well apart from ongoing engagement with the other. Exegesis and dogmatics have apostolic mandate for the church's ongoing intellectual life as disciples of the Word of God; ancillary helps such as biblical theology or theological interpretation of Scripture may serve at times to reorient or infuse missing elements and recalibrate the scriptural texture of exegesis and dogmatics, though we do well to remember that in so doing they are functioning as an intellectual therapy or crisis intervention, not a long-term regimen.[94]

---

94. My thanks to Wesley Hill, Jono Linebaugh, Scott Swain, Liam Goligher, and Carl Trueman for help with this chapter.

Chapter 6

ON APOCALYPTIC THEOLOGY

Recent remembrances of the Protestant Reformation frequently marked with sorrow the splintering of the Western church in the sixteenth century. With some regularity such remembrances also observed ways in which Protestantism helped speed up or even to spawn the rise of modern individualism, liberalism, and secularism. Martin Luther's fixation upon the human soul needing justification before God, and his single-minded focus upon the texts of Romans and especially Galatians, serves as a focus for this kind of worry. For a variety of political and ecclesiological reasons, Protestantism has been much maligned in recent days.

How interesting it is, then, that one of the most significant movements in contemporary theology has been a determined focus upon a distinctly Protestant theology practiced in a mode drawn uniquely out of Galatians and related Pauline imagery. Theology has taken an apocalyptic turn in recent decades, owing to the influence of Schweitzer, Barth, and Käsemann and then especially to J. Louis Martyn and a number of those influenced by him. In days when Protestant theology has sometimes lacked nerve, whether owing to historiographic debates about the new perspective(s) on Paul, the Finnish reading of Luther, or ecumenical conversations about pursuing churchly unity, a concerted attention to Paul's most radical imagery as an orienting lens for Christian theology stands out as a jarring proposal for contemporary theological construction.

What is this apocalyptic turn? And, does this represent a viable way forward for a Protestant theology in the twenty-first century? In what ways does this approach represent a pastoral or prudential judgment regarding the specific needs of a particular *chronos*? And in what respects might it herald promise for a viable Protestantism which may have recovered its nerve for the days ahead? While the apocalyptic turn has drawn the attention of interpreters working in the ecumenical or postliberal world, it has also occurred amongst those who would seek to draw on the radical Lutheran vision of a Rudolf Bultmann.[1] So it also must

---

1. See, e.g., Douglas Harink, *Paul among the Postliberals: Pauline Theology Beyond Christendom and Modernity* (Grand Rapids: Brazos, 2003); David Congdon, *The Mission of Demythologizing: Rudolf Bultmann's Dialectical Theology* (Minneapolis: Fortress Press, 2015), 357–9. Congdon has rightly shown that Bultmann has an apocalyptic strand in his own thought: see especially idem, "Apocalypse as Perpetual Advent: The Apocalyptic

be asked what kinds of Protestant vision and what sorts of Christian theology can be furthered by such an apocalyptic turn.

Philip Ziegler's *Militant Grace: The Apocalyptic Turn and the Future of Christian Theology* provides the most programmatic proposal for answering these questions and deserves careful attention. The book contains thirteen essays (all previously published elsewhere) relating to apocalyptic from biblical, theological, historical, and ethical angles.[2] In that regard, it is the most wide-ranging analysis of apocalyptic and the future of theology yet available. If one listens carefully, it offers an assessment of the apocalyptic turn in theology thus far, proffers a way to shore up some of its most notable weaknesses, and manifests tensions that remain latent in the enterprise and in any future developments. Wrestling with Ziegler's argument surely aids in weighing the merits and limits of the apocalyptic turn.

What Is the Apocalyptic Turn? from Pauline Studies to Christian Theology

First, Ziegler speaks of an "apocalyptic turn" in recent theology which deserves attention. "The apocalyptic eschatology, language, and imagery of the New Testament is integral to its witness to the accomplishment of God's salvation in Jesus Christ, representing a primary idiom by which faith sought to attest the gospel and conceive its consequences" (p. xiii). Using the language of what is "primary" and "integral," Ziegler seeks to point not only to what is communicated but also to how it is communicated; form and content cannot be neatly divided or separated. Methodological concerns must attend to biblical idioms then: "The overarching argument of this book is that in pursuit of renewed accountability to the apocalyptic gospel, theology is required to think again about its own forms, methods, and foci precisely in virtue of its distinctively eschatological *content*" (p. xv). Not surprisingly, a number of those interested in the apocalyptic Paul and his consequence for Christian theology are also influenced by postliberalism (with its scripture-shaped vision of the church, as in Frei and Lindbeck).

How do these apocalyptic forms serve integrally to commend the good news of Christ? "For theology to take an 'apocalyptic turn' of this kind means undertaking to discern and inhabit forms of thought that eschew conformity with the schema of that old 'world which is passing away' because they seek to accord with the

---

Sermons of Rudolf Bultmann," *Theology Today* 75, no. 1 (Apr. 2018), 51–63. Not for nothing, Congdon sees Bultmann's apocalyptic account evident in his engagement of John's teaching on Advent; outside Paul, no other text so significantly presents a potentially dualistic portrayal of the children of light and the children of darkness (on which see Stephen Barton and especially Miroslav Volf, "Johannine Dualism and Contemporary Pluralism," in *The Gospel of John and Christian Theology* [ed. Richard Bauckham and Carl Mosser; Grand Rapids: Eerdmans, 2008], 3–18 and 19–51).

2. Grand Rapids: Baker Academic, 2018. Citations will be offered parenthetically.

world graciously remade by God in Christ" (p. xv). Language of grace and of the good news is repeated throughout, frequently tethered to this confession of a world remade or recreated. Such is the value of apocalyptic categories which attest disruption and intervention and newness and describe disjunction and transformation and triumph. Ziegler even asks if these categories have a singular sufficiency in this regard: "Might we agree that the eschatological categories provided by the New Testament—casting forward to the future while anchored christologically—are finally the only ones adequate to trace the lineaments of the gospel and to 'render to reality its due', as Käsemann once put it"? (p. 12). May grace really be confessed apart from the language of militancy?

Ziegler claims a singular role for this idiom because he offers a substantial reading of this apocalyptic news, and readers do well not to miss the gravity of his claim or its purported implications. Drawing especially on the writings of Paul, in particular texts such as Galatians and to some extent Romans, Ziegler captures the distinctiveness of an apocalyptic approach by offering six theses which are worth quoting in full:

"1. A Christian theology funded by a fresh hearing of New Testament apocalyptic will discern in that distinctive and difficult idiom a discourse uniquely adequate both to announce the full scope, depth, and radicality of the gospel of God, and to bespeak the actual and manifest contradiction of that gospel by the actuality of the times in which we live" (p. 26). He will go on to speak of how this "uniquely adequate" word about God and his works: "The apocalyptic idiom strains to articulate the gratuity of divine sovereignty and the sovereignty of divine grace" (p. 26).

"2. A Christian theology funded by a fresh hearing of New Testament apocalyptic will turn on a vigorous account of divine revelation in Jesus Christ as the unsurpassable eschatological act of redemption; its talk of God and treatment of all other doctrines will thus be marked by an intense Christological concentration" (p. 26).

"3. A Christian theology funded by a fresh hearing of New Testament apocalyptic will stress the unexpected, new, and disjunctive character of the divine work of salvation that comes on the world of sin in and through Christ. As a consequence, in its account of the Christian life, faith, and hope, it will make much of the ensuing evangelical 'dualisms'" (p. 27).

"4. A Christian theology funded by a fresh hearing of New Testament apocalyptic will provide an account of salvation as a 'three-agent drama' of divine redemption in which human beings are rescued from captivity to the anti-God powers of sin, death, and the devil. In addition to looking to honor the biblical witness, this is also, it is wagered, an astute and realistic gesture of notable explanatory power" (p. 28).

"5. A Christian theology funded by a fresh hearing of New Testament apocalyptic will acknowledge that it is the world and not the church that is the ultimate object of divine salvation. It will thus conceive of the church as a creation of the Word, a provisional and pilgrim community gathered, upheld, and sent to testify in word and deed to the gospel for the sake of the world. Both individually and corporately, the Christian life is chiefly to be understood as militant discipleship in evangelical freedom" (p. 29).

"6. A Christian theology funded by a fresh hearing of New Testament apocalyptic will adopt a posture of prayerful expectation of an imminent future in which God will act decisively and publicly to vindicate the victory of Life and Love over Sin and Death. The ordering of its tasks and concentration of its energies will befit the critical self-reflection of a community that prays, 'Let grace come and let this world pass away'"! (p. 30).

While apocalyptic does refer to a literary genre and certain concomitant literary features, it has been transmuted or developed to attest with its idiom the word of eschatological disruption in Jesus Christ. Indeed, a commitment to revert neither to creational metaphysics nor to historical chronology alone marks out this program from others. A "christological concentration" and these "evangelical dualisms" will shape a disruptive and downright polemical theological posture. Ziegler will later claim: "Soteriology must increase; anthropology as such must decrease" (p. 166). Grace quite literally cannot be evident apart from the militancy of redemption from sin.

The apocalyptic turn magnifies elements of both the works of God and the ways of the Christian. First and foremost, apocalyptic accents the agency of the transcendent God in his disjunctive, world-transforming militancy (pp. 6, 10). Whereas theologies built on creational metaphysics may seek to show the smooth transition from nature to grace and eventually unto glory, an apocalyptic theology will always identify the created order outside Christ with the terrain pulverized by sin, death, and the devil. Insofar as attention to the linear progress of redemptive history can easily become speculative projection of anthropological ideals, the apocalyptic turn summons us back to the singular revelation of God in Christ Jesus. Like Barth's early reflections on the Epistle to the Romans, then, the apocalyptic turn has sought to call the church back to the God who acts. Second, apocalyptic resituates the Christian on the far side of a battle with a need to declare allegiance and to suffer the loving sovereignty of God. The possibility of a quiet disposition before the ways of this death-dealing world is rendered null and void by the actuality of citizenship in the kingdom governed by the Lamb. Not only God's works but also the ways of the Christian are refashioned owing to this new action of God in Christ. Whether written by Barth, Martyn, or Ziegler, the apocalyptic Paul offers a bracing retort to well-trained intuitions about human progress and the moral limits of a thoroughgoing historicism.[3]

---

3. For analysis of historicism in the modern academy see Frederick Beiser, *The German Historicist Tradition* (Oxford: Oxford University Press, 2015).

How Does Philip Ziegler Advance the Apocalyptic Cause?
Reflections on the Christological and Ethical Arguments

The first part of Ziegler's book surveys scholarship in recent decades on the apocalyptic Paul and its potential for Christian theology, yet *Militant Grace* devotes the better part of its attention to shoring up two areas that are frequently underdeveloped in this apocalyptic conversation: Christology (part two) and discipleship (part three). In so doing, he not only sums up a conversation that has been ongoing but also seeks to channel and direct it in a more sustainable path and to equip it with deeper resources. The turn began as an effort to discern the center of Paul's theology (Ernst Käsemann, J. Louis Martyn, Douglas Campbell, etc.) and has branched out to engage recent continental philosophy (Douglas Harink, Joshua Davis, Travis Kroeker, Nathan Kerr, etc.). With Ziegler's book, the apocalyptic turn is taken into the work of Christian dogmatics more fully.

First, Ziegler provides a more substantive Christology than has hitherto been included in apocalyptic theologies. For all their talk of a "christological concentration," apocalyptic theology has frequently tended to assume rather than commend a particular Christological account (a thinness that Barth recognized in his own earlier, more apocalyptic work). In its material claims, apocalyptic theology has fixed upon a narrow range of claims (tightly wrapped around key terms like event or crucifixion/death), to which Ziegler now seeks to offer a broader placement and by implication a more textured description. While he does make use of the language of the Christ event regularly (as this has been a staple of apocalyptic rhetoric), he turns to more substantive terms such as "office" to provide a habitat of reference and theological conceptuality for the more dynamic language native to the apocalyptic idiom.

This major infusion to apocalyptic Christology involves retrieval of the specific language of Christ's royal office (a hallmark especially of Reformed Christology since Calvin). Christ reigns as king, and in so doing he transforms expectations regarding the figure at the center of God's kingdom. Interestingly, Ziegler sometimes moderates the apocalyptic movement's tendency to stand over against the dogmatic tradition, acknowledging instead that "Historic Reformed sources, much to their credit, track these Pauline emphases quite closely" (p. 75). Nonetheless, it is worth paying attention to what he suggests are the most central facets of an apocalyptic understanding of sin and of grace, of the royal Christ and of the coronation gift of his Spirit. "First, Reformed theology advances a doctrine of sin whose seriousness is only overreached by the seriousness of its doctrine of salvation, including its account of conversion to faith" (p. 75). "Second, we do well to avoid truncated understandings of the Spirit's work that too narrowly identify it with the 'interior' call to faith in contrast to the 'external' call of the gospel" (p. 76). "Third and finally, the distinctive Reformed doctrine of effectual calling is liable to a similar kind of pneumatological restatement along these same lines" (p. 77). While appreciative of the Reformed tradition here, Ziegler wants to accent what are sometimes atrophied elements of its confession. He seeks to relocate Christ, Spirit, and faith in a thoroughly eschatological milieu.

What is the value of these three emphases? "It is the task of Protestant theology generally, and of its account of the Christian life in particular, to demonstrate that such a life is 'an impossible newness given as an unfitting gift' by the Spirit, so that the 'potency of [divine] grace should be made perfect in our weakness'" (p. 79). Here again he will regularly invoke the language of the Christ event and of the inbreaking of God's eschatological deliverance. The "impossible newness" marks out the way in which this triumph is transcendent and not according to the ways of this world. The "unfitting gift" goes further to attest the manner in which this transformed reality does not sit easily alongside the sin-riddled existence of the children of Adam. Reformed Christology and Pneumatology are turned here to gesture toward not only an eschatological context but one that accents the soteriological discontinuity of nature and grace.

Second, apocalyptic theology has commended the dualistic posture of the disciple as one who lives this side of a definitive invasion. Yet the apocalyptic turn has so majored upon disruption that concrete ethical proposals have not always been forthcoming. The language of event can register change, but it suffers to signify order or structure with the same degree of rigor. It can also be developed in such a way that perhaps ironically threatens the triumphant distinction of divine King and his creaturely disciples.[4] In the final part of *Militant Grace*, then, Ziegler also seeks to widen the ethical project of apocalyptic theology. Ziegler shows that the apocalyptic turn has not only generated a vibrant focus upon divine agency but also upon ethics. What of its unique emphases for Christian practice? Apocalyptic idioms bring out the rhythms of prayer with a special verve: "I suggest that praying 'Thy Kingdom Come' faithfully means inhabiting an eschatological field shaped decisively by both Christological and apocalyptic coordinates, and that petitioning God in just this way is properly constitutive of the very fundaments of Christian faith" (p. 82).

Prayer—specifically invocation of the kingdom—is definitive for the way of discipleship. "To pray for the coming of the Kingdom is to beg that God would come upon the world as God" (p. 84). Ziegler draws the reader's attention to the focal images in play here as well. "In the parabolic idiom of the Gospels, what is in view is the arrival of the bridegroom (Mt. 25.1-13), the return of the master (21.33-44), the coming of the thief in the night (24.42-44), the inescapable final assize (25.31-46), the threshing of creation's harvest (3.12), the apocalypse of the Son of Man (Lk. 17.30), and so, in short, the accomplishment of 'that destiny toward which the whole of time is directed'" (p. 84). The cry of anticipation will be one that speaks of human rejection of epistemological control, of revelational clarity, and of political power. The prayer of the disciple will mark out one who

---

4. For example, Shannon Nicole Smythe's language of "Spirit-led kenotic practices" may push the language of kenosis to its breaking point, given that it is there applied to human religious practice ("The Way of Divine and Human Handing-Over: Pauline Apocalyptic, Centering Prayer, and Vulnerable Solidarity," *Theology Today* 75, no. 1 [2018], 85 [77–88]).

waits and observes and looks to the clouds. The language of human control has been subverted by the call to redeemed confession.

The kingdom cry also involves prophetic speech. "Apocalyptic theology will be a non-speculative, concrete, and practical form of knowing, committed to the work of discerning the signs of the times by Scripture and Spirit" (p. 30). Describing prayer for the reign of God by means of attending to the varied and concrete images of the parables manifests this tinge of an apocalyptic discipleship. In watching the clouds, the disciple relativizes the events of the day. In waiting for the second advent, the Christian acknowledges that time has been remade. And all this because faith has already come, Jesus has appeared, and revelation has been made known. The invasion of the sin-riddled cosmos has recast all times and places due to the eschatologically impactful insurgency of King Jesus.

Divine agency and prophetic discipleship are given vitality in this apocalyptic news: "[A]s Carl Braaten once observed, while other theological idioms are not incapable of giving voice to such truths, apart from an apocalyptic perspective their expression is readily and all too often obstructed and rendered 'sterile or inactive'" (p. 69). Ziegler commends an apocalyptic posture of theology that recurs constantly to a word of grace and yet discerns grace in its militant manner of subverting the ways of this world, as "the kingdoms of this world become the kingdoms of our Lord and of his Christ." *Militant Grace* wagers that the apocalyptic turn helps better attune theologians to the necessary disjunction of Christ's work and of Christ's call to discipleship.

What Future Might There Be for a Protestant Theology? Reflections on Hermeneutical Consistency

Like many participants in the apocalyptic turn, Ziegler self-identifies as bearing a distinctly and radically Protestant concern.[5] He says:

> For my own part, I am certainly drawn to the task of envisaging an apocalyptic theology for 'ardently Protestant' reasons. For it seems to me that, understood as it is here, apocalyptic is a discursive idiom uniquely suited to articulate the

---

5. See also Nathan Kerr, *Christ, History, and Apocalyptic: The Politics of Christian Mission* (London: SCM, 2008). Ry O. Siggelkow has juxtaposed the apocalyptic turn as an alternative to what Siggelkow deems the "ecclesial turn" in recent Protestant theology ("Ernst Käsemann and the Specter of Apocalyptic," *Theology Today* 75, no. 1 [2018], 37–50): "in such accounts, the pressing theological task is fundamentally and primarily a matter of the maintenance of the church and its institutions and traditional practices" (pp. 46). For an analysis of what prospects an apocalyptic theology may well have within Roman Catholic theology in both Augustinian and non-Augustinian modes, see Cyril O'Regan, "Two Forms of Catholic Apocalyptic Theology," *International Journal of Systematic Theology* 20, no. 1 (2018), 31–64.

radicality, sovereignty, and militancy of adventitious divine grace; just so it is of real import to the dogmatic work of testing the continued viability of Protestant Christian faith.

(p. xvii)

Yet any viable theological future must be held by a particular sort of Protestant theology. "It is the task of Protestant theology generally, and of its account of the Christian life in particular, to demonstrate that such a life is 'an impossible newness given as an unfitting gift' by the Spirit, so that the 'potency of [divine] grace should be made perfect in our weakness'" (p. 79). Such alertness to invasive grace has not been dominant in modern Protestant theology. Ziegler reminds us that "Robert Jenson has argued that 'modernity's great theological project was to suppress apocalyptic, and to make messianism into guru-worship'" (p. 25). In other words, Jenson faults modern theological projects for receding from historical claims and settling for abstract principles, what maxims might be offered by a mere guru. Nineteenth-century archaeologists of religion might have offered the grandest of such accounts, whereby the Christian faith could be plotted among the evolution of human religiosity, but the temptation has remained and spread much more widely in pietistic, psychological, and political directions.

Over against such abstractions, Ziegler suggests that an apocalyptically shaped theology will be "non-speculative, concrete, and practical" (p. 30). In other words, the apocalyptic turn may involve repenting of historicist attention to the things of this world and recurrence unto those eschatological disruptions of Christ's advent and its victorious imprint on the cosmos. Thus, the apocalyptic theologian does not speculate, fixes upon the eschatologically concrete, and points to practical judgment. All three descriptors can be helpful emphases, to the extent that they fix one's attention upon receptive reflection on God's self-revelation and God's own works. In so doing, they chart a pathway at odds with the idol-making pretensions of human ingenuity.

Yet the concrete and the practical can easily morph into the speculative if they are insufficiently broad in dogmatic scope and are canonically malnourished in their hermeneutical function. Indeed, a tension can arise if the concrete and the practical are not held in seamless unity with contemplation of the full range of God's works and the depths of God's own self-revelation. It is quite possible for a theology of the economy or of soteriology to remain at the level of benefits or the soteriological *pro me*. If not the way of the reformers, then such is at least the pathway of Ritschl, and such is a tempting path. Does the apocalyptic intensity of focus upon soteriology actually keep the human too much in the center of things? Might this narrowing of dogmatic range keep us in the outer courts and fail to draw us into the holy of holies where the divine glory actually dwells? Can such a principled posture make sense of the Scriptures, the testimony of both prophets and apostles as they unveil the "whole counsel of God" (Acts 20.27)? What might be its hermeneutical implications and its dogmatic limitations?

The apocalyptic turn may be a broader, more nuanced hermeneutic than, say, the Radical Lutheran rendering of the law-gospel distinction inasmuch as it locates judgment more broadly: "A forensic emphasis on saving divine judgment admits and demands this crucial cosmological supplement" (p. 100). Salvation will be more than merely moral in such an approach and will also exceed the existential. "Envisaged in this way, salvation can come only through a divine incursion from without, the invasion of divine grace, because what humanity needs is ontic and ontological rescue, 'not merely repentance and forgiveness, but liberation from its captivity and, indeed, new creation'" (p. 107). The apocalyptic turn locates the typical forensic concern of Protestant theology amidst a militant fight between light and darkness. In that sense, it thickens the kind of hermeneutical distinctions exercised by those hewing more closely to the earlier Lutheran and Reformed distinction.

Like the law-gospel distinction, though, the extent of its systemic and structural import may vary a good deal. So here with the apocalyptic turn, exactly how radical a lens the apocalyptic may be is debated. Martyn employs the lens in an operative and functional manner such that other key idioms are reshaped. For instance, he renders the term *dikaiosune* "rectification" so as to modify its declarative form and augment its effective or transformative impact; Ziegler depicts this shift as such: "The aim is to connect talk of justification so closely with talk of death and life along these lines that they become identified, as indeed they were by Luther" (p. 7). While justification stands upon Christ's death and life and bears upon our own, Martyn's translational transition here is not innocuous. Bruce McCormack has also argued that Martyn morphs the cross into a place of triumph rather than of death and suffering.[6] Again, the death of the king is necessary unto his victory over sin, death, and the devil, but it is not in and of itself a victory with regard to these cosmic foes.[7] In his essays as well as his commentary on Galatians, Martyn clearly uses apocalyptic as a *discrimen* for interpreting Paul's texts.

Other accounts are on offer regarding the relationships of apocalyptic to Christian theology construed more broadly, such as Joseph Mangina's far more measured approach that celebrates apocalyptic for its unique contributions and yet locates it amongst other canonical idioms.[8] Having considered Galatians in particular, Mangina relates the apocalyptic form as a pastoral response to a particular historical challenge, rooting it in the first commandment and thus expounding it as a reminder that "*Chronos* is no god" over against what he deems

---

6. Bruce L. McCormack, "Can We Still Speak of 'Justification by Faith'? An In-House Debate with Apocalyptic Readings of Paul," in *Galatians and Christian Theology: Justification, the Gospel, and Ethics in Paul's Letter* (ed. Mark W. Elliott et al; Grand Rapids: Baker Academic, 2014), 168.

7. Though Wesley Hill reminds me that the Gospel according to John certainly identifies the cross with Jesus' glorification (12.23; 13.31).

8. Grant Macaskill also describes how Richard Hays's work functions alongside certain other postliberal readers of the Old Testament (and by implication Paul and the Gospels) to offer a more canonical version of an apocalyptic Paul ("History, Providence, and the apocalyptic Paul," *Scottish Journal of Theology* 70, no. 4 [2017], 421–2).

the one modern heresy: historicism. In the face of historicist narratives and materialist imagination, "an apocalypse is what happens when the whole world has a hole in its roof."[9] Mangina concluded that "The appeal to apocalyptic cannot solve all our theological problems. It is only one among a number of idioms employed in Scripture and the dogmatic tradition and needs to find its place in a diverse ecology that includes creation, law, wisdom, sacrifice, worship, and for that matter Scripture's narrative element—the stories of Jesus and Israel and the church."[10] Apocalyptic here functions as a necessary prompt and a crucial piece of the canonical puzzle, but Mangina suggests that it is not meant to be load-bearing or foundational, at least not by itself. He specifically notes that the apocalyptic moments of Paul (and, we might add, John) need to be read alongside the narrative accounts of Luke (and, we should note, the other synoptics).

If the apocalyptic turn is to have productive gains to offer Christian theology, then it must find a way of avoiding any conceptual overconcentration that prompts a hermeneutical and canonical constriction. In that regard, Mangina's exegetical proposal seems far more promising than that of Martyn, and Ziegler's theological framing offers more viability than that of other such accounts in recent years which bespeak of apocalyptic "without reserve" (e.g., Kerr, Lowe).[11] If apocalyptic is taken to be the only form of Christian theology come fully into its own, then it will surely have a parasitic effect wherein a purportedly nonspeculative concentration upon God's revelation in Jesus Christ guarantees a need for a projectionist approach to cosmology and anthropology, much less the doctrine of God. As Barth soon found when he took up the task of dogmatics, God's divine unveiling in the incarnation of Jesus Christ is invariably bound up with a simultaneous veiling, in as much as this was not pure divine translucence but divine incarnation. And such developments will necessarily involve parsing out the canon within a canon.[12]

Herein we might identify tensions within even Ziegler's salient depiction of the apocalyptic turn. On the one hand, apocalyptic is all about "the ends" of the

---

9. Joseph Mangina, "Apocalypse Now: On Doing Theology at a Time Near the End of the World," p. 7.

10. Ibid., 11.

11. Kerr, *Christ, History, and Apocalyptic: The Politics of Christian Mission*; Walter Lowe, "Prospects for a Postmodern Christian Theology: Apocalyptic Without Reserve," *Modern Theology* 15, no. 1 (1999), 17–24; see also the many significant essays in Joshua B. Davis and Douglas Harink (eds.), *Apocalyptic and the Future of Theology* (Eugene, OR: Wipf & Stock, 2012).

12. Siggelkow reminds us that, for Käsemann, "the New Testament is a battleground: far from presenting a unified theological front, it represents a collection of documents that contain glimpses into serial conflicts, quarrelling theological factions, and opposing theological perspectives" ("Käsemann and the Specter of Apocalyptic," 47–8). Even if one finds "a unified theological front" to be too homogenous a portrayal, it is a significant jump to move to describing the New Testament canon as involving conflicts that are "serial," factions, and "opposing theological perspectives." Indeed, Käsemann is committed to reading perpetual and perennial challenge internal to the church.

gospel (p. 11). Indeed, his pursuit of this project is "to argue for the adequacy of a Christian doctrine of salvation whose central motif is the eschatological struggle and victory of God over Sin for the sake of his beleaguered creatures" (p. 54). And yet the depiction of this end focuses upon its emergence rather than its nature. Edwin Chr. van Driel has suggested that this may be paired with a similar failure of apocalyptic theology to reckon Christ himself as "plan A," God's original intention for his creation.[13] Does Christ define the ends of human being or is Christ not defined—dominated—to some extent by the plight or problem to which he is the soteriological and triumphant answer? Can a thoroughgoing soteriological reframing of theology actually sustain even a specifically Christological concentration with its full range of concerns or are they all truly reduced to soteriology?

An ethical tension arises by implication. First, Ziegler suggests that

> the universality that our contemporary Christian ethicists seek by a retrieval of natural law could be secured not by appeal to creation per se but rather by appeal to the one reality of the one world that has been remade at the turning of the ages, the reality of the twice-invaded world, and so by appeal to the 'universality of the revealed God', to use Wolf Krötke's phrase.
>
> (p. 137)

But, second, his emphasis remains upon "discontinuity [which] is the dominant motif" (p. 134). In discussing ethics, he will also say that "a Protestant Christian ethic should take its first and defining cues from a dramatic theological account of fall and redemption" (p. 151), moving ahead of orders of creation, natural law, or any primal design to straightforward teaching on redemptive history. For all his language about universality and its present deployment via militant imagery, Ziegler continues to speak of the cosmos as terrain war-torn and divided by forces of sin and redemption. We may well ask if the hamartiological and soteriological framing of all cosmology has not actually generated a portrait that centralizes creaturely being, both of the world as such and of its human occupants in particular.

Does This Apocalyptic Turn Reintroduce Speculation?

The apocalyptic reader of Paul seeks to work nonspeculatively. Yet in so doing the hermeneutical function played the apocalyptic framing of the gospel can have a constricting effect upon the scope and sequence of Christian doctrine. A question must be posed: Is not a broader scope of Christian theology and a more restrained emphasis upon the apocalyptic idiom to re-introduce speculation into

---

13. Edwin Chr. van Driel, "Christ in Paul's Narrative: Salvation History, Apocalyptic Invasion, and Supralapsarian Theology," in *Galatians and Christian Theology*, 235; see also Edwin Chris Van Driel, "Climax of the Covenant vs Apocalyptic Invasion: A Theological Analysis of a Contemporary Debate in Pauline Exegesis," *International Journal of Systematic Theology* 17, no. 1 (2015), 6–25.

the praxis of theological construction? Remember the epistemological concern of the apocalyptic turn which is voiced early by Ziegler: "[I]t seeks to answer the questions 'where am I?' and 'what time is it?' in ways that simultaneously acknowledge that the theologian is decisively placed—not only conceptually, but also actually—by the gospel" (pp. 12–13). So does a resituating maneuver place the theologian otherwise than by the gospel? Must it?

If apocalyptic attests disjunction and event to the exclusion of nature and order, then the jarring and novel and even heavenly character of grace is highlighted. Ziegler's book shows such a militancy to confess grace with vigor and verve. Yet one is left wondering where grace takes us, not to mention where sin has brought us from. To know there is a change is one thing, to believe that there is a triumph is no small matter. But a question arises regarding the character of that glory. If the apocalyptic framing of antagonizing dualisms filters all theological accounts, then the Christian will need to turn elsewhere for such answers. In other words, it appears that a radically consistent application of an apocalyptic hermeneutic—that is, an application that takes the seemingly all-encompassing claims of Martyn and others at face value—may well plunge us right back into speculation in the name of being concrete and practical and pegging a Christological concentration so tightly upon the categories of a militant soteriology.

Where does Ziegler's project sit among this range of accounts? It is not entirely clear. On the one hand, he broadens the concerns christologically and ethically and does not even hesitate to note occasions where the Reformed tradition has preceded apocalyptic concerns in its own way. True, he will often use more innovative language of recent years (such as the "dative self" on p. 159 fn. 26), but he is asserting the vital pneumatology of the earlier Reformed (and Augustinian) tradition for understanding not merely life in Christ but even the activity of faith itself. While freshened up, such concerns are classically Reformed and sit snugly with a host of threads regarding pneumatology, providence, and the gift of faith.[14] On the other hand, he concurs with Martyn regarding the seeming disruption to theology: "In a notable understatement, Martyn once observed that if Käsemann's thesis concerning the eschatological character of divine rectification is correct, then 'not a little of the discussion among systematicians will have to be changed'" (p. 56). Perhaps exactly where we plot *Militant Grace* on the spectrum of hermeneutical consistency is less significant than that we wrestle with ways in which the apocalyptic Paul might reshape not only the Christian kerygma but also the scope and sequence of Christian theology.

In the end apocalyptic is about faith rather than sight, divine grace and not human works. "Christian dogmatics must be eschatological if it is to do justice to the very logic and form of divine grace as such" (p. 11)—but does eschatology

---

14. For further elaboration of how providence can and should frame apocalyptic theology more broadly, see Macaskill, "History, Providence, and the apocalyptic Paul," 409–26.

require apocalyptic as its summit and *sine qua non* not only literarily but materially? Readers of Ziegler's book will rightly be prompted to examine the significance of this mandate and of the severity of its implications, though they ought to consider whether it is textured enough to serve as a true discrimen not only for portions of Paul's writings nor even the totality of his thought but for the Christian *kerygma* more broadly and what would be the implications of such a foreshortening of the theological register.[15]

---

15. My thanks to Wesley Hill, Jonathan Linebaugh, R. David Nelson, Ryan Peterson, and Scott Swain for reading and offering feedback.

Chapter 7

DISPUTATION *FOR* SCHOLASTIC THEOLOGY: ENGAGING LUTHER'S 97 THESES

In fall 1517, a German monk offered theses for disputation which would shake the faith and practice of the world around him. They cut against the grain of ecclesiastical and theological practice and would set a course for ongoing reform and challenge according to God's Word. We do well to consider afresh those principal concerns at the root of the Protestant Reformation. So we turn again to Wittenberg, to Luther, and to the 97 theses. That's right. On September 4, 1517, Luther participated in a disputation regarding sin and the will, nature and the experience of Christian salvation. This academic disputation, (much) later dubbed the "Disputation against scholastic theology," has not gained the level of acclaim garnered by the later "95 Theses or Disputation on the Power and Efficacy of Indulgences," but they will capture our attention and prompt some thinking regarding what shape theological practice might take this side of Luther's witness.[1]

These theses actually cut right to the heart of so many of Luther's abiding concerns. Far more than the focus on indulgences to come two months later, these theses turn directly to issues of human nature and divine salvation. They forecast in many ways that great text which would so mark Luther's legacy, his 1525 response to Erasmus entitled *The Bondage of the Will*. They thread the needle of assaulting the latent tradition which he finds so marred by hubristic excess without shirking his abiding commitment to learn from Augustine, who had himself been a formative thread of that late medieval fabric.[2] In many ways, these theses, like the

---

This chapter was delivered as an inaugural lecture for the John Dyer Trimble Chair of Systematic theology at Reformed Theological Seminary in Orlando on September 6, 2017. Many thanks to Scott Swain, Jono Linebaugh, and Ryan Peterson for feedback.

1. Martin Luther, "Disputation Against Scholastic Theology, 1517," in *Career of the Reformer 1* (Luther's Works 31; ed. Harold J. Grimm; trans. Harold J. Grimm; Philadelphia: Fortress, 1957), 3–16; see *WA* 1, 221–8 for the German original. Numbering varies in editions as Thesis 55 has been divided into two theses in the work of Vogelsang, leading to a total of 98 theses.

2. On the complicated legacy of reading Augustine on all sides, see now Arnoud S. Q. Visser, *Reading Augustine in the Reformation: The Flexibility of Intellectual Authority in Europe, 1500–1620* (Oxford Studies in Historical Theology; New York: Oxford University Press, 2011).

Heidelberg Disputation of the following year, will do the hard work of beginning to connect the emerging Reformational vision of sin and grace with matters of intellectual authority and theological formation. Here we see the force and the tension of Luther's theology.

In this chapter I want to argue with Luther seemingly against Luther; that is, tracing Luther's anthropology and soteriology through, I will seek to show that today a scholastic theology with certain disciplined protocols in place prompts us to lean against our sinful proclivities and to linger longer before the life-giving Word of God. In so doing, however, I will seek to sketch an approach to scholastic theology which ties its task to the pursuit of theological discipleship and even intellectual asceticism. To do so means that the description offered here differs from some lingering assumptions about scholasticism and about the practice of systematic theology today and challenges the disciplinary *status quo* in some fundamental ways. As much as the argument seeks to argue for the ongoing need for the theological calling, then, it also aims to reorient the way in which that practice follows in much of its modern exercise by reorienting systematic theology as a form of intellectual asceticism.[3] In so doing Luther is a genuine prompt, in as much as he not only reflected upon the stranglehold of sin (in the 97 theses) but also sought in multiple ways to orient theology around his account of sin and grace (in various texts). While arguing with Luther regarding our sinful proclivities and our dire need for God's gracious intervention even in the life of the mind, then, we will also turn beyond and, to some extent, against Luther to espouse an argument for a distinctly scholastic practice of theology so as to further those spiritual ends. Four specific aspects regarding the shape of a sanctifying approach to scholastic theology will conclude the proposal.

Unto those ends, the chapter first seeks to unpack the anthropological and soteriology teaching of Luther's diatribe "against scholastic theology," that is, against Semi-Pelagian or Pelagian moral anthropology in his 97 theses. Second, the chapter turns to ways in which the theological task is located by Luther in the history of sin and grace, thus connecting his teaching against the anthropology of the scholastics with his methodology for studying theology academically and clarifying the precise nature of the objections to scholasticism raised by Luther and other reformers (such as Calvin). Third, the chapter concludes by charting a set of four protocols for systematic or scholastic theology today, so as to reconfigure the intellectual practice as an exercise in intellectual asceticism or discipleship that is part of the broader process of the sanctification of human reason.

---

3. Sarah Coakley has also sought to reorient the discipline in an ascetic register, albeit in a very non-scholastic fashion (see her *God, Sexuality, and the Self: An Essay "On the Trinity"* (Cambridge: Cambridge University Press, 2014]). For interaction with her proposal and an argument that a more focused scholastic protocol might more effectively serve her stated purgative-spiritual goals, see Michael Allen, "Dogmatics as Ascetics," in *The Task of Dogmatics: Explorations in Theological Method* (ed. Oliver Crisp and Fred Sanders; Grand Rapids: Zondervan Academic, 2017), 189–209; repr. as Chapter 8 in this volume.

With Luther Against Semi-Pelagian or Pelagian Moral Anthropology: Analysis of the 97 Theses of September 1517

Luther did not pull punches. Whether in woodcuts or theses, homilies or treatises, he was not hesitant to name names and give addresses. So here in his 97 theses from September 1517, he took many luminaries to task: Aristotle and Ockham, the Cardinal and Gabriel, Porphyry and the philosophers, the Scholastics and Scotus.[4] Take Aristotle alone as an example. "Virtually the entire *Ethics* of Aristotle is the worst enemy of grace," Luther claims "in opposition to the scholastics" (Thesis 41). He will specifically oppose the Philosopher's contentions regarding happiness (Thesis 42), but more often ranges rather widely by saying, first, that "it is an error to say that no man can become a theologian without Aristotle" (Thesis 43); second, that "no one can become a theologian unless he becomes one without Aristotle" (Thesis 44); third, "briefly, the whole Aristotle is to theology as darkness is to light" (Thesis 50); and fourth, "even the more useful definitions of Aristotle seem to beg the question" (Thesis 53). He only comes up for air, as it were, to offer Porphyry similar, even if more abbreviated, treatment, saying that "it would have been better for the church if Porphyry with his universals had not been born for the use of theologians" (Thesis 52). Yet "in these statements," he concludes, "we wanted to say and believe we have said nothing that is not in agreement with the Catholic church and the teachers of the church" (conclusion).[5]

Knowledge, lies, and exaggeration—these terms frame the beginning of Luther's theses. "To say that Augustine exaggerates in speaking against heretics is to say that Augustine tells lies almost everywhere. This is contrary to common knowledge" (Thesis 1). To fall foul of this problem would grant victory to Pelagius and the heretics (Thesis 2) and make "sport of the authority of all doctors of theology" (Thesis 3). While Luther begins widely, using generalities such as

---

4. On the scholastic backdrop of the disputation, see especially Heiko Oberman, *The Harvest of Medieval Theology: Gabriel Biel and Late Medieval Nominalism* (Cambridge, MA: Harvard University Press, 1963); David C. Steinmetz, "Luther among the Anti-Thomists," in *Luther in Context* (2nd ed.; Grand Rapids: Baker Academic, 2002), 47–58; Brian Gerrish, "Luther Against Scholasticism," in *Grace and Reason: A Study in the Theology of Luther* (Oxford: Clarendon, 1962), 114–37. Jared Wicks has addressed a "Wittenberg Augustinianism" evident in these early texts (*Man Yearning for Grace: Luther's Early Spiritual Teaching* [Washington: Corpus, 1968], 178, 197). Indeed, Luther spoke of a theology shared with Andreas von Karlstadt as "our theology" and of their community as "us Wittenberg theologians." His first thesis given in this disputation was adapted from a line by Karlstadt (Lyndal Roper, *Martin Luther: Renegade and Prophet* (New York: Random House, 2017], 209).

5. Unfortunately we do not possess further argumentation or qualification for these theses (as with either the famous 95 theses regarding indulgences or those prepared later for the Heidelberg Disputation in 1518), on which see the helpful assessment of Jared Wicks, *Man Yearning for Grace*, 372–3.

"against heretics" or even employing the phrase "almost everywhere," it becomes plain that his eye is upon the Pelagian controversy, for he shifts immediately and without comment to say, in Thesis 4, that "It is therefore true that man, being a bad tree, can only will and do evil." Over against "common opinion," he adds that "the inclination is not free, but captive" (Thesis 5). Nor can the will regulate or reform itself, as if its ill bent were merely a temporary conundrum, for "it is false to state that the will can by nature conform to common precept" (Thesis 6). "As a matter of fact," Luther states, "without the grace of God the will produces an act that is perverse and evil" (Thesis 7). Long before Erasmus's writings on freedom provoke Luther's 1525 *Bondage of the Will*, he warns lest the church be tempted into giving any quarter to ideas of innate moral neutrality or goodness. Thus lies the path of Pelagius.

Luther walks a tightrope here in affirming the depravity of the human creature. Over against the Manicheans, he first states that "it does not, however, follow that the will is by nature evil, that is, essentially evil" (Thesis 8). "It is nevertheless innately and inevitably evil and corrupt" (Thesis 9).[6] Somehow essential or natural evil is excluded, while innate and inevitable evil is affirmed. A good while later, Luther will speak "in opposition to the philosophers" by saying that "We are not masters of our actions, from beginning to end, but servants" (Thesis 39). He later gives a concrete example, speaking of anger and lust (cf. Mt. 5.21-30). "Outside the grace of God it is indeed impossible not to become angry or lust" (Thesis 65), but "it is by the grace of God that one does not lust or become enraged" (Thesis 67). Luther offers a summative remark and then a further clarification. First, the summative remark: "Therefore it is impossible to fulfill the law in any way without the grace of God" (Thesis 68). Then the further clarification: "As a matter of fact, it is more accurate to say that the law is destroyed by nature without the grace of God" (Thesis 69). If Thesis 8 said that the will is not naturally, that is, essentially evil, then Thesis 69 plainly must speak of nature in a different vein, circumscribed by the fuller phrase "nature without the grace of God." This depiction of graceless nature riffs not on that described in Thesis 8 (nature or essence) but on what appeared in Thesis 9 (the innate and inevitable evil and corruption of the will). Luther plainly wants to affirm the created goodness of the human will, as well as its utter derangement and degradation with the onset of evil and the loss of grace.

Where then comes hope? Can such a vivid depiction of sinfulness find its way beyond utter despair and misanthropic despondency? Luther gestures toward grace at this point as a way of pointing ultimately unto God. "The best and infallible preparation for grace and the sole disposition toward grace is the eternal election and predestination of God" (Thesis 29). Luther not only affirms the divine prevenience here but also goes on to deny certain assumed qualifications or supplements. First, "on the part of man, however, nothing precedes grace except

---

6. On the anti-Manichaean and anti-Pelagian readings of Augustine's corpus, see Steinmetz, "Luther and Augustine on Romans 9," in *Luther in Context*, 21.

indisposition and even rebellion against grace" (Thesis 30).⁷ Second, human struggle does not identify its own need or the divine remedy, for Luther goes on to say that "this is false, that doing all that one is able to do can remove the obstacles to grace" (Thesis 33).⁸ Our problem is twofold: "in brief, man by nature has neither correct precept nor good will" (Thesis 34). Humans not only walk in what he deems an "invincible ignorance" or perceptional darkness but they are also disinclined to the true, the good, and the beautiful.

Grace does not come at the prompting of human ingenuity, nor does the human even incline themselves to its provision. But grace does provide. Indeed, over against all the language of inability and of darkness, one must cast Luther's powerful affirmation of the reality of grace. "The grace of God is never present in such a way that it is inactive, but it is a living, active, and operative spirit; nor can it happen that through the absolute power of God an act of friendship may be present without the presence of the grace of God" (Thesis 55).

Friendship proves to be a central term in the argument here. "An act of friendship is not the most perfect means for accomplishing that which is in one," nor even "for obtaining the grace of God or turning toward and approaching God" (Thesis 26). Yet "an act of friendship is done," though Luther is impelled to clarify "not according to nature, but according to prevenient grace" (Thesis 20). And this prevenient grace really affects the will. While "everyone's natural will is iniquitous and bad" (Thesis 88), "grace as a mediator is necessary to reconcile the law with the will" (Thesis 89). "The grace of God is given for the purpose of directing the will, lest it err even in loving God" (Thesis 90). Luther here notes the shadow side of the bound will, namely, that human distortion can mar even that which is pious. Even love of God can be inflected in such a way that it ceases in so doing to follow the direction of the one whom it is thereby loving.⁹

Underneath all this talk of willing and of warfare, of friendship and of formation, Luther eventually comes to talk of loves. He does so by asking, "what is the good law?" He offers two demurrals. First, "not only are the religious ceremonials not the good law and the precepts in which one does not live (in opposition to many teachers)" (Thesis 82), "but even," second, "the Decalogue itself and all that can be taught and prescribed inwardly and outwardly is not good law either" (Thesis 83). Human custom nor even divine mandate does not in and of itself constitute the good law, not until one presses further to the true definition. "The good law and that

---

7. Luther consistently reads Gregory of Rimini as the one scholastic theologian avoiding the error of Thomas, Scotus, and Ockham (as in his 1519 "Resolutions on Propositions debated at Leipzig"); see Steinmetz, "Luther among the Anti-Thomists," 57. Cf. Risto Saarinen, "Weakness of Will: Reformation Anthropology between Aristotle and the Stoa," in *Anthropological Reformations: Anthropology in the Era of Reformation* (ed. Anne Eusterschulte and Hannah Wälzholz; Refo500 28; Göttingen: Vandenhoeck & Ruprecht, 2015), 17–32.

8. Latin: *facere quod in se est*.

9. The issue of hypocrisy arises regularly in the theses (see theses 76–8 especially).

in which one lives is the love of God, spread abroad in our hearts by the Holy Spirit" (Thesis 84). Love fulfills the law (Rom. 13.8), yet law forms love (Jn. 15.7, 10).

Indeed, the need for law from the outside matches disordered love. "Anyone's will hates it that the law should be imposed upon it; if, however, the will desires imposition of the law it does so out of love of self" (Thesis 86). Indeed, "anyone's will would prefer, if it were possible, that there would be no law and to be entirely free" (Thesis 85). The human desires to go their own way.[10] This waywardness takes a particularly disturbed tack when it comes time to reflect on human efforts to reform or revitalize our problematic proclivities. Even—perhaps especially—in our moral programs, our own self-direction becomes most apparent and harmful.

Luther accents this ironic fate when coming to the conclusion of the disputation where he offers his final two theses regarding the proper relation of our will and God's own will. First, "we must make our will conform in every respect to the will of God" (Thesis 96, explicitly disagreeing with Cardinal Cajetan). Second, we conform our will unto God's "so that we not only will what God wills, but also ought to will whatever God wills" (Thesis 97). In other words, it is not enough to bring our questions to the surface and to conform to God's answers. We must do the difficult work of self-examination and of intellectual and moral repentance such that we trace God's direction still further unto the very questions up for consideration. God not only answers the need but defines the need itself. Not only moral energy but also a distinctly Christian epistemology, swirling round the vocation of theological discernment, marks the dependent yearning of the sin-sick human. God does not merely give truthful answers but he provides the life-giving questions.

Perhaps an analogy will help. Imagine struggle with a severe course of an autoimmune disease. Months of struggle do not go as one would have expected, for the normal rhythms of palliative and medical care had not offered reprieve from ills. Typical remedies actually worsened the situation, and finally one was shipped to the emergency room in a truly dire situation. When clarity came, the takeaway was rather direct: the immune system is one's own worst enemy, for its efforts to protect and to strengthen are actually precisely what undercuts one's own flourishing. So ongoing care requires scaling down the strength of the immense system, a bombardment of force meant to weaken the defenses which themselves weaken the self. What might strike us is the way in which this is true spiritually as well. Not only our moments of utter disinterest in God or even of stick-necked insouciance but also our pious and zealous attempts at reform actually further our sin-sick struggles. We demand the recalibration of our wills by God's own will, so that we no longer harm ourselves by inclining toward rhythms of evil excess or of moral malpractice. As Luther says, we need a mediator (Thesis 89). And as he insists, resting on that mediator will involve professing that "to love God is at the same time to hate oneself and to know nothing but God" (Thesis 95).

---

10. See Theo Dieter, *Der junge Luther und Aristoteles. Eine historisch-systematische Untersuchung zum Verhältnis von Theologie und Philosophie* (Theologische Bibliothek Töpelmann 105; Berlin: De Gruyter, 2001), 80–107.

We suffer inability not only in addressing but also in identifying the actual character of our plight.

With that finale in mind, we do well to turn to ask how Luther's theses might help prompt us to consider the task of academic, that is, scholastic theology today. Luther not only alerts us to the stranglehold of sin and the need for grace, but he gestures toward the way this must shape the practice of theological work also. Because the theologian is a moral agent before God—a sinsick sinner panged by death, Devil, and the depravity within—his protest of Semi-Pelagian and Pelagian anthropology and his celebration of God's radical grace must impinge on the process of divine revelation and of God's sanctification of human reason.

With Luther For Scholastic Theology: Theological Parameters for Intellectual Discipline

Theology does not hold a monopoly on concerns regarding moral formation. In his 1911 Cambridge Inaugural Lecture as Kennedy Professor of Latin at the University of Cambridge, A. E. Housman addressed "The Confines of Criticism."[11] He began with survey, noting the ways in which British and German literary criticism had drifted into non-critical forms of analysis. "In short, while the English fault is to confuse this study with literature, the German fault is to pretend that it is mathematics."[12] Each tendency marked a drift toward an extraneous mode of mental functioning, either that of literary creation or that of sequential and numerical method. Both ruin literature in their own way by pressing it into another mission, whether of a sociopolitical, moral, or scientific tilt. When Housman probes the root of these tendencies, he says "there is a very formidable obstacle: nothing less than the nature of man himself."[13] And "our first task is to get rid of them, and to acquire, if we can, by humility and self-repression, the tastes of the classics."[14] To this anthropological diagnosis, Housman also offered a prescription: "we must be born again."[15] But what hope or future expectation can be offered by this moral critic? Housman concludes only with this offering: "It is well enough to inculcate the duty of self-examination, but then we must also bear in mind its difficulty, and the easiness of self-deception."[16]

Luther's anthropology seems to agree with Housman regarding the "nature of man himself" and the fundamental need to be born again, lest we take up the task of theology and comport it toward the protocols of other fields, whether of the

---

11. A. E. Housman, *The Confines of Criticism* (Cambridge: Cambridge University Press, 1969).
12. Ibid., 37.
13. Ibid., 40.
14. Ibid., 34–5.
15. Ibid., 35.
16. Ibid., 43.

politeia or the *psyche*. But Luther and the Reformed Christian are not left with mere self-examination, not even primarily with self-examination. In the remainder of this chapter, I want to explore the ways, first, in which the divine discipleship of our theological reason is necessitated by Luther's anthropology and, second, the manner in which a particular form of scholastic theology may help channel such reform and maturation of the theologian.

Martin Luther knew that theological practice must be defined with distinctly theological categories. This could be his undoing, of course, as he sometimes reduced theology to the topics of the justifying God and the sinning human in his extrapolations on Psalm 51.[17] In that kind of claim, he clearly locates the theological task within the orbit of sin and redemption; indeed, sufficiently and solely within such an orbit.[18] His constriction there—tying theology notably and narrowly to justification—evidences a concern to think the theological task within the matrix of redemption from slothful or hubristic reason. In another notable text, the Heidelberg Disputation of 1518, he offered his perceptive vision of the difference between the theologian of glory and the theologian of the cross. Again, questions might be raised regarding whether or not this is an overly constricted breadth—with "cross" standing in for the posture of faith in its full range and perhaps with an overly lush antipathy to the full spectrum of revealed media for theological contemplation—but we can appropriate this approach without falling into any latent historicism. Michael Korthaus has shown this theme to be one that attains any methodological significance only in the twentieth century, as it appears only six times in this small portion of the early Luther's corpus.[19] While it has been cherished by those who have sought to tether metaphysical contemplation

---

17. Martin Luther, *LW* 12:305; see *WA* 40II, 319; see also Oswald Bayer, *Martin Luther's Theology: A Contemporary Interpretation* (ed. Thomas H. Trapp; Grand Rapids: Eerdmans, 2008), 38–9.

18. Otto Hermann Pesch has argued that this approach to theology varies greatly from that of Thomas Aquinas. One need not affirm Pesch's distinction to affirm that Luther rightly locates theology amidst the vagaries and valleys of the spiritual journey, the gifts and the grain of the economy of redemption. See Otto Hermann Pesch, "Existential and Sapiential Theology—The Theological Confrontation Between Luther and Thomas Aquinas," in *Catholic Scholars Dialogue with Luther* (ed. Jared Wicks; Chicago: Loyola University Press, 1970), 61–81; see also Michael Root, "Continuing the Conversation: Deeper Agreement on Justification as Criterion and on the Christian as *simul iustus et peccator*," in *The Gospel of Justification in Christ: Where Does the Church Stand Today?* (ed. Wayne Stumme; Grand Rapids: Eerdmans, 2006), 42–61.

19. Michael Korthaus, *Kreuzestheologie: Geschichte und Gestalt eines Programmbegriffs in evangelischen Theologie* (Tübingen: Mohr Siebeck, 2007), 405. See Martin Luther, "Heidelberg Disputation, 1518," in *Career of the Reformer 1* (Luther's Works 31; ed. Harold J. Grimm; Philadephia: Fortress, 1957), 35–70; cf. *Lectures on Genesis 1-5* (Luther's Works 1; ed. Jaroslav Pelikan; St. Louis: Concordia, 1958), 11, 13, 14 (on 1:2), 45 (on 6:5-6), 72 (on 6:18).

rather constrictively to the historically immanent, it need not take such a parasitic approach to the classical tradition of Christian dogma. In a more chastened form focused on the question of the theological practitioner (rather than so much on the object of that theological practice), the theology of cross serves as yet another reminder that we deal here with the sanctification of reason.[20] In at least these two ways, then, Luther was committed to locating the practice of theology amidst the valleys of human sin and the vista of divine grace.

Luther sought to address the practice of theology in light of sin and grace in a still third frame. Luther identified three rules for theology in his comments on Psalm 119, where David heralds the law of the LORD as life-giving. Luther identified the call to *oratio*, first, wherein "you should immediately despair of your reason and understanding…. But kneel down in your little room and pray to God with real humility and earnestness, that he through his dear Son may give you His Holy Spirit, who will enlighten you, lead you, and give you understanding."[21] Luther next summoned us to *meditatio*, a second action wherein the theologian joins with David to "talk, meditate, speak, sing, hear, read, by day and night, and always about nothing except God's Word and commandments."[22] Oswald Bayer says here that "Luther swims against the tide of common opinion in not seeing the process of listening turned inwards but rather opened outwards." Rather, "when we meditate," he says, "we do not listen to our inner selves, we do not turn inwards, but we go outside ourselves. Our inner beings live outside themselves in God's Word alone."[23] Third, the monk calls us to *tentatio* that we might find suffering to be our teacher. Spiritual attack (*Anfechtung*) will come for the little Christian who meditates on God's Word, for the one who meditates will say, with David in Psalm 119 and elsewhere, that the Word drew enemies of varying sorts. But the student will also be able to say of those enemies what Luther spoke of the papists and the fanatics, namely, that "they have made a fairly good theologian of me, which I would not have become otherwise."[24]

Prayer and suffering are worthy topics, yet we will focus our attention now upon meditation as Luther's second concern for true theology.[25] In particular, we want to consider what it means to lead a life ordered to the external Word of God and in what ways this shapes the academic practice of theological contemplation or meditation. In his 1535 *Lectures on Galatians*, Luther would say: "And this is the

---

20. John Calvin also offers something of a *theologia crucis* in his reading of the Corinthians Epistles, on which see Michael Allen, "John Calvin's Reading of the Corinthians Epistles," in *Reformation Readings of Paul: Explorations in History and Exegesis* (ed. Michael Allen and Jonathan Linebaugh; Downers Grove, IL: IVP Academic, 2015), 175–81.

21. LW 34:285f. (translation altered by Oswald Bayer); WA 50:659, 5–21.

22. LW 34: 286; WA 50: 659, 22–35.

23. Bayer, *Theology the Lutheran Way*, 53.

24. LW 34: 286f.; WA 50:660, 1–16.

25. See especially Ronald Rittgers, *The Reformation of Suffering: Pastoral Theology and Lay Piety in Late Medieval and Early Modern Germany* (Oxford Studies in Historical theology; New York: Oxford University Press, 2012), esp. 111–24.

reason why our theology is certain: it snatches us away from ourselves and places us outside ourselves, so that we do not depend on our own strength, conscience, experience, person, or works but depend on that which is outside ourselves, that is, on the promise and truth of God, which cannot deceive."[26] How do we contemplate these promises and that truth such that we are taken out of ourselves and offered true certainty?

Before we conclude by suggesting four protocols of scholastic reflection and its attention to the external, life-giving Word of God, we do well to linger briefly over the adjective "scholastic." In either the post-Reformation or the post-manualist moments, for Protestants and Roman Catholics, respectively, scholastic can sometimes be taken simply as a prompt for traditional or historic protocols. Along those lines, we do well to observe that the dominant tradition of the late medieval university and the *via moderna* (Gabriel Biel especially) were opposed ardently by Luther.[27] But we dare not read his opposition as a global dismissal of tradition or of medieval academic culture. In a letter penned to Johannes Lang on May 18, 1517, Luther had offered this assessment of changes afoot at the University of Wittenberg: "Our theology and St. Augustine are by God's help prospering in our university, while Aristotle descends gradually toward a coming everlasting oblivion. The lectures on the *Sentences* are being despised, and no one can hope to have hearers unless he lectures on Scripture, on St. Augustine, or on some other ecclesiastical doctor."[28]

Luther was not assaulting tradition as tradition nor even the protocols of academic theology but a specific set of anthropological judgments that he deemed to be out of step with Augustine and, more significantly, the soundings he had made in lecturing on Holy Scripture (especially on Romans, the Psalms, and Hebrews at this point). More significantly, though, scholasticism defines a method which is matched to and prompted by the material under examination. As L. M. De Rijk defined it, scholasticism in either its medieval or later Protestant forms is "a collective noun denoting all academic, especially philosophical and theological, activity that is carried out according to a certain method, which involves both in research and education the use of a recurring system of concepts, distinctions, proposition-analyses, argumentative strategies, and methods of disputation."[29] Historiography of scholastic method has taken a markedly contextual turn in the last fifty years, observing ways in which the moniker "scholastic" related to protocols and methods rather than any particular ideological inflection. The

---

26. Luther, *Lectures on Galatians*, 387; W XL: 589–90.

27. On the prevalence of Biel behind the disputation, see especially Leif Grane, *Contra Gabrielem: Luthers Auseinandersetzung mit Gabriel Biel in der Disputatio contra scholasticam theologiam, 1517* (Acta Theologica Danica 4; Kopenhagen: Gyldendal, 1962), 371–85.

28. WBr1, 41,8; 99 (translation by Jared Wicks).

29. L. M. De Rijk, *Middeleeuwse wijsbegeerte: Traditie en vernieuwing* (Assen: Van Gorcum, 1977), 25 (cited in Martin Bac and Theo Pleizier, "Reentering Sites of Truth: Teaching Reformed Scholasticism in the Contemporary Classroom," in *Scholasticism Reformed: Essays in Honour of Willem J. Van Asselt* [ed. Maarten Wisse, Marcel Sarot, and Willemian Otten; Leiden: Brill, 2010], 36).

methods were meant to vary by way of subject matter, so that the object delimits its approach and defines its analysis.

Particular protocols follow from this material-molded approach to theology. To take but one example: in his forays into assessing John Calvin's relationship to the practice of scholastic thought, Richard Muller has identified four features of this sort of academic theology in the late medieval or early modern university context: scholastic theology identifies an order and mental pattern suitable to the debate at hand, uses the thesis or *questio* to frame discussion, orders theses to be discussed by way of thesis and standard objections, and then refutes objections and provides exposition of the correct answer.[30] These protocols in varying ways belie a commitment to follow the organization of the subject matter, not one's own predilections, and to remain alert to opposing viewpoints lest one drift into myopic narrowness or remain in unchallenged confusion. A look to other settings of a scholastic order would accent different protocols, and theological students will rejoice to learn that this need not involve reinstituting the public disputation as the chief protocol for examining students of divinity.

A commitment to tradition will come only indirectly then, to the extent which tradition or traditions are themselves overt prompts from the subject of theology itself, namely, divine self-revelation. In the case of theological contemplation, the triune God, upon whose face we seek to gaze and whose name alone we seek to exalt, has given birth not only to our wisdom but to a whole host of heavenly confessors and a lively communion of saints, within whose chorus we take our part. So scholastic commitment is not inherently opposed to the textualism of humanistic studies in the sixteenth century, though it would come into conflict with iterations of literary study that refused to read those texts as apostolic scripture and insisted on orienting its focus upon them in the guise of comparative religious literature of the ancient world.[31] A fully orbed Trinitarian theology of revelation will insist that

---

30. Richard A. Muller, "Scholasticism in Calvin: A Question of Relation and Disjunction," in *The Unaccommodated Calvin: Studies in the Foundation of a Theological Tradition* (Oxford Studies in Historical Theology; New York: Oxford University Press, 2000), 28. The literature on scholasticism in its medieval and post-Reformation settings has burgeoned in recent years; for introduction and survey, see especially Ulrich G. Leinsle, *Introduction to Scholastic Theology* (trans. Michael J. Miller; Washington, DC: Catholic University of America Press, 2010); and Willem. J. Van Asselt, with T. Theo J. Pleizier, Pieter L. Rouwendel, and Maarten Wisse, *Introduction to Reformed Scholasticism* (trans. Albert Gootjes; Grand Rapids: Reformation Heritage, 2011).

31. On this adaptation of reading strategies, see Michael Legaspi, *The Death of Scripture and the Rise of Biblical Studies* (Oxford Studies in Historical Theology; New York: Oxford University Press, 2010); Jeffrey Morrow, "The Politics of Biblical Interpretation: A 'Criticism of Criticism,'" *New Blackfriars* 91, no. 1035 (Sept. 2010), 528–45; idem, "The Bible in Captivity: Hobbes, Spinoza and the Politics of Defining Religion," *Pro Ecclesia* 19, no. 3 (Summer 2010), 285–99. The significant shift here is the tilt toward historicism, on which see now Frederick Beiser, *The German Historicist Tradition* (Oxford: Oxford University Press, 2015).

the prophet ministry of the Risen Christ involves the unique instrumentality of the words of his prophets and apostles (Heb. 4.12-13), as well as the realization that his "Word dwells richly" amidst the testimony of the whole company of the redeemed (Col. 3.16-17). Any scholastic or tradition-marked characteristics of theology, then, ought to flow from the entailments of divine action and its promised forms, not from some presumption of the antique or exotic bearing intrinsic force. The rule of faith and rule of love govern the protocols of our intellectual life and the way in which we presently honor the past and look unto the future. In a sense, then, a scholastic bent to theology follows from a spiritual vision regarding the intellectual life. If we are to throw ourselves into the tasks of the academic life, then we want to do so out of an abiding commitment to the cause of intellectual asceticism.[32]

Without suggesting that disputations or a question-and-answer format is necessary, a scholastic or academic study of theology helps frame and form our spiritual contemplation of the God who has revealed himself climactically in Jesus Christ and in his life-giving Word. While scholasticism defines the procedures and not necessarily any predetermined philosophical results of our academic inquiry, these methods are themselves motivated by certain anthropological and moral principles. Indeed, there are specifically theological reasons for accenting particular academic protocols as they help foster theological virtues, habits, practices, and order that marks the well-equipped man or woman of God (2 Tim. 3.16-17). Those working recently in intellectual history and the history of the university have rightly noted that scholasticism does not reduce to a particular philosophical, ethical, or theological commitment, over against some older suggestions in the nineteenth and twentieth centuries that scholastic method carried with it a full bore commitment to a particular set of material principles. While a scholastic method does not necessarily equate to a full bore philosophy, and while scholastic method is not homogenous, we do well to note nonetheless that intellectual protocols match anthropological and theological *principia*.

---

32. Language of intellectual discipleship or asceticism has been helpfully unpacked in Fergus Kerr, "Tradition and Reason: Two Uses of Reason, Critical and Contemplative," *International Journal of Systematic Theology* 6, no. 1 (2004), 37-49; Frederick Christian Bauerschmidt, *Thomas Aquinas: Faith, Reason, and Following Christ* (Christian Theology in Context; Oxford: Oxford University Press, 2013), 36, 81, 140. Some parallel approaches in medieval literature are thoughtfully analyzed by Peter M. Candler Jr., *Theology, Rhetoric, Manuduction, Or Reading Scripture Together on the Path to God* (Radical Traditions; Grand Rapids: Eerdmans, 2006), with regard to the use of the language of *ductus*, *skopos*, and an *itinerarium*, though his theological account fails to press on to offer much covenantal or Christological specificity in its broadly participationist metaphysics and also offers a severely mangled reading of early Protestant theology and the development of *sola Scriptura* (esp. 13-16); similarly inclined, though overly focused on categories of embodiment, is Nathan Jennings, *Theology as Ascetic Act: Disciplining Christian Discourse* (New York: Peter Lang, 2010).

Scholastic Protocols for Sanctifying Systematic Theology: Four Practices for Theology Today Prompted by Luther's Reformational Teaching on Sin and Grace

If not *quodlibet* or recitations of catechisms, then what might scholastic protocols look like today? I conclude by suggesting four patterns of scholastic or systematic theological procedure for our consideration today.[33] These principles flow from two realities attested in Luther's theses: first, that human being is marked by a need for sustenance from beyond and further imprinted by a sinful distortion to close in upon itself and, second, that the triune God acts so as to give and to glorify life in Christ. These are meant to be protocols for theological practice in the land of the gospel and this time of God's patience, a time which the apostle Peter tells us is meant for intellectual repentance (2 Pet. 3.15). Luther's theses may well fund certain scholastic disciplines, but these protocols and the theology espoused by Luther would summon much common description and practice of "systematic theology" to account. It is not the status quo but a spiritual quest of intellectual asceticism and theological repentance before God's life-giving Word that we wish to describe here.

First, a scholastic approach to theological reflection will seek to draw our attention to the breadth of God's Word. Concern for order and scope matches the Pauline claim regarding the value of the "whole counsel of God" (Acts 20.27). The Marcionite challenge was the first threat to the Christian faith in the post-apostolic era, and it struck at the roots of the canonical form of the Christian way. In that second-century challenge, Irenaeus and others had to manifestly demonstrate that the prophetic witness of the Old Testament and the scripturally infused texts of the apostles were bound together with the witness of Paul and the other evangelists.[34] The early theologians commended the catholic faith by attesting the wholeness (lit. *kata holos*) of Scripture, namely, that the triune confession of one God in three persons was an achievement of a two testament canon and that, apart from the perduring pressure of the prophets of Israel, the doctrine of God would take quite different form.[35]

---

33. The concept of systematic theology is not without debate regarding definition either. For a survey of recent approaches and a proposal with which I am largely sympathetic, see John Webster, "Introduction: Systematic Theology," in *The Oxford Handbook of Systematic Theology* (ed. John Webster, Kathryn Tanner, and Iain Torrance; New York: Oxford University Press, 2007), 1–15.

34. Irenaeus, *On the Apostolic Preaching* (trans. John Behr; Crestwood, NY: St. Vladimir's Seminary Press, 1997), 68.

35. See esp. Brevard Childs, *Biblical Theology of the Old and New Testaments* (Minneapolis: Fortress, 1992), 376; C. Kavin Rowe, "Biblical Pressure and Trinitarian Hermeneutics," *Pro Ecclesia* 11, no. 3 (2002), 295–312; Christopher Seitz, *The Character of Christian Scripture: The Significance of a Two-Testament Bible* (Studies in Theological Interpretation; Grand Rapids: Baker Academic, 2011).

Biblical breadth may be lopped off or excised in a variety of ways. Canonical amputation can occur in other areas—anthropological and sexual matters being particularly obvious instances in contemporary discourse[36]—but this matter of the being of God is surely the most salient and significant. Scholastic theology prompts us to read and then to read on, not to get snagged merely in the genre, corpus, or epoch that transfixes our curiosity or encourages our ecclesiastical niche or comports most with pertinent issues in our cultural moment. Rather, scholastic theology disciplines us to be alert to the whole counsel of God, for "*all* Scripture is breathed out by God and profitable" (2 Tim. 3.16, emphasis mine). In so doing the scholastic prompt of exploring biblical breadth pushes against any parochialism (of the denominational tradition, of one's socio-political formation, or of personal predilection) and pressures toward a catholic theology of the whole.

Second, a scholastic approach to theological reflection will summon us to fix anew our emphases and priorities in the places where God's own Word draws our attention. The question of order and sequence, as well as the attendant concern for proportion, helps alert us to another area of biblical formation. Because even our love can go awry by perhaps willing with God though not, as Luther put it, willing "whatever God wills," we must be reoriented to the north star of God's own light. Invariably our experience raises questions and our reason sees connections, but our own forays into intellectual reflection must always be taken before the Word's own self-presentation. What does the whole counsel of God commend? What bears "first importance" (1 Cor. 15.3) over against its secondary and tertiary matters? We can go astray not only in misperceiving an element of the biblical tapestry but in failing to distinguish the foreground from the background. Only attention to the whole canonical canvas will bring into relief the relative emphasis and consequent prioritization that best conveys the elements of biblical doctrine.

An exercise in Luther reception can illustrate the point. How might priorities go haywire? One need only prioritize justification as the criterion of the gospel and

---

36. Luke Timothy Johnson, *Scripture and Discernment: Decision Making in the Church* (Nashville: Abingdon, 1996), 70–5; Stephen Fowl, *Engaging Scripture: A Model for Theological Interpretation* (Oxford: Blackwell, 1998), 97–127; Sylvia Keesmaat, "Welcoming in the Gentiles: A Biblical Model for Decision Making," in *Living Together in the Church: Including Our Differences* (ed. Greig Dunn and Chris Ambidge; Toronto: Anglican Book Centre, 2004), 30–49, for a supposedly pneumatologically prompted counterargument to Israelite Scripture regarding same sex unions in Acts 10–15. For a critical reply, see Michael Allen and Scott Swain, *Reformed Catholicity: The Promise of Retrieval for Theology and Biblical Interpretation* (Grand Rapids: Baker Academic, 2015), 74–8. Such canonical reconfiguration began prior to debates regarding gender identity or same-sex unions, in discussions regarding gender and ecclesiastical office (see, e.g., Mark Husbands, "Reconciliation as the Dogmatic Location of Humanity: 'Your Life is Hidden with Christ in God,'" in *Women, Ministry, and the Gospel: Exploring New Paradigms* (ed. Mark Husbands and Timothy Larsen; Downers Grove, IL: IVP Academic, 2007], 127–47).

treat it ahead of the person of Christ, that is, the whole Christ. In the approach of Gerhard Forde and the self-proclaimed "Radical Lutherans" we can see the kind of disorder caused by treating one crucial strand of Christology and soteriology as if it were the leading and lone article of that confession. Christ becomes functionally a cipher for the balm of the conscience. Such approaches may lay claim to following the (early) words of Philipp Melanchthon: "to know Christ is to know his benefits."[37] But Melanchthon presumed a Trinitarian and Christological metaphysics—and a contemplative focus in liturgy and theology upon the triune God's perfection—that his post-Kantian and post-Ritschlian heirs no longer embody. Failing to proclaim Christ in his fullness and eternity before Christ in his justifying capacity leads not only to a misprioritization but an outright distortion of the doctrine of justification.[38] The justifying word easily becomes the affirming conscience, rather distant from the concrete life, death, and resurrection of the Redeemer. A response to these "radical" readings of Luther that have flowed from the early twentieth-century Luther renaissance need not in any way renege on the sufficiency of Christ or the peace that he brings, but it will take the form of always tethering peace and reconciliation to his concrete action and union with his person. By refusing to sever the person and work of Christ, theology can accent the whole Christ and insist that the gift of his person marks a higher priority than any single blessing found therein, whether justification or sanctification. Only by attending to priorities will we be alert to the manifold principles of divinity.

Third, a scholastic approach to theological practice provokes us to attend to the ways in which the Holy Scriptures take common terms and employ them to fundamentally singular purposes. Luther turned toward the way in which Aristotelian thought had been brought into the fold of Christian divinity in the late medieval period. After running the gauntlet of critical analysis in the twelfth and thirteenth centuries (with the input of Averroes and Avicenna, as well as Albert and Thomas), the philosopher's categories were employed in Christian ethics and theology. Luther retorts: "It is an error to maintain that Aristotle's statement concerning happiness does not contradict Christian doctrine" (Thesis 42). The notion of beatitude apparently suffered from definitional ambiguity and an overly pacific posture by the schoolmen toward the descriptions of the philosopher. Indeed, Luther says that "it is very doubtful whether the Latins comprehended the correct meaning of Aristotle" (Thesis 51). But the error was not only theirs, for "even the more useful definitions of Aristotle seem to beg the question" (Thesis 53). In challenging reason and its absorption by the contemplation of faith in recent Latin theology, Luther reminds us that terms do not come in self-explanatory, singular fashion. They must be defined, and Christian divinity must turn to the

---

37. Philipp Melanchthon, *Loci Communes* in *Melanchthon and Bucer* (ed. Wilhelm Pauck; Library of Christian Classics; Louisville: Westminster John Knox, 1969), 21.

38. See the penetrating analysis of David Yeago, "Gnosticism, Antinomianism, and Reformation Theology: Reflections on the Costs of a Construal," *Pro Ecclesia* 2, no. 1 (1993), 37–49.

Word of God for such direction in discerning whether the language of the Gentiles can be employed in a given instance or whether there must be a distinction drawn.

Scholastic theology serves a crucial missiological purpose, therefore, in casting light upon the ways in which we have only human words to use in our testimony of God and our pointing to his own Word. Common terms are employed, to be sure, yet the divine communication through ordinary human language transfigures and puts the common to a sacred use, and our own witness must regularly return to reflect on the ways in which latent assumptions about the meaning of stock language can tempt or incline us to misperceptions. Our vocabulary draws on adoption and marriage to convey fellowship with God, though the divine family cannot be construed along sociological lines. We do know the love of God, so rich and full that Song of Songs can employ erotic imagery to convey it, and yet it is qualitatively distinguished from and analogically related to other experiences of love shown and love lost.[39] Particularly in a culture marked more and more by biblical illiteracy, we must observe how even colloquial engagement of the biblical writings is cross-cultural. We must be alerted to ways in which God cannot be constrained within the bounds of our terms as common construed. Systematic theology's scholastic mode serves missiological purposes, in as much as we are increasingly alert to the fact that the claims of the gospel and the categories of the "whole counsel of God" are "foolishness to the Greeks."[40]

Fourth, a scholastic approach to theological practice demands of us an accounting for what manner of cohesion may be observed in our pilgrim state, lest we be satisfied with a fragmented witness to the way in which Christ speaks his Word (Heb. 1.1-2). We can be tempted perhaps to itemize the themes and the idioms of scripture as an index of distinct topics to be accessed each in their own distinct manner. Perhaps the need to think coherently becomes most apparent when addressing the moral entailments of the way of Jesus. Whereas our contemporaries might be prone to assess the virtues of discipleship as nothing more than social mores or group preferences, these moral entailments extend from basic Christian confessions.[41]

So Paul's words in Romans 4 manifest the way in which the posture of faith befits the human creature who has been created wholly by God's life-giving Word,

---

39. Similar concerns could be raised regarding so many other biblical and doctrinal terms, as, e.g., Richard Hays raises the now popular term "liberation" as another pertinent illustration (*The Moral Vision of the New Testament* (New York: Harper, 1995], 203-4).

40. See Lesslie Newbigin, *Foolishness to the Greeks: The Gospel and Western Culture* (Grand Rapids: Eerdmans, 1988); John Webster, *Holiness* (Grand Rapids: Eerdmans, 2003), 4-5.

41. See especially Oliver O'Donovan's repeated argument that moral theology is neither an addendum to nor a mere repetition of Christian doctrine but is a thinking out or unfolding of the moral involvements of various doctrinal claims (e.g., "Sanctification and Ethics," in *Sanctification: Explorations and Proposals* (ed. Kelly M. Kapic; Downers Grove, IL: IVP Academic, 2014], 150-66).

resurrected in the Spirit's raising of Jesus from the dead, and now also justified and granted the full rights and privileges as an heir of Abraham. Faith ethically matches the metaphysical frame of these creational and covenantal actions by the triune God.[42] Apart from viewing the summons to trustful existence in such a doctrinal frame, the call to conversion becomes something without depth and meaning, a reduction to arbitrary moral posturing. Indeed, apart from a fit with the metaphysical and moral frame of elemental Christian doctrines, the summons to faith actually suggests a potentially misanthropic calling for the human. Such was Nietzsche's judgment. Yet we do not view the call of Jesus in a vacuum. The one who beckons us to follow is the one who made us, the one raised by the Father's power, and the one who names us as righteous and well-pleasing in union with him. Thus, his call that we submit our will unto his own and that with him we journey through the valley by faith *en route* to the paradise of the redeemed is no summons to slavish surrender and no manifesto for misanthropic misery. Rather, the call of Jesus—the morals of life in this one—is the most elemental and glorifying of any humanisms, because the human has been viewed first and only within a theological matrix marked by inflections across the scope and sequence of the divine economy. God gives life. Live by borrowed breath. God raises the dead. Live by his power. God justifies the ungodly and adopts the orphan. Live by his declaration. Appreciating the links between creation and new creation, as well as the delightful news of Jesus' resurrection that stitches them together, helps grant depth and beauty to his summons to us. Scholastic theology does not tuck items away in boxes, but it does prompt us always to ask how the varied divine works manifest God's being and pressure us to work by way of reduction (*reductio*), that is, of tracing all truths back unto God. Scholastic theology will demand of us questions of a metaphysical register, lest morality and the salvific economy flit around like disjointed phenomena.

These comments are mere sketches of four principles for a scholastic theology today. Even when extended more fully, these four moves will not erase questions or remove quandaries. In each respect, these protocols of a scholastic or systematic theology call for us to remain alert and to stay vigilant—indeed, that is precisely the point of scholastic practice as a protocol for pilgrim theology. This attentiveness takes a particular form. We are neither emboldened to spiritual self-mastery nor to intellectual self-defense, as if fear of ignorance or incoherence calls for us to be on guard. Just the opposite. In these ways, we have been sketching how the "fear of the LORD is the beginning of wisdom" (Ps. 111.10) and beginning to tease out protocols by which that fear might take disciplinary shape in our academic enterprises. Luther has reminded us of our terrible need for that formative discipline given our sin-sick and death-doused condition, where even our efforts at intellectual repentance remain hamstrung by self-direction. Affirming that kind

---

42. See the repeated emphasis on this connection as viewed through three doctrinal lenses (creational, Christological, and eschatological) in David Kelsey, *Eccentric Existence: A Theological Anthropology* (Louisville: Westminster John Knox, 2009).

of reformational or Augustinian anthropology has prompted an argument for the significance of theological practice taking scholastic shape as a means of turning outward and entrusting one's intellectual journey unto the source of all wisdom. If we want our theology to be not only a practice of methodological competence and material conversation but ultimately a formation of Christian wisdom, then our alertness to the anthropological condition in Luther's "Disputation *against* Scholastic Theology" should be paired with a concerted vision for theological contemplation by also offering a "Disputation *for* Scholastic Theology."

Chapter 8

DOGMATICS AS ASCETICS

*Worship, Discernment, and Theology: Can Dogmatics
Serve These Sanctifying Ends?*

I appeal to you therefore, brothers, by the mercies of God, to present your bodies as a living sacrifice, holy and acceptable to God, which is your spiritual worship. Do not be conformed to this world, but be transformed by the renewal of your mind, that by testing you may discern what is the will of God, what is good and acceptable and perfect (Rom. 12.1-2 ESV).

Paul's well-known appeal involved a call to "spiritual worship" by way of "living sacrifice" of one's whole self (Rom. 12.1). And to that liturgical and spiritual end, he identified a need for "discern[ing] what is the will of God, what is good and acceptable and perfect" (12.2). Worship is not only bodily but also intentional, rational, reflective. Discernment by means of testing shapes and sustains that course of self-sacrifice. Paul also warns of a twofold threat to this discerning offering of one's own body: warning, first, that we might be "conformed to the world" (12.2) or led astray by cultural malformation; and, second, that we might simply remain where we are and as we are or left in our own calcifying darkness. Indeed, it is crucial to observe that he not only calls for a stiff-arm to be thrown to the whelming flood of cultural pressures but that he then presses away from the spiritual status quo as well: "be transformed by the renewal of your mind" (Rom. 12.2). So Paul's call to worshipful discernment must press away undue influence but cannot rest content there; it must also press in the sanctifying, renewing work of God upon our own minds.

Theology must serve spiritual purposes. Theology leads to praise, and theology shapes wise and prudential reasoning.[1] But to those ends, Christian theology first

---

1. For helpful guidance in this regard, see especially Kevin J. Vanhoozer, *The Drama of Doctrine: A Canonical-Linguistic Approach to Christian Theology* (Louisville: Westminster John Knox, 2005); Daniel J. Treier, *Virtue and the Voice of God: Toward Theology as Wisdom* (Grand Rapids: Eerdmans, 2006); Michael Horton, *The Christian Faith: A Systematic Theology for Pilgrims on the Way* (Grand Rapids: Zondervan Academic, 2011), 13–34; Kevin J. Vanhoozer, *Faith Speaking Understanding: Performing the Drama of Doctrine* (Louisville: Westminster John Knox, 2014); Kevin J. Vanhoozer and Daniel J. Treier, *Theology and the Mirror of Scripture: A Mere Evangelical Account* (Studies in Christian Doctrine and Scripture; Downers Grove, IL: IVP Academic, 2015), 131–57.

cuts against the cultural grain and cuts across our own sinful selves. The question for us becomes: can dogmatic theology with its focus upon seemingly settled resources be a practice of unsettling our sinful ways? Might this most ecclesiastical of Christian intellectual enterprises be a tool for the "renewing of our minds" or must it inherently privilege the status quo? We do well to note that suspicions have arisen in recent years regarding the supposedly ontotheological, hegemonic, and phallocentric tendencies of systematic theology in contemporary theological discussions.[2]

Perhaps unsurprisingly, another pathway has dominated theological discourse in recent years as a purported means to address this stultifying status quo: "Theology and ... " Many such pairings have garnered significant attention in recent decades: theology and economics, theology and gender, theology and literature, perhaps more obviously theology and politics. Drawing on other realms of thought has been seen as a way of enlivening the doctrinal task, loosening the stultifying grip of old orthodoxies, fostering a more faithful humanism. And the following chapter might be thought to offer yet another pairing, theology and ascetics. Perhaps ascetics is simply another conversation partner which can—must!—leaven dogmatics. In such an approach, ascetics would add moral and self-renunciatory facets to a dogmatics which is itself anything but. But I wish to suggest that dogmatics hold a unique place in the intellectual work of the Christian church. It is not superior work; in many ways, it is subservient to other tasks, for instance, the discernment and worship which Paul attests as of penultimate and ultimate significance in Romans 12.1-2; and its practitioners, as officers of the church, serve to equip the saints for the work of ministry (Eph. 4.11-12). Worship and witness are the first-order activities of Christian language, but the wisdom won by being wrestled to the ground with God's truth serves as an instrument and means of intellectual discipleship without which we dare not journey.[3] Construed as a tool of discipleship, then, Christian dogmatics plays a

---

2. Sarah Coakley, *God, Sexuality, and the Self: An Essay "On the Trinity"* (Cambridge: Cambridge University Press, 2013), 42.

3. Language of intellectual discipleship has been helpfully unpacked in Fergus Kerr, "Tradition and Reason: Two Uses of Reason, Critical and Contemplative," *International Journal of Systematic Theology* 6, no. 1 (2004), 37–49; Frederick Christian Bauerschmidt, *Thomas Aquinas: Faith, Reason, and Following Christ* (Christian Theology in Context; Oxford: Oxford University Press, 2013), 36, 81, 140. Some parallel approaches in medieval literature are thoughtfully analyzed by Peter M. Candler Jr., *Theology, Rhetoric, Manuduction, Or Reading Scripture Together on the Path to God* (Radical Traditions; Grand Rapids: Eerdmans, 2006), with regard to the use of the language of *ductus*, *skopos*, and an *itinerarium*, though his theological account fails to press on to offer much covenantal or Christological specificity in its broadly participationist metaphysics and also offers a severely mangled reading of early Protestant theology and the development of *sola Scriptura* (esp. 13–16); similarly inclined, though overly focused on categories of embodiment, is Nathan Jennings, *Theology as Ascetic Act: Disciplining Christian Discourse* (New York: Peter Lang, 2010).

unique role in the rhythms of Christian sanctification and, by God's grace, does so with its own disciplinary integrity.

To offer something approximating an argument for this claim, I will begin by considering what likely seems to be the most companionable approach to an ascetical theological method today, namely, the *théologie totale* articulated by Sarah Coakley in her systematic theology. I will then compare and contrast Coakley's account of desire and knowledge with the way in which the late John Webster articulated the "holiness of theology." In so doing, I will seek to show that Webster sustained the spiritual and even ascetical intuitions so powerfully articulated by Coakley, though he did so by pressing beyond mere systematic theology to the task of Christian dogmatics. I will gesture still further in concluding the chapter with some principles for envisioning Christian dogmatics as a practice of intellectual asceticism and discipleship.[4]

Theology, Desire, Asceticism: Sarah Coakley on théologie totale

Purgation and desire go together, at least that is the wager of Sarah Coakley, who has previously argued so poignantly that power and submission are necessary bedfellows.[5] In the much acclaimed first installment of her systematic theology, entitled *God, Sexuality, and the Self*, Coakley argues that "theology involves not merely the metaphysical task of adumbrating a vision of God, the world, and humanity, but simultaneously the epistemological task of cleansing, reordering, and redirecting the apparatuses of one's own thinking, desiring, and seeing."[6] Theology does address metaphysics, with the divine and the creaturely realm coming in for assessment together, sure enough, but such ontological talk simultaneously concerns purifying the mind, the heart, and the eyes.

Theology, then, is "fundamentally purgative of idolatry."[7] This purifying is no small matter for Coakley attends to three looming threats, each of which are oftentimes presumed to render systematic theology invalid. First, ontotheology supposedly flattens the categories of the divine and the creaturely in a totalizing and, thus, blatantly idolatrous fashion.[8] Second, hegemony lurks as a threat whereby the powers and principalities can bend discourse and shape its very questions to prop up their own interests, suggesting that the system, as it

---

4. I hope thus to extend the arguments offered years ago in J. I. Packer, "An Introduction to Systematic Spirituality," in *Serving the People of God: Collected Shorter Writings on The Church, Evangelism, the Charismatic Movement, and Christian Living* (Collected Shorter Writings of J. I. Packer 2; Vancouver: Regent College Publishing, 1998), 305–16.
5. See Sarah Coakley, *Powers and Submissions: Philosophy, Spirituality, and Gender* (Challenges in Contemporary Theology; Oxford: Blackwell, 2002), esp. ch. 2.
6. Coakley, *God, Sexuality, and the Self*, 20.
7. Ibid., 20.
8. Ibid., 44–7.

were, determines what is systematic, even in theology.[9] Third, a specific feminist concern about the more subtle hegemony of male dominance—what might be called theology's phallocentric form—has so permeated the Western tradition, at least, as to inscribe a male imaginary into the confessions and expositions of theology.[10] These three threats are actually one in manifold form: "each presumes that the systematician idolatrously desires mastery: a complete understanding of God, a regnant position in society, or a domination of the gendered 'other'; and each presumes that the same systematician will thereby abuse his knowledge, his power, or his 'male' mode of thinking, for purposes of intellectual, social, or sexual dominance."[11]

Theology cannot be severed from contemplation, if such threats without and within are to be exposed and defeated by grace. "[T]he very act of contemplation—repeated, lived, embodied, suffered—is an act that, by grace, and over time, inculcates mental patterns of 'un-mastery,' welcomes the dark realm of the unconscious, opens up a radical attention to the 'other,' and instigates an acute awareness of the messy entanglement of sexual desires and desire for God."[12] Contemplation proves crucial here, for Coakley inverts one maxim of Freud, arguing instead that "desire is more fundamental than sex," while affirming another such principle of his, namely, that sublimation of such desires is essential.[13] Theology "comes, that is, with the urge, the fundamental desire, to seek God's 'face,' and yet to have that seeking constantly checked, corrected, and purged."[14] Those urges are not merely false judgments but, indeed, urges or desires: "To speak theologically: unredeemed desire is at the root of each of these challenges to the systematic task."[15] And such needed checks and balances take the form of systematic concern: "wherever one desires to start has implications for the whole, and the parts must fit together."[16] They not only fit together but form one in that manner, for "the contemplative task, which rightly sustains systematics, is itself a progressive modulator and refiner of human desire: in its naked longing for God, it lays out all its other desires ... and places them, over time, into the crucibles of divine desire."[17]

Contemplation cannot be myopic, then, but must be drawn upward and out to consider not only God and certain divine things of spiritual prestige. No, such would be to set the gaze upon the easily ossified. Coakley calls for a *théologie totale* which "makes the bold claim that the more systematic one's intentions, the more necessary the exploration of such dark and neglected corners" as those found in the nooks and crannies of the scriptures, the etchings of the catacombs,

---

9. Ibid., 47–9.
10. Ibid., 49–50.
11. Ibid., 51.
12. Ibid., 43.
13. Ibid., 7–8.
14. Ibid., 45.
15. Ibid., 51–2.
16. Ibid., 41.
17. Ibid., 52.

and the prayer-life of charismatic sects. And so the scope and sequence of her first volume—an "essay 'on the Trinity'"—moves from two chapters which offer a programmatic and methodological entryway to the multivolume project toward a sequence of chapters on "praying the Trinity" in patristic texts on desire (ch. 3); on fieldwork investigations of English congregations in the charismatic world (ch. 4); on iconographic representations of the triune God (ch. 5); and then two final chapters addressing her own account of patristic trinitarianism (ch. 6) and the interplay of desire, Trinity, and apophaticism (ch. 7).

The title of her volume—*God, Sexuality, and the Self*—is not mere hodgepodge. She really does articulate a rather cogent, seamless garment wherein an account of the Trinity and an understanding of desire (in God and in humanity) move back and forth. She sublimates gender breakdowns or dichotomies, for example, in the triune account of God, avoiding a common move (by supposed conservatives or purported liberals) to pattern social practice on the triune life.[18] Rather, "twoness [of gender], one might say, is divinely ambushed by threeness [of triune reflexivity]."[19] And this third, the Holy Spirit, is thus determinative, for the Holy Spirit is the "inherent reflexivity in the divine."[20] The Trinitarian account shares much with recent revisions regarding doctrinal history. She disputes the dominant East/West dichotomy of the late nineteenth and twentieth centuries.[21] She opposes the proposals of so-called doctrinal critics, expounding the ascetical, exegetical, and simultaneously apophatic accounts of triunity found in Nyssa and others.[22] She even defends the traditional naming of the triune God as Father, Son, and Holy Spirit, over against largely feminist concern about its gendered connotations.[23]

Yet she also turns trinitarianism somewhat on its head. Coakley operates with a strict dichotomy of her own, opposing what she calls an "incorporative" or "reflexive" model of the Trinity over against the "linear" schema. The linear model, so focused on processions and missions, finds its fullest expression in the Gospel according to John and bears within it the tendency toward an orthodoxy that may subordinate the Spirit, the other, the dark margins that alone can purge us.[24] A "prayer-based" and "Spirit-leading" approach will take up an incorporative or reflexive view of the trinity, drawn primarily from Romans 8. Origen holds both views,[25] and writings of Nyssa and others (especially in oft-overlooked texts)

---

18. Ibid., 270–1. She points out further that we may imitate the incarnate Son (in as much as he is human) though not the triune Godhead as such (ibid., 309).

19. Ibid., 58.

20. Ibid., 56.

21. Ibid., 269–70.

22. See, e.g., ibid., 105–11. Hans Boersma has raised significant questions regarding the viability of her employment of Nyssa in this regard (see *Embodiment and Virtue in Gregory of Nyssa: An Anagogical Account* [Oxford Early Christian Studies; New York: Oxford University Press, 2012]).

23. Ibid., 324–7.

24. Ibid., 101 (esp. fn. 1), 105, 111 fn. 12.

25. Ibid., 140 fn. 42.

gesture toward this more enfolding approach, wherein the hope for our desire being retooled and recast comes from our being caught up in the divine life through the reflexively incorporative mission of the Divine Spirit. Not only are we caught up but she speaks of a "divine force" to overthrow our divine desire. We do contemplate the divine, so real agency is espoused of the human practicing such intellectual and erotic purgation. Yet divine agency of a particularly intrusive sort is affirmed herein as necessary due to an affirmation of an Augustinian doctrine of sin.[26]

Coakley rightly treats mind and will together, although one will have to wait for her second and third volumes to see if her desire-tilted anthropology and Trinitarian schematic are balanced by a needed intellectualism rooted in the Logos of God. Even now, her blending of spirituality and theology can be perceived clearly and appreciated. Further, her commitment to a robust doctrine of sin and a concomitant account of divine agency in transforming, even purifying human selves and longings, calls for profound gratitude. How rare to have someone, cognizant of the dangers of power and self-delusion alike, speak of the shape of submission or of asceticism in the midst of being enfolded or incorporated into the divine life.[27] We do well to explore, then, if a commitment not to systematic theology simply, much less to *théologie totale*, but to Christian dogmatics can also offer an account of intellectual asceticism and a spiritual vision of doctrine as a chastening instrument in the purgative work of God's sanctifying presence.

"The Holiness of Theology": John Webster on the Eschatological Sanctification of Reason

In a lecture given in the late 1990s at the University of Otago, a theologian addressed the "culture of theology" and in so doing called for "attentive, ascetic reading" of Holy Scripture and the classics of the Christian tradition.[28] The language occurs amids discussion of what he calls the "rhetoric of effacement," itself a correlate to "Christian eschatological culture" wherein "attention dispossesses us of our expectations; it involves self-renunciation, so that the gospel itself may speak of its own presence and vitality." The language sounds ascetical: effacement, self-renunciation, dispossession, attentiveness unto the eschatological. In years when theology had been dogged by so-called doctrinal criticism and was beginning to be shaped by the emboldened claims of Radical Orthodoxy, such calls sounded a markedly different note. Several years later, John Webster took up those concerns

---

26. Ibid., 299; see also 6.

27. Further analysis is owed to Sarah Coakley, *The New Asceticism: Sexuality, Gender, and the Quest for God* (London: Bloomsbury, 2015).

28. John Webster, "Texts: Scripture, Reading, and the Rhetoric of Theology," *Stimulus* 6, no. 4 (Nov. 1998), 14 (10–16); now published as Webster, *The Culture of Theology* (ed. Ivor J. Davidson and Alden C. McCray; Grand Rapids: Baker Academic, 2019), 76.

again in the first chapter of his book *Holiness*, an essay entitled "The Holiness of Theology."[29] That essay's very existence is telling, in as much as Webster addressed the holiness of God, of the church, and of the Christian in later chapters only after first characterizing the very task of intellectual reflection in a certain way by attentively noting the holiness of theology.

What demanded sustained attention in this quest to practice theology in a holy posture? Like Coakley, Webster attended to the ever-present threat of idolatry and its mental or intellectual forms. Thinking about the divine is not inherently good unless one thinks about the true God in a faithful way. As this is not the only option in the religious market or even in the dark recesses of our hearts, "we need to make sure that we are thinking about the true God, and not about some God of our own invention."[30] Webster was drawing on specifically Reformed resources, such as Calvin's keen eye toward idolatry, in offering such a theological stiff-arm to undue speculation or underdisciplined theological exuberance.[31] Webster introduced this book, of which "The Holiness of Theology" serves as the introductory essay, as a "Trinitarian dogmatics of holiness."[32] It, thus, provides a helpful point by which we might assess how a specifically dogmatic theology may or may not flow from and further fund a pursuit of intellectual asceticism. We must assess in what ways Webster's project moved with and diverges from that of Coakley. A sketch of his approach sets the stage, then, for such comparison.

He offered a thesis:

> *A Christian theology of holiness is an exercise of holy reason; it has its context and its content in the revelatory presence of the Holy Trinity which is set forth in Holy Scripture; it is a venture undertaken in prayerful dependence upon the Holy Spirit; it is an exercise in the fellowship of the saints, serving the confession of the holy people of God; it is a work in which holiness is perfected in the fear of God; and its end is the sanctifying of God's holy name.*[33]

A number of elements therein deserve expansion. First, this theological enterprise—the *very act of considering* what it means to be holy—is itself "an exercise of holy reason," for "like all other aspects of human life, reason is a field of God's sanctifying work."[34] Contrary to the idealized view of knowledge and understanding in the Enlightenment era and as entrenched in modern rationalism, thinking is affected by sin and, thus, must be sanctified by God. Dogmatics begins with recognition, gleaned not from feminist or postcolonialist theory but from Holy Scripture itself, that our minds are darkened and we are wise only in our own eyes (e.g., 1 Cor. 2.14; Isa. 5.21; Prov. 3.7). But dogmatics affirms that God

---

29. John Webster, *Holiness* (Grand Rapids: Eerdmans, 2003).
30. Ibid., 9.
31. John Calvin, *Institutes of the Christian Religion*, I.xi.8.
32. Webster, "Holiness of Theology," 1.
33. Ibid., 9–10.
34. Ibid., 10.

does not leave us to our sinful selves; God sanctifies or sets apart our reason, and dogmatics is an instrument or tool in that divine work (Rom. 12.1-2). The first rule of such thinking laid out by him noted the significance of this move: "theological thinking *about* holiness is itself an exercise *of* holiness. Theology is an aspect of the sanctification of reason, that is, of the process in which reason is put to death and made alive by the terrifying and merciful presence of the holy God."[35]

Second, this theological enterprise—the *very act of considering* what it means to be holy—"has its context and content in the revelatory presence of the Holy Trinity."[36] That God reveals himself provides the context for theology's possibility; not only that but God's revelation of himself is the very content of theology's consideration. In other words, theology is a "positive science" which thinks after (*nachdenken*) that which God has revealed, working "both from and towards" the given. So "holy reason is not a *poetic* but a *receptive* enterprise; indeed, in Christian theology, poetics is tantamount to idolatry."[37]

Webster labors at just this point, for it is in his diagnosis and prescription against idolatry that his project differs from so much of the contemporary scene: "theology is nothing other than an attempt to repeat the name which God gives to himself as he manifests himself with sovereign mercy, 'I am the Lord, your Holy One' (Isa. 43.15)."[38] Two attending claims follow by necessity: first, theology is not religious phenomenology or, specifically in this case, the *very act of considering* what it means to be holy does not focus upon a human experience of the "tremendous mystery" (as in R. Otto) or the numinous; second, theology attends to Holy Scripture as its norm and limit.[39] We might ask why that negation and that affirmation are so central. In so doing, we can see that Webster locates intellectual self-renunciation in a more densely defined context, it seems, than does Coakley.

Idolatry is not something which we bat off with our own two hands, as if we were the last line of defense. We do not defeat the gods, whether of the world or of our own imagining. Like Coakley's affirmation of divine agency here, Webster speaks of God's encountering us and refusing to be mastered.

> Because God is majestic and therefore to be feared before all things, to encounter him is to be encountered by that which we can never master, which can never become an object, an idea or pattern of words or experience that we can retrieve and inspect at will ... Reason can only be holy if it resists its own capacity for idolatry, its natural drift towards the profaning of God's name by making common currency of the things of God. A holy theology, therefore, will be properly mistrustful of its own command of its subject-matter; modest; aware that much of what it says and thinks is dust.[40]

35. Ibid., 8.
36. Ibid., 12.
37. Ibid., 16.
38. Ibid., 16–17.
39. Ibid., 18–19, 19–21.
40. Ibid., 28.

And Webster also offers an ecclesial location for this intellectual chastening; he speaks of theology as "*an exercise in the fellowship of the saints, serving the confession of the holy people of God.*"

Precisely here Webster's ecclesiology and concomitant methodology diverge from Coakley. Coakley attends to the "dark corners" of the church, turning not to Trinitarian treatises much less the creeds and confessions of the church but to indirect attestation in individual writings on virginity and asceticism, to assessment of icons, and to fieldwork in a smattering of British charismatic communities. This *théologie totale* values breadth and catholicity, but it is questionable to what extent apostolicity proves to be an animating principle. Dogmatic theology, however, fixes first upon the apostolic writings and their prophetic precursors as the norm and limit to theological reflection and then upon the ecclesiastical rules which function as a guide for rightly dividing the word. It does so precisely because these texts are the embassies of divine self-revelation, taken up and sent out by the Risen Lord Jesus himself.[41]

So we have a divergence between extensive and intensive postures, conversational or dogmatic theology. Admittedly, Webster noted, "a good deal of contemporary systematic or dogmatic theology tends to be conversational or comparativist in approach. 'Conversational' theologies ... construct Christian theology by drawing on a wide range of cultural, philosophical and religious sources to build up an account of the Christian faith through elaborating the associations and interrogations which occur as Christianity talks to others."[42] Coakley's volume draws primarily on resources from the Christian faith, whether icons or fieldwork, exegesis or patristic *ressourcement*. Compared to, say, the various iterations of the Workgroup on Constructive Theology, her *God, Sexuality, and the Self* may well appear remarkably antiquarian and ecclesiastical in tone, resources, and claims.[43]

---

41. For a mature exposition of Holy Scripture as apostolic embassy in God's divine economy, see John Webster, "The Domain of the Word," in *The Domain of the Word: Scripture and Theological Reason* (London: T&T Clark, 2012), 3–31.

42. Ibid., 4.

43. See, e.g., Peter Hodgson and Robert King (eds.), *Christian Theology: An Introduction to Its Traditions and Tasks* (Minneapolis: Fortress, 1982); Rebecca Chopp and Mark L. Taylor (eds.), *Reconstructing Christian Theology* (Minneapolis: Fortress, 1994); and Serene Jones and Paul Lakeland (eds.), *Constructive Theology: A Contemporary Approach to Classical Themes* (Minneapolis: Fortress, 2005). David Ford has written of the widespread significance of "conversational theology" in modern British systematics in "Theological Wisdom, British Style," *Christian Century* 117 (2000), 388–91. For critique, see John Webster, "David F. Ford: *Self and Salvation*," *Scottish Journal of Theology* 54, no. 4 (2001), 548–59; and response in David F. Ford, "Salvation and the Nature of Theology: A Response to John Webster's Review of *Self and Salvation: Being Transformed*," *Scottish Journal of Theology* 54, no. 4 (2001), 560–75. One longer attempt to broker this disagreement may be found in Michael Allen, "Divine Transcendence and the Reading of Scripture," *Scottish Bulletin of Evangelical Theology* 26, no. 1 (2008): 32–56; repr. as Chapter 4 in this volume.

Yet it is similarly driven in many ways by questions, concerns, animating principles from other fields, not least feminist and gender studies. Even in her inversion of some of these fields, Coakley has privileged their concerns and questions in constructing her theology. If ever there was an example of extensive theology, this *théologie totale* must be it.

How did Webster describe his dogmatic approach? "By contrast, the kind of theology attempted here is less sanguine about the prospects for such exchanges. It more naturally thinks of its host culture, not as Athens, but as Babylon. It is acutely conscious of the menace of wickedness in the life of the mind."[44] Initially, Webster may sound like Coakley, but the divergence comes quickly thereafter. "And it is intensive before it is extensive. That is, its work is focused upon a quite restricted range of texts (the biblical canon) as they have been read and struggled with in the complex though unified reality which we call the tradition of the Church."[45] He admits, of course, that such may seem stultifying. "Such an understanding of theology enjoys rather little contemporary prestige, and is commonly judged to be naïve, assertive, authoritarian, above all, closed."[46] But it is worth noting that his claim runs just the opposite way. "Yet although it is in intensive in this way, it is not stable or settled. The persistence with which it returns to its singular theme is an attempt to face the reality of the gospel as a permanent source of unsettlement, discomfiture and renewal of vocation."[47] And he locates this rattling of the intellectual sabers within the action of the very present God: "The intensity of this kind of theology is not the internally-directed energy of an achieved, separated world of ideas, but that of a way of thinking which might be called eschatological—always, that is, emerging from its own dissolution and reconstitution by the presence of the holy God."[48]

So Webster's Reformed approach to catholic doctrine shares a self-renunciatory and purgative facet with Coakley's project. The two projects also share a common commitment to an Augustinian hamartiology and its necessary overcoming by the gracious missions of Son and Spirit. Webster's approach fixes more concretely upon scriptural authority and hearing the Word of God, whereas Coakley's approach ranges widely to "dark corners" and disciplinary conversation partners as ways of jarring the spiritual status quo of Christian intellectual life. That principled difference is ultimately rooted in a different notion, it seems, of the character of God and the consequent covenantal shape of ordered life with God for those human creatures who participate by grace in the full life that is his alone by nature. Might we even say that Webster's approach offers a divinely provided and ordered means of ongoing ascetical discipline, by means of the Reformed Scripture principle, which is only somewhat contingently matched by Coakley's

---

44. Ibid., 4–5.
45. Ibid., 5.
46. Ibid., 4.
47. Ibid., 5.
48. Ibid.

dependence upon intellectual scavenging for unsettlement? Might it be the case that dogmatics actually offers a sustained and structured approach to intellectual asceticism that outpaces the desires of even a *théologie totale*? We do well to attend to some principles for such a path forward by way of conclusion.

Ascetical Dogmatics: Reformed Catholic Theses for a Spiritual Theology

Dogmatics serves discipleship, providing a register whereby the intellectual life (as with the bodily and relational facets of human existence) may be governed by the Word of God. Frequently, contemporary theologians have estimated dogmatics impotent to such ends and felt the need to enlist other disciplines as ancillaries, handmaids, or, perhaps at times, tutors to school dogmatics in its ethical responsibilities. We do well to conclude with some principled theses for how such a dogmatics might undertake its labors, aware that it must remain earnest at all times lest it drift from a posture of faith into an arrogance of sight and of closure. Four concerns deserve our consideration: the Trinitarian matrix of ascetical dogmatics, the perfection of God and its formative shape in giving birth to the Reformed Scripture principle, the relationship of contemplation and radically anti-speculative theology, and the difference between intensive and extensive (or interdisciplinary) theology.

First, an ascetical dogmatics must be grounded in the biblical trinitarianism of the catholic creeds if it is to be a protocol of God's grace, flowing from his own triune perfection and unto self-displacing and renewing discipline, rather than a posture of self-mastery, accenting our autonomous intellectual projects. Here we need not deny what is affirmed by Coakley, though we must walk back some of her suggested negations and contextualize her account to make it serviceable. Remember that she has argued in favor of an incorporative approach to the Trinity rooted in Romans 8 over against the linear structure which she deems to be founded in Johannine trinitarianism and developed later in the official creedal texts of the fourth century. Again, such claims are not an analytic commentary on implicit judgments but are her own explicit statements regarding what is to be affirmed, what must be denied, and where they are both rooted in scripture and tradition. She does note that "distinction between the two models is not necessarily absolute," but she speaks only of the negative potentiality of the linear model.[49] Why does she go this route? The incorporative model draws us into the very life of God through prayerful incorporation of the human self and their desire into the triune movement, specifically through the reflexive posture of the Spirit. The linear model involves a hierarchical approach that invariably minimizes the Spirit's role of return unto Father and Son.

A classical account of the Trinity might affirm the incorporative work of the Trinity and might show its eternal roots by locating it amid the so-called linear

---

49. Coakley, *God, Sexuality, and the Self*, 111.

model which Coakley denies. Indeed, the linear model shows that the missions of Son and Spirit are rooted in God's own life (*theologia*) and do not merely express some economic reality (*oikonomia*).[50] That the Spirit flows forth or proceeds eternally from the Father and (through) the Son (*filioque*) serves to root the spiritual ascent of humans ultimately and eternally in God's own being and action, willed from all eternity. Such claims do not undermine the economic reality of spiritual incorporation; far from it, for their purpose is to characterize and specify such ascent as truly willed by the one true God according to triune order befitting and expressive of God's eternal character.[51] Still further, Matthew Levering helpfully reminds us that incorporation cannot be an undifferentiated experience. As he says, "[t]he emphasis on the order of origin—on the Father begetting the Son and the Father (and Son) spirating the Spirit—enhances the incorporative model by showing us that our unexpected entrance into the divine life means not pure relationality but an ordered relationship."[52] Incorporation occurs through the Son by the Spirit; even Coakley's preferred passage in Romans 8 manifests a precise concern to offer what can be deemed prepositional theology, and these distinct prepositional monikers mark out a specific order (*taxis*) to the divine economy and its attendant spiritual implications for human incorporative ascent.

Why is this pertinent here? Why are such matters of triune being and action pertinent to a discussion of dogmatics as ascetics? Why do they in any way relate to the question of whether or not dogmatics can sustain a self-renunciatory pattern of intellectual discipleship? Trinitarian order helps displace the self-directed approach to God in one's own manner.[53] God defines the terms of approach. Just as the God of Israel sketches the contours of holiness by which priests might enter his presence in the book of Leviticus, so the Trinitarian logic of the Gospel according to John and of Romans 8 provides a paradigm fully of God's design for covenant life with him. Union and communion with God occur by our desire, but only secondarily, for God has first desired or elected life with us. Further, this incorporative ascent occurs only by his design and as revealed in his own

---

50. See esp. Scott R. Swain, "Divine Trinity," in *Christian Dogmatics: Reformed Theology for the Church Catholic* (ed. Michael Allen and Scott R. Swain; Grand Rapids: Baker Academic, 2016), 103–5.

51. John Webster, "'It Was the Will of the Lord to Bruise Him': Soteriology and the Doctrine of God," in *God Without Measure*, Volume 1: *God and the Works of God* (London: T&T Clark, 2015), 143–58.

52. Matthew Levering, *Engaging the Doctrine of the Holy Spirit: Love and Gift in the Trinity and the Church* (Grand Rapids: Baker Academic, 2016), 37–8 (see 36–40 for wider reflection upon Coakley's proposal); see also Christopher Holmes, *The Holy Spirit* (New Studies in Dogmatics; Grand Rapids: Zondervan Academic, 2015), 33–42 for critique of a "Spirit-leading approach."

53. Similarly, ascetical implications are drawn out of Irenaeus's focus on the divine economy by John Behr, *Asceticism and Anthropology in Irenaeus and Clement* (Oxford Early Christian Studies; Oxford: Oxford University Press, 2000), ch. 1.

triune self-disclosure. The transcendentals might be pursued in various modes; the idol might be approached willy-nilly; the triune God, however, brokers only one pathway into his presence. Much more could and should be said here regarding displacement via dogmatic discipline—for instance, to take up Otto Hermann Pesch's terms, that a dogmatic theology will not sacrifice existential concern in its pursuit of sapiential ends, but will pursue existential discipline and grace precisely in and by the discipline of a de-centering vision that Pesch terms sapiential.[54]

By enabling wisdom (*sapientia*), reduction (*reductio*) of one's presenting concerns to theological *principia* serves not only intellectual but ascetic or self-displacing ends.[55] Augustine of Hippo infamously taught that we may enjoy (*frui*) God and must use (*uti*) all other things and then nuanced his distinction, in a positive rhetorical way, to help us sketch what it means to love God for his own good and to love all else for God's own sake, thus avoiding idolatry.[56] In other words, in loving other persons or goods, we must love them in such a way that we still love God and that our fulfillment of the second facet of the great love commandment does not negate the ever-looming command of its first facet. To honor this distinction demands resolute discernment. Henry Chadwick observed, "In 'correct use' there is an implication of reflective detachment, whereas by contrast what is enjoyed is all-absorbing."[57] That use of other goods is not merely detachment from them, but reflectively or intentionally (even if subconsciously) so, suggests the need for intellectual formation. Formation in tracing all things back to God helps one discern what is itself divine and worthy

---

54. For the distinction between sapiential and existential theology, see Otto Hermann Pesch, *Theologie der Rechtfertigung bei Martin Luther und Thomas von Aquin: Versuch eines systematischtheologischen dialogs* (Mainz: Matthias Grünewald Verlag, 1967), 918–48; idem, "Existential and Sapiential Theology—The Theological Confrontation between Luther and Thomas Aquinas," in *Catholic Scholars Dialogue with Luther* (ed. Jared Wicks; Chicago: Loyola University Press, 1970), 61–81.

55. On *reductio* in dogmatics, see not only Bonaventure, *Itinerarium Mentis in Deum* (Works of St. Bonaventure II; ed. Philotheus Boehner; trans. Zachary Hayes; St. Bonaventure, NY: Franciscan Institute, 2002); but also Herman Bavinck, *Reformed Dogmatics*, Volume 2: *God and Creation* (ed. John Bolt; trans. John Vriend; Grand Rapids: Zondervan Academic, 2004), 29: "All the doctrines in dogmatics ... are but the explication of the one central dogma of the knowledge of God. All things are considered in light of God, subsumed under him, traced back to him as the starting point."

56. See Augustine, *De vera religione*, 12.24; and idem, *De doctrina christiana*, 1.3–40.

57. Henry Chadwick, "Frui-uti," *AugLex* (Basel/Stuttgart: Schwabe, 1986); see also especially William Riordan O'Connor, "The *Uti/Frui* Distinction in Augustine's Ethics," *Augustinian Studies* 14 (1983), 45–62; Oliver O'Donovan, "*Usus* and *Fruitio* in Augustine, *De doctrina christiana* I," *Journal of Theological Studies* 33 (1982), 361–97; Gerald Boersma, *Augustine's Early Theology of Image: A Study in the Development of Pro-Nicene Theology* (Oxford Studies in Historical Theology; New York: Oxford University Press, 2016), 240–2.

of enjoyment in and of itself and, by contrast, what deserves love only for its use unto love of God. Dogmatics, then, reduces all things unto God that we might know when and how to love rightly. In Paul's terms, "the renewal of your mind" leads to moral discernment of that which is "good and acceptable and perfect" (Rom. 12:2).

Second, the perfection of God serves a fundamental role not only in identifying God but in rooting the ordered form of God's sanctification of human reason and demonstrating that we are disciplined by direction unto the very means of our intellectual-spiritual discipline in Holy Scripture, as our only final authority in his fatherly hands. In other words, the doctrine of God is not only a doctrine of God but of God's works, which include the way in which God puts to death and makes alive human reason. The Reformed Scripture principle serves a pivotal role here in Webster's own theology that is not matched by the prolegomenal materials marshalled by Coakley, and this shapes the eschatological and ascetical vigor of the two accounts.[58] Whereas she turns to "dark corners," he calls for a focus upon the light of the inscripturated Word.[59] Verbal descriptions of theology, then, must note the way in which it follows always responsively to God's revelation: "theology as holy reason finds its completion in such acknowledgment and indication."[60] Verbs matter, and we must observe that "acknowledgment" and "indication" are not akin to the far more active verbs of contemporary intellectual culture, especially in its activistic register. Yet these verbs season the language of Zion, of a people who have been illumined from outside and led from on high through the murky and dangerous wilderness. The people of God are decentered by the life-giving agency of the God who takes center stage.

A deeper point dare not be missed either, namely, that the Reformed Scripture principle flows from a radicalizing of the catholic doctrine of divine perfection as applied to our intellectual provision. Christians have for centuries attested God as the perfect one, fully sufficient in and of himself. The Reformed tradition has not involved an augmenting or supplementing of those claims but, rather, a consistent application of God's triune fullness to the whole of theology. Indeed, Herman Bavinck argued beautifully that the varied distinctives of Reformed theology can,

---

58. For assessment of the shape and development of Webster's own theological principles, and the place of the Reformed Scripture principle therein, see Michael Allen, "Toward Theological Theology: Tracing the Methodological Principles of John Webster," *Themelios* 41, no. 2 (2016), 217–37 (esp. 225–6 fn. 45 on his bibliology). For his most thorough, mature accounts of this terrain, see "Biblical Reasoning" and "Principles of Systematic Theology," in *The Domain of the Word: Scripture and Theological Reason* (London: T&T Clark, 2012), 115–49.

59. Nathan Eubank has shown that Nyssa's Life of Moses moves from the moment of darkness to that of the tabernacle, such that it does not end with sheer apophaticism ("Ineffably Effable: The Pinnacle of Mystical Ascent in Gregory of Nyssa's *De vita Moysis*," *International Journal of Systematic Theology* 16 [2014], 25–41).

60. Ibid., 29.

each in their own way, be related or traced back to a fundamental radicalizing of divine fullness, which he terms its "root principle."[61] Note that Bavinck is not arguing for a so-called central dogma from which we might somehow logically deduce attendant doctrinal claims. The nineteenth-century typologies that suggested a Reformed rooting of all dogma in predestination, perhaps over against a Lutheran rooting in justification by faith alone, mangle not only the architectural shape of Reformed dogmatics but also the varied seams connecting one piece to another. Yet Bavinck is right to note that an unstinting perception of God's fullness, his perfection, what might be termed his self-sufficiency and immensity, has shaped the way in which the many works of God are viewed. Each of them flows from and manifests the God who has all within himself; none, therefore, marks out a terrain wherein God is completed, augmented, supplemented, corrected, or even approached from without.

A doctrine of divine perfection has been matched, of course, by an attendant participatory construal of creaturely reality and of human moral agency. Some Reformed theologians—not least John Webster—have been leery of the language of participation. Their concern, as stated pointedly at times by Webster, was that participation is easily heard in ways that elide the profound distinction between created and uncreated being.[62] Over against participation, then, language of covenant fellowship was often suggested as a means of affirming a dogmatics of divine perfection that did not cease to be truly ethical and to give real legitimacy to human moral responsibility. Affirming Webster's worry without necessarily following his terminological hesitancy, I think we can appreciate how creaturely being participates in the perfect God's life and how that participatory fellowship is ordered according to the biblical categories of covenant.[63] Webster and the Reformed tradition make a much bigger deal of divine perfection—and its other related divine attributes—than does Coakley, in whose volume they receive no focused attention. And a corollary, I believe, is a similar focus upon participatory rest being covenantally ordered and, as structured by God's lead, as shaped

---

61. Herman Bavinck, "The Future of Calvinism" (published 1894 in *The Presbyterian & Reformed Review*: http://scdc.library.ptsem.edu/mets/mets.aspx?src=BR1894517&div=1).

62. See, e.g., John Webster, "Perfection and Participation," in *The Analogy of Being: Invention of the Antichrist or the Wisdom of God?* (ed. Thomas Joseph White; Grand Rapids: Eerdmans, 2011), 379–94. In more recent works, especially some as yet unpublished essays on creation and providence, Webster had tilted toward a more assertive use of categories that parallel or involve participatory language.

63. Such approaches are not foreign to the early Reformed tradition, on which see J. Todd Billings, *Calvin, Participation, and the Gift: The Activity of Believers in Union with Christ* (Changing Paradigms in Historical and Systematic Theology; Oxford: Oxford University Press, 2007); more recent expansion may be found in Michael Allen, *Justification and the Gospel; Understanding the Contexts and the Controversies* (Grand Rapids: Baker Academic, 2013), chs. 1–2.

authoritatively by Scriptural guidance.[64] We have seen then two principles regarding how the doctrine of God shapes the principles of an ascetical dogmatics, corresponding to the Trinitarian order and the perfect character of the God of the gospel. We must now turn briefly to two corresponding anthropological principles, pertaining to the ends and the manner of such a dogmatics.

Third, an ascetical dogmatics walks the careful line of pursuing contemplative ends while maintaining a radically anti-speculative posture. Metaphysics serve contemplation, even as exegesis shapes metaphysics.[65] We must clarify, therefore, the two ways in which theology can be speculative, only one of which is salutary. Katherine Sonderegger has helped greatly in this regard.[66] Early on in the first volume of her systematics, we encounter the claim that "metaphysical claims about Oneness and idolatry go together."[67] One might think that this would prompt a protocol of specification for the sake of avoiding idolatry, commending a theology with strict contours and sharp edges so as to avoid veering into paganism. Without detracting from edges and specifications, Sonderegger points to a more startling reality: the call to honor the divine mystery. "Divine mystery is not a sign of our failure in knowledge, but rather our success. It is because we know truly and properly—because we obey the axiomatic First Commandment—that we can know God as mystery. His metaphysical predicate of Oneness, when known, yields mystery."[68] Elsewhere the point is repeatedly pressed home that mystery is an intellectual achievement flowing from divine presence, not a limit owing to divine absence.[69]

Radically anti-speculative theology rooted in exegesis of the scriptural testimony of the triune economy generates the focal point of such contemplation of the

---

64. I have tried to sketch these connections between the doctrine of God, the doctrine of the covenant, and the doctrine of Holy Scripture in Michael Allen, "Knowledge of God," in *Christian Dogmatics: Reformed Theology for the Church Catholic* (ed. Michael Allen and Scott R. Swain; Grand Rapids: Baker Academic, 2016), 7–29; see also Scott R. Swain, *Trinity, Revelation, and Reading: A Theological Introduction to Scripture and Its Interpretation* (London: T&T Clark, 2012), chs. 1–2.

65. For more on the contemplative ends of theology, see Matthew Levering, *Scripture and Metaphysics: Aquinas and the Renewal of Trinitarian Theology* (Challenges in Contemporary Theology; Oxford: Blackwell, 2004), 23–46; Karen Kilby, "Aquinas, the Trinity, and the Limits of Understanding," *International Journal of Systematic Theology* 7, no. 4 (2005), 414–27, seeks to reorient theology in a grammatical and apophatic fashion. Her concerns are significant, though they need not be juxtaposed with Thomas's contemplative commitments (which are fundamentally purgative).

66. My reflections here are drawn from http://zondervanacademic.com/blog/commonplaces-engaging-with-kate-sonderegger-the-one-and-the-many/.

67. Katherine Sonderegger, *Systematic Theology*, Volume 1: *The Doctrine of God* (Minneapolis: Fortress, 2015), 19.

68. Ibid., 24.

69. Ibid., 40, 42, 50, 87, 460.

divine mystery. Mystery does not equal abstraction in the sense of nonspecificity. Mystery relates to the super-saturated shape of the divine self-revelation in the full scope and sequence of biblical attestation. Contemplative theology attends to the "whole counsel of God" (Acts 20.27), tracing or reducing all topics back to their end in God without becoming speculative in any unloosed manner but remaining tethered to the canonical form of spiritual presentation. With Bavinck, we can attest that

> Mystery is the lifeblood of dogmatics ... In truth, the knowledge that God has revealed of himself in nature and Scripture far surpasses human imagination and understanding. In that sense it is all mystery with which the science of dogmatics is concerned, for it does not deal with finite creatures, but from beginning to end looks past all creatures and focuses on the eternal and infinite One himself.[70]

Fourth, dogmatics fixes its eyes intently upon a very limited set of resources, providing a lens whereby Christians might then engage other intellectual sources. Dogmatics is not an interdisciplinary activity in the sense of connecting Christian theological analysis with that of other fields. Such work is not illegitimate; intellectual conversation proves essential on many fronts, for Christ is Lord of all, and his children are called both to learn of him from his book of nature as well as his apostolic emissaries (Psalm 19) and also to seek the welfare and benefit of spheres beyond the churchly (Jer. 29.5-7).

Sarah Coakley's project may seem resolutely theological, in that its presenting problems (all in the realm of sex, gender, and self) are resourced by averting attention toward church fathers, biblical exegesis, and congregational fieldwork. But it is worth noting the kind of attention given here. Kevin Hector has commented that

> the idea here, again, is that theologians are constantly tempted to self-deception, bias, partiality, and so forth, and that they can effectively resist such temptations only on the basis of a sort of principled interdisciplinarity, the aim of which is to force oneself to remain open to other points of view, to loosen the grip of one's prejudices and presumptions, and, in sum, to make it more difficult for one to see objects as corresponding to one's desire-inflected preconceptions of them.[71]

One can perhaps appreciate the method by considering the two facets of "sanctity of mind" in Thomas Aquinas that are highlighted in Bauerschmidt's apt study: "Thomas's particular sanctity of mind combined both intellectual openness and unswerving evangelical purpose. Thomas believed in following arguments where they led, but he also believed that truthful arguments could never lead us away

---

70. Bavinck, *Reformed Dogmatics*, II: 29.

71. Kevin Hector, "Trinity, Ascesis, and Culture: Contextualizing Coakley's *God, Sexuality, and the Self*," *Modern Theology* 30, no. 4 (2014), 564.

from Christ."[72] Coakley's project does not seek to shirk Christ, of course, though it is arguable that her first volume's focus on intellectual openness, both to many extra-canonical discourses and to a strand of canonical reasoning found in Romans 8, leads to a loss of that evangelical purpose (exemplified so by her shirking of the witness of Johannine trinitarianism). Here we surely have Christ with extension, but I fear we may also have only a Christ without absolutes.[73]

Again in the realm of interdisciplinary attempts to stave off self-satisfaction in the status quo, Trinitarian matters are not far from the surface. Eugene Rogers asks, "[I]s the Christology to be all eschatological, all in what the Spirit will work, and not historical, in what the Spirit has already conceived? Perhaps Coakley will say that only after we train our eyes to see Christ in our neighbor are we really able to see Christ anew in Jesus."[74] Coakley has responded that the delay of a proper Christology is intentional and that "my main interest in vol. 1 is deliberately to destabilize any complacent sense that we can get our hands around 'Jesus' without prior pneumatological displacement."[75]

One element here is that her interdisciplinary effort to hear the Spirit in various discourses raises the question of targets and of breadth. Has she listened in the right places? And has she listened widely enough?[76] Truthfully, I am not sure how such questions could ever be satisfied given her protocol. But a more fundamental question raised by Rogers haunts more profoundly: Can we really expect to hear the Christ of Scripture only after hearing the Spirit in his world? Is this not exactly the reverse of what Calvin taught regarding the need for a scriptural set of lenses through which we might glean how the whole world serves as a theater of God's glory?[77] Why would we expect and structure our theological approach to "pneumatological displacement" around nontheological theories or disciplines? Why the focus on "dark corners" and distant lands rather than illumined hallways and the churchly homestead? A more densely developed Christology and pneumatology would provide resources for a more intensive

---

72. Bauerschmidt, *Thomas Aquinas*, 36.

73. See Sarah Coakley, *Christ Without Absolutes: A Study of the Christology of Ernst Troeltsch* (Oxford: Oxford University Press, 1988).

74. Eugene F. Rogers Jr., "Prayer, Christoformity, and the Author: New Sites of Discussion for Theology," *Modern Theology* 30, no. 4 (2014), 558.

75. Sarah Coakley, "Response to Reviewers of *God, Sexuality, and the Self*," *Modern Theology* 30, no. 4 (2014), 592.

76. Mary Catherine Hilkert has asked, "how a different location for pastoral fieldwork or qualitative social research might have affected some of her theological conclusions" ("Desire, Gender, and God-Talk: Sarah Coakley's Feminist Contemplative Theology," *Modern Theology* 30, no. 4 [2014], 580). Similarly, Katherine Sonderegger has stated that a grateful reading of this volume with its many forays is nonetheless left demanding, grasping, desiring more ("Review Article: *God, Sexuality, and the Self*," *International Journal of Systematic Theology* 18, no. 1 [2016], 98).

77. John Calvin, *Institutes of the Christian Religion*, I.vi.

focus, I think, upon Holy Scripture and, subserviently, the church's attention to that revelation in her witness and wisdom, from which we can then turn to assess the illumination thrown on all the world as God's own theater (as suggested by Calvin's favored image).

In sum, I hope that this sketch of the terrain and these brief theses help suggest that the seemingly establishmentarian might just be the most eschatological, for dogmatics serves within the triune economy, by God's mortifying and vivifying grace, to discipline our minds and hearts. Not burning down the house, in a fit of vibrant revolt, but finding the fire of the tabernacle to light our very minds unto holiness. Dogmatics does so precisely by decentering our own presenting questions and assumptions, reducing all data and questions unto the triune God. Such intellectual discipline, however, demands a careful walk toward contemplative wisdom rooted in a radically anti-speculative approach to biblical reasoning. While dogmatics shapes and forms one to engage in interdisciplinary reasoning and extensive conversation, the discipline itself fixes its sights intensives upon a certain set of divinely gifted resources and angles of inquiry.

Chapter 9

THE CONTEMPLATIVE AND THE ACTIVE LIFE

The Practice of Theology as Intellectual Asceticism in Thomas's Writings

Assessing the theology of Thomas Aquinas is no simple matter. Difficulty resides not only with the reception of Thomas but also with the textual corpus he left behind. When considering a theme such as his theological method or his principles of biblical interpretation, for example, we might turn to a number of resources. First, he wrote a number of doctrinal *summae* which would offer contributions to the topic at hand: not only his initial commentary upon the Lombard's Sentences but also his *Summa contra gentiles, Summa theologiae,* and *Compendia*. Second, he interpreted a large body of Holy Scripture and various portions of that expository work inform his approach to the theological task. Third, he participated as an academic in the University of Paris in a number of disputations wherein theological prolegomena were discussed and his fundamental commitments might be gleaned. In the foreword to his *Summa theologiae*, Thomas comments: "We have considered how newcomers to this teaching are greatly hindered by various writings on the subject." He sketches a number of these hindrances: the "swarm" of unnecessary questions or discussions, the misshapen outline that may be occasioned by following the format of a text or a debate, the dangers of repetition, and so forth. The same questions and concerns might be raised to gleaning from Thomas as well: how does one interact with his corpus in a way that does not swarm with its size, misdirect with its varied formats (marked by different genres and conceptual structures), or breed muddle by reason of repetition.

Typically, debate about theological prolegomena in Thomas fixes upon the first question of the *prima pars* in his magisterial *Summa theologiae*.[1] In that question

---

1. e.g., M. D. Chenu, *La Théologie comme science au xiii siècle* (Paris: J. Vrin, 1942); G. F. Van Ackeren, *Sacra Doctrina: The Subject of the First Question of the Summa Theologica of St Thomas Aquinas* (Rome: Catholic Book Agency, 1952); Erik Persson, *Sacra Doctrina: Reason and Revelation in Thomas Aquinas* (trans. Ross Mackenzie Oxford: Blackwell, 1970.); F. Van Steenberghen, *La philosophie au XIII Siécle* (2nd ed.; Louvain: Éditions Peeters, 1991); for a refreshingly different approach, see Frederick Christian Bauerschmidt, *Thomas Aquinas: Faith, Reason, and Following Christ* (New York: Oxford University Press, 2013), 46–51.

Thomas addresses a number of definitional matters regarding the discipline which the entire text of the *Summa theologiae* exemplifies. Many matters can be gleaned from such an approach, and it has borne much fruit in diverse studies. Yet I wish to propose a different approach to retrieving Thomas's contributions regarding the method of Christian theology, a path that begins not with initial statements on prolegomena but that moves backward from his final observations and provides a matrix within which we might make sense of those methodological principles. In a sense, my approach will move backward twice over: first, from his *Compendia* to the *Summa Theologiae*; second, from his eschatology back to his prolegomena within the *Summa Theologiae*. Finally, we will conclude with a backward survey and a forward sketch of what might be involved in appropriating his insights with respect to theological method for a Reformed Thomism today. In so doing we will focus on the decisive significance of the beatific vision as an eschatological hope and the contemplative life as a moral commitment. Rather than allow an intellectual or cultural context to overdetermine the methods of theology, a Reformed Thomism does well to relocate the exercise of theological reason in the economy of the gospel and to re-envision its practice as an exercise of intellectual asceticism in the contemplative life.

Thomas Aquinas on Human Intellectual Life in the Divine Economy

First, we do well to consider the final theological project of Thomas, his *Compendia*, and note the way in which it introduces the theological task:

> Faith is a certain foretaste of that knowledge which is to make us happy in the life to come. The Apostle says in Heb. 11.1 that faith is "the substance of things to be hoped for," as though implying that faith is already, in some preliminary way, inaugurating in us the things that are to be hoped for, that is, future beatitude. Our Lord has taught us that this beatific knowledge has to do with two truths, namely, the divinity of the Blessed Trinity and the humanity of Christ. That is why, addressing the Father, He says: "This is eternal life: that they may know Thee, the only true God, and Jesus Christ, whom Thou hast sent." All the knowledge imparted by faith turns about these two points, the divinity of the Trinity and the humanity of Christ. This should cause us no surprise: the humanity of Christ is the way by which we come to the divinity. Therefore, while we are still wayfarers, we ought to know the road leading to our goal.[2]

A number of observations can be made. First, knowledge has an end: "our goal" in which "we come to the divinity" and enjoy "eternal life," "which is to make us

---

2. Thomas Aquinas, *Light of Faith: The Compendium of Theology* (trans. Cyril Vollert St. Louis: B. Herder, 1947); (repr. Manchester, NH: Sophia Institute Press, 1993), 4–5.

happy in the life to come." These "things which are to be hoped for, that is, future beatitude" constitute a *telos* for theological knowledge. Second, knowledge has a movement: "the way" as well as "the road" to such knowledge is sketched here. Knowledge has not arrived; knowledge is sought. The imagery remains that of the pilgrimage for those who "are still wayfarers." The idiom is not stasis, nor is it consummation; the conceptuality comes from the realm of the journey. Third, this knowledge has a particular shape or form: "All the knowledge imparted by faith turns on these two points, the divinity of the Trinity and the humanity of Christ." Note that these two doctrines are not the totality of knowledge but the "hinge" upon which all knowledge turns. They constitute the focal point and the singular shape of Christian knowledge. We see, then, that knowledge has a *telos* which is an eschatological hope and that this hope must be attained through a particular journey.

Thomas presses still further, however, to match his eschatological reflections with further comments about theology. He does not merely address the question "what is theology?" but also inquires regarding "how does theology come to happen?" Fourth, he notes that God provides for theological knowledge: here Thomas alludes to the divine missions (in quoting Jn. 17.3, he speaks of the sending of the Son) whereby God makes himself known. He comments on the instrumentality of the humanity of Christ, specifically, inasmuch as the economy of gospel revelation centers on this revelation, for "the humanity of Christ is the way by which we come to the divinity." Fifth, Thomas not only identifies theological knowledge as a lingering hope for the finale of gospel history but also characterizes it as a present anticipation that can be enjoyed proleptically. "Faith is a certain foretaste of that knowledge"; that is, "faith is already, in some preliminary way, inaugurating in us the things that are to be hoped for." So Thomas not only flavors his theological method with eschatological imagination but also locates the practice of theology—and its present exercise, particularly—in the economy of the gospel.

In the *Compendia*, then, Thomas prompts us to think of theological methodology in the context of eschatology, ethics, and the economy of the gospel. In so doing, Thomas reminds us of the importance of locating intellectual practices within the prior matrix of an intellectual ontology, that is, a depiction of the reality wherein and whereby knowledge arises. To understand the practice of intellectual work focused upon the knowledge of God, one must attend to the figures involved and the relations whereby they communicate (or "make common") such knowledge. Thomas's observations, however, do not remain at the formal level; he presses these formal, analytic concerns in a specific material direction. Theology must be defined in light of the gospel of Jesus Christ. His emphasis upon not only the singularity of the one triune God but also his commitment to the humanity of Christ as "the way by which we come to the divinity" prioritizes the missions of the Triune persons in this regard.

Second, we will take the most fruitful course through Thomas's wider corpus if we follow the sketch provided, albeit briefly, in this final methodological introduction, namely, by noting the ways in which ethical and eschatological categories flavor the practice of theology itself. These connections are not as overt or immediate in the *Summa theologiae*, wherein Thomas's comments regarding them are found emerging as he works his way through the various topics. In suggesting that we follow a path charted by the *Compendia's* introduction, though, I do not mean to suggest that Thomas has changed his method or has altered his general approach to theological principium.[3] Far from it. Thomas has made overt and immediately explicit what was only patiently and with some difficulty seen over the course of reading his wider *Summa theologiae*.

In the space that remains, then, we consider the eschatological imagination provided by Thomas in the *prima secundae* wherein he describes beatitude (*ST.* 1a2ae.1-5).[4] Then we consider the ethical distinction that marks Thomas's theological method more than any other, namely, the distinction between the active life and the contemplative life (*ST.* 2a2ae.179-182). Finally, I offer a reading of his discussion of the discipline or science of theology as it appears at the beginning of the *prima pars*, considering that famous entryway in light of these eschatological and ethical concerns (*ST.* 1a.1).

Thomas Aquinas on Beatitude and Our Spiritual End (ST. 1a2ae.1-5)

"There can be no complete and final happiness for us save in the vision of God" (*ST.* 1a2ae.3.8). Thomas has affirmed that all humans have a desire for happiness, at least in the abstract, though not all desire its concrete particularization in the enjoyment of God (1a2ae.5.8). But Christians know and hope in this joy, looking for and journeying toward this blessed sight. While the beatific vision will be enjoyed by all glorified believers in Christ, it will not be uniform in its exercise. For one, "joy can be deeper because he is more open and adapted to receive it" (1a2ae.5.2) (cf. 1a2ae.5.2; 1a2ae.4.1). This adaptive openness stems from "the degree of sharing in this good" (1a2ae.5.2 *ad* 3).

What do we see in seeing God? Thomas speaks to our vision of God's own being in his singular identity but then surveys more broadly how we see all things in his light (cf. 1a2ae.4.3 *ad* 1). First, we participate in God or share in God through this vision. Herein our Godward focus crystallizes: "Manifestly man is destined to an end beyond himself, for he himself is not the supreme good [*non enim homo est summum bonum*]" (1a2ae.2.5). While "happiness is a real condition of soul, yet is founded on a thing outside the soul" (1a2ae.2.7). Thomas offers a discussion of the various options to satisfy that soul-ish desire: riches, honors, fame, power, bodily vitality, pleasure, soulish gifts, or, finally, any created value whatsoever (see 1a2ae.2.1-8). Fundamental to appreciating his argument is its baseline that runs through exegesis of Ecclesiastes throughout 1a2ae.2. Thomas sums up the vanity

---

3. See Michel Corbin, *Le chemin de la théologie chez Thomas d'Aquin* (Paris: Beauchesne, 1974), 713–27.
4. All citations of the *Summa Theologica* will appear in parentheses.

of created objects in this way: "For man to rest content with any created good is not possible, for he can be happy only with complete good which satisfies his desire altogether: he would not have reached his ultimate end were there something still remaining to be desired" (1a2ae.2.8). What, then, may be the satisfying object of our desire? "The "good without reserve" (*universale bonum*) fulfills the human appetite or will, while the "true without reserve" (*universale verum*) satisfies the mind's search; both of these are "found, not in anything created, but in God alone" (1a2ae.2.8). Not just in God but we must go further and say that "complete happiness requires the mind to come through to the essence itself" (1a2ae.3.8).

But our blessed vision of God centers on sight of God without being reduced to mere vision of the Almighty. In him we see all other things. While Thomas insists that its object is divine ("man's ultimate end is uncreated good, namely God"), its exercise is human ("man's ultimate end is a creaturely reality in him, for what is it but *his* coming to God and *his* joy with God"); he clarifies that "with respect to its object or cause happiness is uncreated reality, while with respect to its essence it is a creaturely reality" (1a2ae.3.1; see also 1a2ae.2.7: "happiness is a real condition of soul, yet is founded on a thing outside the soul"). Our human exercise is complex: the human will moves us toward happiness; this beatitude consists of an act of the mind, and this beatific intellection leads to pleasure in the will (1a2ae.3.5). Further, the object of this human, creaturely vision is not simply God, though it is singularly God; by that I mean to note that Thomas believes we see all other things inasmuch as they relate to God. We see God and his many-splendored works in our glorious vision.

How can we characterize this beatific vision as an act? It is a created act, that is, an act performed by creatures. Thomas prioritizes this act by its contemplative or intellectual character. He does so for exegetical reasons, citing Jn. 17.3 at a decisive point to note that "eternal life" is "to know thee, the one true God," which he identifies there as "an activity of the mind" (1a2ae.3.4, *sed contra*; he also explains the significance of this scriptural passage in 1a2ae.3.2). He does so for anthropological reasons. We can trace his argument in three steps. "First, given that happiness is an activity, then it ought to be a man's best activity, that is to say when his highest power is engaged with its highest object." Second, "man's mind is his highest power, and its highest object is divine good, an object for its seeing, not for its doing something in practice." Third, then, "the activity of contemplating the things of God is principal in happiness" (1a2ae.3.5). His language in this discussion is not exclusive, however, as he speaks of "man's last and perfect beatitude ... wholly centred on contemplation."

Human vision of God, then, remains human. Indeed, Thomas will later distinguish between the varied knowledge of God available to figures in glory. "In this respect ends are diverse for lower and higher natures according to their various relationships to that one thing. So therefore God's happiness in comprehending his essence is higher than the happiness of men and angels, who see but do not comprehend him" (1a2ae.3.8 *ad* 2; see also 1a2ae.1.8). A hierarchy has been sketched: God's knowledge, glorified human's knowledge, angelic knowledge. The creatures in glory "see but do not comprehend." Later scholastics would draw out distinctions between archetypal and ectypal theology, that is, between God's own knowledge of himself and that knowledge of him which he shares with creatures, and then between the diverse forms of ectypal theology: that of those in glory (beatific knowledge or that of the comprehensors) and that of those still on the journey (wayfaring knowledge).

What of the body and its pleasures? Thomas offers a qualified affirmation of their benefits to the person. "Bodily well-being, then, is a consequent condition, for the happiness of soul overflows into the body, which drinks of the fullness of soul" (1a2ae.4.6). Yet Thomas presses still further: "Happiness is not centered on bodily good as its object, but can be endowed with a certain glow and beauty by it" (1a2ae.4.6 *ad* 1). The language of center here beckons to be yoked with its paired term—circumference—to lay out a portrait whereby soulish contemplation of God provides the center of our happiness, around which other delights make up a wide circumference. The imagery of the center not only speaks to the primacy of the contemplative joy of the soul but also to its productivity, for Thomas does speak of bodily pleasure as a "consequent condition" and an "overflow" from the soul. Sensitive activity may not be a constituent of our happiness but it is an "antecedent" and "preliminary" to our "partial happiness" now and a "result" of the "perfect happiness hoped for in heaven" (1a2ae.3.3; see also 1a2ae.4.2).

What of external goods? They are presently necessary; indeed, they are "required for the imperfect happiness open to us in this life, not that they lie at the heart of happiness, yet they are tools to serve happiness which lies ... in the activity of virtue" (1a2ae.4.7). But they will not always be necessary: "Nowise are they needed for the perfect happiness of seeing God .... Perfect happiness, however, is for a soul without a body or a soul united to a body which is no longer animal but spiritual" (1a2ae.4.7). In addressing the intermediate state of presence unto the Lord and the resurrected state of the glorified body, Thomas comments that external goods which presently sustain the body (e.g., food, drink) will no longer be needful. Similarly, while friends are presently necessary, they will later be an added benefit though not a strict need (1a2ae.4.8).

Our *telos* shapes our behavior now. "The end is not altogether extrinsic to the act, but is related to it as its origin and destination, and so enters into its very nature, for as an action it is from something and as a passion it is towards something" (1a2ae.1.3 *ad* 1; 1a2ae.1.3 *ad* 2 presses further: "the end affects the will as prior by intention"). "And in this life as we draw nearer to it by the felicity of the contemplative life rather than of the active life, and grow more like God ... so do we become less dependent ... on these external bodily goods" (1a2ae.4.7). Our pursuit of this blissful end in God, then, renders our actions valid (at least with regard to their goal, though their manner and form are also pertinent matters). Beatitude does not simply follow our lives as a consequence; the blessed vision of God constitutes our actions as a final cause and goal, a chief end which we pursue in all sorts of varying ways (affections, thoughts, words, deeds). And this constitutive function plays an increasingly formative role, as we are weaned off other affections and drawn more deeply into communion with the one true God.

Yet Thomas does not suggest that contemplation might overwhelm or remove our need for activity in this era. Indeed, even our thoughts (the very realm of the contemplative) cannot be circumscribed by the spiritual; "we are not expected always to be thinking of our last end whenever we desire or do something in particular." He even gives an example of this principle: "For example, in walking somewhere one does not have to be reminding oneself of one's destination at every step" (1a2ae.1.6 *ad* 3). The journey provides the context for one's every action, though it may not be the overt content of every thought or maneuver. He derives a principle: "The force of our first intention with respect to it persists in each desire of any other thing, even though it is not adverted to" (1a2ae.1.6 *ad* 3).

We do well, then, having considered our beatific end, now to turn to reflection on the ways in which the contemplative life draws us unto that glorious goal. We have seen in Thomas's eschatological comment that contemplation plays a central, that is, a prioritized and productive, role in our future hope of glory with God, and we have seen that it shapes our behavior now. In turning to his material on ethics and human behavior in light of the gospel, we can consider in greater detail the distinction between our contemplative life and the active life.

Thomas Aquinas on the Contemplative and the Active Life (ST. 2a2ae.179-182)

Theology constitutes a spiritual practice and, thus, an ethical agency borne of the divine economy. We do well, then, to think more directly about pertinent ethical categories that shape how he views the theological task by providing something of a spiritual-relational framework for its definition and exercise. Perhaps most significant in this regard is his division of human life into the active and the contemplative life (see *ST.* 2a2ae.179-182).

The division finds affirmation in a common-sense manner: "Since some men especially dedicate themselves to the contemplation of truth while others are primarily occupied with external activities, it follows that human living is correctly divided into the active and the contemplative" (2a2ae.179.1). Of course, Thomas is not making a personal judgment regarding empirical observation; he has already cited the authoritative judgment of Gregory the Great, having alluded to his use of this distinction between the active and the contemplative, and he will allude throughout to symbols of these two facets of life in scripture (e.g., Leah and Rachel, Mary and Martha) (see 2a2ae.179.1 *sed contra*; 2a2ae.179.2 *sed contra*). While this division would not apply to other forms of life, it marks out key facets of human life, which is distinguished by its rationality (see 2a2ae.179.1 *ad* 2).

It is worth noting, first of all, that this division is complete inasmuch as it describes the intellectual function of humans. It is not complete, however, as a total description of everything that encompasses human life, not only in its distinction from other animals by way of rationality but also in its commonality with the animals in its animality. For example, Thomas will cede the point that humans do pursue the "life of pleasure" as do the "beasts" (2a2ae.179.2 *ad* 1). So

Thomas notes that bodily loves shape human action now, but these pursuits are distinctly human (even if they are also, nonetheless, actually human). As noted earlier, Thomas defines distinctly human life by its highest apogee, in this case, by its intellectual exercise or rational functioning.

Thomas describes the contemplative life as an intellectual activity which, nonetheless, "consists in love" and "terminates in delight … This in its turn intensifies love." Whereas debates had swirled regarding whether the contemplative life was a function of the intellect or the will, Thomas proffers: "as regards the very essence of its activity, the contemplative life belongs to the intellect; but as regards that which moves one to the exercise of that activity, it belongs to the will, which moves all the other faculties, and even the intellect, to their acts" (2a2ae.180.1; see also 1a2ae.9.1). In other words, while contemplation is an intellectual act, it is moved by love and results in delight and, by extension, deeper love. It is not love or delight per se, but it exists only in their wake and for their sake (see also 2a2ae.180.7). Similarly, Thomas notes that the moral virtues are not a part of the essence of the contemplative life, though they dispose one for this life; here he develops a distinction between something being essential or being dispositive (2a2ae.180.2; cf. 2a2ae.181.1).[5] So contemplation, for Thomas, flows from love, has been disposed for by the moral virtues, actualizes the intellect, culminates in delight, and results in deepening love. Also the intellectual actualization occurring in contemplation "has only one activity in which it finally terminates and from which it derives its unity, namely the contemplation of truth, but it has several activities by which it arrives at this final activity," and he sketches them briefly: understanding epistemological principles, deduction from those principles (which he later suggests [2a2ae.180.3 *ad* 1] has been termed meditation and consideration), and contemplating that truth deduced (2a2ae.180.3).[6] Thus far, his description of the subject and exercise of the contemplative life.

What of the object of the contemplative life? Thomas has much to commend here as well. He will chart "four things [that] pertain in a certain order to the contemplative life: first, the moral virtues; secondly, certain acts other than contemplation; thirdly, contemplation of divine effects; and fourthly, the complement of all, namely the contemplation of divine truth" (2a2ae.180.4). It is plain from his prior discussion that the first two components pertain to preparations for contemplation: disposing oneself morally unto such intellectual communion with God by way of virtue or fittingness; certain mental acts, not themselves contemplative, which serve, nonetheless, to prompt one to contemplation, that is, consideration of first principles, deduction, prayer, and so on. The third and fourth components involve consideration of the divine effects or economy and, most fundamentally, of God in himself.

---

5. One wonders why this essential/dispositive distinction might not be put to use in 2a2ae.179.2 regarding the relationship of pleasure to the contemplative life.

6. Later he maps the various intellectual motions along circular, straight, and spiral images (2a2ae.180.6.3, reply and *ad* 2).

Thomas argues that "we can arrive at the contemplation of God through divine effects ... so the contemplation of them also pertains to the contemplative life, because through them man is led to a knowledge of God" (2a2ae.180.4). The works of God, however, make up part of the contemplative life in a penultimate or improper manner, namely, inasmuch as "David sought a knowledge of God's works so that through them he could be led to God" (2a2ae.180.4 *ad* 1; see also 1a.1.3-4, 7). Thomas uses the language of primary and secondary objectivity to note that God is the primary object of contemplation and knowledge of all things in God is only a secondary object of contemplation.

How do we fare in terms of enjoying this contemplative life to the full in this life, namely, by partaking of the beatific vision? Thomas observes that both Gregory and Augustine limit beatific vision to life after this bodily and mortal life (2a2ae.180.5). Yet Thomas introduces a further distinction: someone can be in this life either "actually" or "potentially but with suspension of activity" as in rapture (2a2ae.180.5). Inasmuch as someone is living this life actually with bodily and sensory entanglements, he cannot partake of the beatific vision. But "in this second state the contemplation of the present life can attain to a vision of the divine essence," and Thomas considers Paul's rapture described in 2 Cor. 12.2 to be an example. By invoking this distinction, Thomas wants to push the envelope historically regarding the way in which we might categorize someone partaking of the beatific vision in this life (and, notably, he will extend this approach to his reading of Christ's continuous beholding of the divine essence during his incarnate life along the lines of an extended rapturous experience: 3a.9.2 and 3a.10).

Thomas describes the active life as that which is "occupied with external activities" (2a2ae.179.1). The active life involves thought or knowledge but such reflection is directed not to the goal of "the knowledge of truth as such" but the goal of "some external action, which engages intellect as practical or active" (2a2ae.179.2; see also 2a2ae.181.1). Inasmuch as our present state brings with it many needs, Thomas can assert that "in a qualified sense or in a special case the active life is to be preferred, in view of the needs of the present life" (2a2ae.182.1). His depiction of how the active life connects to the contemplative life manifests an asymmetry. While one may be called into active exercise, this summons always supplements and never should substitute for one's contemplative activity. He argues that activity can be a mandate "not done by way of subtraction but by way of addition" (2a2ae.182.1 *ad* 3). Whereas he will not say the opposite, he here insists on the priority of the contemplative to the active.

Thomas relates the two divisions of life, evincing a consistent though complex concern to affirm this asymmetry. First, the active life can inhibit the contemplative life: "external occupation prevents a man from considering matters of thought, which are removed from the concrete affairs with which the works of the active life are concerned" (2a2ae.181.2 *ad* 2). Inasmuch as external necessities distract from fundamental reality—God—they hinder human contemplation in the present. Second, the active life can actually enhance the contemplative life, as described in the vein of teaching. Teaching, inasmuch as it involves interior contemplation, is contemplative; teaching, inasmuch as it finds "audible expression," however, makes contribution to the active life (2a2ae.181.3). Audible teaching, itself an active exercise, equips others better for the future exercise of contemplation, though it is itself not contemplation as such. Third, the active life will end, though the contemplative life will continue forevermore (2a2ae.181.4). Thomas then lists nine reasons—as befitting the most excellent things in humanity, as being more continuous, as bringing greater delight, as being more self-sufficient, as loved more for itself, as concerned with higher or greater things, as more proper or distinctly human, and as stated in Jesus' commendation of the way of Mary over that of Martha—why the contemplative life is more excellent than the active life (2a2ae.182.1). These nine reasons are prompted, overtly, by Aristotle in the first eight instances and by Jesus himself in the ninth. However, even those observations regarding the greater excellency of the contemplative life which come from Aristotle's *Ethics* are also yoked in each case to scriptural argumentation. Fourth, the contemplative life, in and of itself, is more meritorious than the active life, considered in and of itself. Admittedly, however, Thomas notes that the way in which someone performs active works of service to his neighbor may well be more meritorious than the way in which someone else merits by way of contemplative activity (2a2ae.182.2).

Ideally, how would the active and contemplative lives relate? Thomas argues that the active life "regulates and directs the internal passions of the soul" and in so doing "fosters the contemplative life, which is impeded by the disorder of the internal passions" (2a2ae.182.4). Inasmuch as the active life involves moral virtue, prudence, and teaching (see 2a2ae.181.1-3), it serves to enhance the contemplative life. However, inasmuch and to the extent that the active life requires attention to external actions, it impedes the exercise of contemplation. Therefore, the ideal scenario would be to minimize such external actions as much as possible, cognizant of the fact that this present life demands such commitments to one degree or another. While some are more or less suited to one or the other life due to innate tendencies either owing to a "spirit of restlessness" or a "naturally pure and calm spirit," Thomas notes that all are intended by God, over time, to "become even readier for contemplation" (2a2ae.182.4 *ad* 3).

Thomas sketches an eschatological end—the blessed vision of God—that only arrives in the state of glory and in this state of grace inasmuch as glory breaks in rapturously yet that, nonetheless, calls for an ethical response whereby we more and more seek to "become even readier for contemplation" here and now, habituating ourselves, as it were, by the exercise of our will and mind and by the gifts of grace to partake of that intellectual communion with God that shall one day be ours.

Thomas Aquinas on Theology (ST. 1a.1)

Eschatology and ethics are yoked together, and Thomas includes the call to contemplation into our summons for this spiritual journey. How do these eschatological, anthropological, and ethical reflections inform theological method? For Thomas, as we will see, *sacra doctrina* unites God's knowledge, human beatific knowledge, and our current intellectual pilgrimage. As Matthew Levering observes: "*Sacra doctrina* both adds this supernatural knowledge and reorders all that can be known naturally in light of the triune God as our beginning and supernatural end."[7]

To appreciate the place of *sacra doctrina*, we do well to note the ways in which Thomas argues that it is necessary alongside the exercise of philosophical reason. First, even where reason is quite capable of rendering judgments that are apt, it is evident only to a few, after much arduous mental exercise, and mixed with many mistakes (*ST*. 1a.1.1). Thus, even where reason can help us to know things—real, significant things—in a valid way, *sacra doctrina* does so in a wider, quicker, more effective way. Here there is a quantitative superiority noted: of the sort of knowledge that might be attained via philosophical reason, *sacra doctrina* gets more of it in a more efficient way. Second, Thomas presses to a qualitative distinction between *sacra doctrina* and philosophical reason by noting that philosophy has limits to its breadth and height which do not similarly bind theology.

> Above all because God destines us for an end beyond the grasp of reason; according to Isaiah, Eye hath not seen, O God, without thee what thou hast prepared for them that love thee. Now we have to recognize an end before we can stretch out and exert ourselves for it. Hence the necessity for our welfare that divine truths surpassing reason should be signified to us through divine revelation.
>
> (1a.1.1)

Divine truths must be revealed divinely—through the instrument of *sacra scriptura*—so that we might know those things which exceed the objects of human reason.

What kind of science is this theological activity? Thomas argues that *sacra doctrina* "takes over both functions," for the precise reason that it involves knowledge of God and all he has made. "All the same it is more theoretical than practical, since it is mainly concerned with the divine things which are, rather than with things men do; it deals with human acts only in so far as they prepare men for that achieved knowledge on which their eternal bliss reposes" (1a.1.4). Thomas characterizes the work of theology, then, as the preparation whereby wayfarers act toward their eternal bliss of beatific knowledge. The superiority of theology flows not merely from its certain roots in divine revelation (which exceeds any certainty in the empirical or philosophical sciences) but especially from its "worth of subject" which is "eternal happiness" in God (1a.1.5). Particular practices (*exercitium*) constitute the theological action of the human wayfarer. Theology

---

7. Matthew Levering, *Scripture and Metaphysics: Aquinas and the Renewal of Trinitarian Theology* (Oxford: Blackwell, 2003), 31; see also Jean-Pierre Torrell, *Recherches thomasiennes* (Paris: J. Vrin, 2000), 132.

calls for investment in these practices of focus upon God's own being as found in God's own self-revelation.

"God is truly the object of this science," though his centrality as its object does not render its circumference narrow. Thomas also affirms: "Now all things are dealt with in holy teaching in terms of God, either because they are God himself or because they are relative to him as their origin and end" (1a.1.7). He observes how a variety of scholastics organized theology according to reality and symbols (Peter Lombard), the works or economy of redemption (Hugh of St. Victor), or the pairing of Christ and the *totus Christus*, his body (Robert Kilwardy). Thomas does not rebuke them, though he seeks to point to deeper organizing principles, namely, that "all these indeed are dwelt on by this science, yet as held in their relationship to God" (1a.1.7).

Theology, for Thomas, involves contemplation of or speculation regarding God and all things in the way in which they relate to God (from whom, through whom, and to whom they exist—Rom. 11.36).[8] Theology is meant to draw us away from lesser goods or less potent ways of knowing the ultimate good (by reason alone) and to draw us to the most potent and primal source of truth, goodness, and beauty. In other words, theology is meant to further our intellectual communion with the triune God. His theological method in *ST*. 1a.1 makes sense only within the spiritual journey bounded by our nature as created by God and intended for glory with this God in the blissful end. Nature and glory, eschatology and ethics, activity and contemplation—each of these pairs speaks into and sets the parameters for Thomas's reflections on theology as a *scientia*, a discipline, a Christian undertaking.

Theology for Reformed Thomists: A Summary and a Sketch

Modern theology oftentimes locates theology and the method of its effective exercise in an intellectual economy. In late modernity, more often than not, these prolegomenal issues have been relocated to cultural and ideological economies. Each has its contributions to make, and we dare not respond to the reductive demands of either approach with a curt dismissal. But the theological reflections of Thomas Aquinas remind us that far more definitive than any intellectual or cultural context is the spiritual matrix within which the exercise of theological reason might transpire.

Charles Taylor has used the language of a "moral ontology" to characterize the time and space within which an agent may exist and act. I suggest we do well to think in terms of an intellectual ontology, that is, a description of the reality

---

8. Gilles Emery reminds us that Thomas tends to employ the term contemplative (*contemplativus*) in texts undergirded by Christian sources and the term speculative (*speculativus*) in texts spawned by commentary on Aristotle, Giles Emery, *Trinity in Aquinas* (trans. Matthew Levering et al; Ypsilanti: Sapientia, 2003), 312–13.

within which intellectual work occurs.⁹ More specifically, we do well to locate the theological task within a reality that has its own order by God's intention. Thus, the category of "ontology" can and must be governed materially by the description of a divine "economy" (*oikonomia*).

If we are not merely to avoid falling into the mires of pluralism and relativism but also lapsing into the muck of modern empiricism, naturalism, and rationalism, then we need to locate the theologian ontologically and economically. The question of what a Reformed Thomist approach to theological method might look like could involve a turning to the works of earlier Protestant Scholastics (whether those who drew eclectically from many but especially from Thomas, as did John Owen, or others who more consistently culled from the angelic doctor, such as Peter Martyr Vermigli) or to John Webster today. For the sake of brevity and clarity, traits especially prized by Thomas's Reformed readers, a few comments along these lines might be useful by way of conclusion.

First, recent scholarship on Thomas has noted the role of narrative in an illuminating manner.¹⁰ More specifically, Matthew Lamb has observed that Thomas's most notable contribution in the realm of eschatology is what he deems his "wisdom eschatology," the way in which the last things center on the beatific vision and the manner by which that terminus reorients all human knowledge in its frame.¹¹ Wisdom comes in the application of truthful judgment in appropriate settings. Thomas exemplifies awareness that widely deploying Christian judgment follows from discerning not simply a narrative within which one fits but, more specifically, a nature and a *telos* which bound that narrative journey. Thomas's approach to exit (*exitus*) and return (*reditus*) may be a far cry from some of the covenantal terminology deployed in the Reformed tradition, but its fundamental judgment remains the same, namely, that humanity (our creation, fall, reconciliation, and restoration in Christ) must be thought eschatologically. Not only that but Thomas, like the later Reformed tradition (though it must be said, unlike Karl Barth's subversion), insists that the state of glory exceeds but befits the state of integrity in creation itself. As Thomas says in this section, grace does not destroy but does perfect nature (1a.1.8 *ad* 2)—understanding grace, therefore, requires knowing both nature and glory (its culmination or maturation in Christ). With respect to our topic, appreciating the role of theology in the Christian life and the church's witness involves appreciating our created nature (as knowers of God) and our intended end (as those who eternally and blissfully contemplate

---

9. Charles Taylor, *Sources of the Self: The Making of Modern Identity* (Cambridge: Harvard University Press, 1989), 8.

10. see especially Levering, *Scripture and Metaphysics*; see also Max Seckler, *Das Heil in der Geschichte: Geschichtstheologisches Denken bei Thomas von Aquin* (Munich: Kösel, 1964).

11. Matthew Lamb. "Wisdom Eschatology in Augustine and Aquinas," In *Aquinas the Augustinian* (ed. Michael Dauphinais et al, 258–75; Washington DC: Catholic University of America Press, 2007), 264–5.

God with his own knowledge in which we graciously participate through Christ and by the Spirit).

Second, "one risks misunderstanding Thomas's intellectual project unless one sees it as a form of discipleship."[12] What does this mean? The theological task must be construed as a process of what Bauerschmidt calls "intellectual asceticism."[13] Theology is inherently confrontational, and Thomas's concern here is matched by the Reformed tradition's emphasis upon theology as an iconoclastic endeavor.[14] In what way does this intellectual ascesis occur? Denys Turner has pointed to what seem to be important features in the work of Thomas: "Thomas is a saint so that theologians might have at least one model within the membership of their guild of a theologian without an ego to promote or protect, who knew how to make holy disappearing into a theological act."[15] Turner describes a Thomas without an ego. From the perspective of genre and literary production, this may seem the case. Thomas does not intrude into the text—he is more personally reticent than even Calvin and, let's call things what they are, a far cry from the self-involving provocateur that was Martin Luther. Thomas seems to pull a John the Baptist: decreasing that another—the subject of theology—might increase.

Yet I think Bauerschmidt argues an even more profound point: it is not simply that Thomas hangs loose from overt personal involvement in the argument but rather that he views theology as a part of the shaping of the self (including the rationality).[16] Again, Bauerschmidt's language of "intellectual ascesis" is terribly helpful here. He teases this out in two directions by which he defines the goal of, as the late Herbert McCabe put it so aptly, "sanctity of mind."[17] The shape of that sanctity, for Thomas, "combined both intellectual openness and unswerving evangelical purpose."[18] Doctrinal particularity is for, not against, intellectual openness, though we may intuit that these two commitments are mutually exclusive or at odds. Thomas speaks of taking "every thought captive to Christ" (2 Cor. 10.5) and then launches into a discussion of grace and nature. Bauerschmidt helpfully shows that grace directs and perfects the function of nature.

Third, Thomas does attempt to honor the activity of will and mind in contemplation, albeit each in its own way. Whereas he and John Duns Scotus disagree over whether or not beatitude is fundamentally knowledge or love, in the mind or in the will, Reformed theologians have been and will surely be compelled to forego such a polarity. Francis Turretin preferred a better way long ago:

12. Frederick Christian Bauerschmidt, *Thomas Aquinas: Faith, Reason, and Following Christ* (New York: Oxford University Press, 2013), x.

13. Ibid., 81.

14. See Michael Allen, *Reformed Theology* (London: T&T Clark, 2010), 12–18.

15. Denys Turner, *Thomas Aquinas: A Portrait* (New Haven: Yale University Press, 2013), 4; cf. 34.

16. See Chapter 8 for further reflection on the pedagogically formative and indeed ascetical aspects of doctrine.

17. Herbert McCabe, *God Matters* (London: Geoffrey Chapman, 1987), 236.

18. Bauerschmidt, *Thomas Aquinas*, 36.

> Some with Thomas Aquinas hold that it is the intellect and maintain the blessedness consists in the vision of God. However, others with Scotus hold that it is the will, who on this account place happiness in the love of him. But both are at fault in this—they divide things that ought to be joined together hold that happiness is placed separately, either in vision or in love, since it consists conjointly in the vision and love of God. Thus neither sight without love, nor love without sight constitutes its form.[19]

Turretin initially seems to suggest that beatitude includes sight and love, mind and will. But he then expands to rephrase "more fully that most blissful state" with three facets: "we think the three things are to united here inseparably cohere with each other in happiness: sight, love, joy." He goes on to sketch out how sight relates to faith, joy answers to hope, and love abides; in other words, the three great theological virtues of 1 Corinthians 13 find their climax in this eternal bliss of human communion with God, making use of every moral and personal faculty that is distinctly human.

This side of not only the sixteenth-century reforms prompted by Luther and others but also especially on the neo-Calvinism of Abraham Kuyper and Herman Bavinck, with all its emphasis upon the breadth of Christ's lordship and the multifaceted nature of grace's restoration of nature, Reformed theologians will want to insist even more that beatitude involves not only every facet of the individual person but every nook and cranny of created existence: not only land, sky, and sea but family, society, and cosmos. To the resurrection of the body, we also add our hope for a new heavens and new earth. Thomas does not glance as widely at the circumference of grace's gift as later Reformed theology would demand. And yet, Thomas does remind us, with a resolve and specificity, that the neo-Calvinist tradition, at least, has hardly mustered, that the center of our hope remains that communion with God that has traditionally been marked out by the beatitude of seeing God's very essence. While our hope takes in the full reach of God's creative resolve, our bliss fixes upon the nearness of our covenant Lord as its anchor and chief mark. While Reformed Thomists will want to supplement and adjust his cosmology and anthropology to attend to wider societal and ecological facets of our eschatological hope, we will want to avoid any denial of or deprioritization of his theocentric focus: for our Christian hope and, by extension, for how we think unto that end as theologians on the journey.

---

19. Francis Turretin, *Institutes of Elenctic Theology*, Volume 3 (ed. James T. Dennison Jr.; trans. G. M. Giger; Phillipsburg: Presbyterian & Reformed, 1997), 609.

Chapter 10

REFORMED RETRIEVAL

Imagine two cities. In one city, the ailing find care within their homes, watched over by their family members; the dying are observed from their final breath until burial, never left alone for even a moment; their bodies will be preserved and buried in the ground, and their graves will be a witness and sign to all, located in church graveyards within the center city bounds. In a second city, the gravely sick are moved from their homes to hospitals for care by professionals; the dying are given over to the funeral service upon bodily expiration, and their bodies will be burned and their ashes scattered.

Historians have noted changing practices with regard to the care of the sick and dying and the treatment of dead bodies by Christians. By and large, the modern era in the Western world has ceased investing in center city graveyards and traditional Christian burials. Instead, bodies are buried in extreme suburbs or exurbs, well outside the daily commute, or, more likely than not, are cremated. For various reasons, the dead no longer function as a costly presence as they used to when they would not merely geographically be present to daily life but also take up valuable real estate. Moderns continue to remember the dead, of course, but that remembrance comes in personal, individual form and finds little structural support or encouragement.

Protestantism has functioned in parallel form to both cities, theologically speaking, with regard to its concern for the dead. Classical Protestantism has tended to the dead, viewed the testimony of this cloud of witnesses as a costly presence. An individualized or radical Protestantism, however, has reduced the presence of the dead to a cost-less memory, whatever occasions for individual remembrance may arise. The issue of cost is not insignificant: moderns remember the dead, of course, though they do not allocate real estate resources in the same way as classicals did for center city graveyards. Having a geographic allocation of capital focused on the location of the dead signals a priority and ongoing necessity of tending to the witness of the dead, exceeding the whim of nostalgia or of personal remembrance, which may come and go.

This chapter seeks to consider the logic of classical Protestantism, specifically of Reformed Protestantism in its classical confessional forms, regarding the role of retrieval in theology. It wagers that there is a distinctly Reformed basis for retrieval in theology. Before we seek to explain that logic, however, we must consider the nature of retrieval in contemporary theological conversation.

Anthropological and Theological Forms of Retrieval

Retrieval might be conceived as archaeological analysis and deemed prudent in light of realities regarding our embeddedness in social and cultural webs of relationships that predate our conscious or subconscious commitments. If the rise of late modernity or postmodernity has meant anything, it has involved the aggravated sense that all knowledge, experience, and action finds its meaning and shape in a context or a nexus of interrelated contexts. Global telecommunications and the ease of international travel made cognizance of diverse cultures more prominent in the Western world. Then the technological advance of the last thirty years has made the experience of men and women more available and accessible than ever before through the internet and social media. While humans may be no more diverse or no more dependent on deeply rooted patterns of social habit than before, we can be more aware now of ways in which various customs, mores, practices, and principles have shaped and do shape the lived reality of men and women around the globe today.

In such a schema, retrieval might be proposed and pursued as a diagnostic tool, a means of excavating underneath the current iterations of human culture or, in our case, theological confession. Retrieval might involve the historical assessment of thought patterns, textual practices, philosophical revolutions, ideological formations, and the like, which have clustered together to shape current engagement in the theological task.[1] In such a scheme, theological retrieval would serve as a parallel to investigation of how economic distribution in nineteenth-century England shaped family structures in the late Victorian period. Such an approach is not directive or prescriptive but descriptive and diagnostic. Retrieval in such a guise becomes simply an assessment of the contextualizations of theology and piety in various eras.

An archaeological approach to retrieval stands or falls with its anthropology. Nothing provides ballast or momentum for its efforts other than the sense that human society and its various forms of production (including the intellectual and theological) show a causal coherence that genuinely runs through its diverse and complex history. Feminist theologians have offered such readings by seeking to show how misogynistic patterns of human organization have bred and entrenched gender binaries that degrade women. The viability of such analysis depends, of course, upon the plausibility of causal demonstration, namely, that something more than mere chronology or parallelism can be shown regarding social precursors or current patterns and their theological confessions. Unless we want to fall into the temptation to simply shout *post hoc, ergo propter hoc*, then we must see deeper evidence of causal influence. Here various genealogies of modernity show not only their vitality but also their severe limits. Consider the

---

1. For an example of such anthropological analysis outside the theological realm, see Paul Connerton, *How Societies Remember* (Cambridge: Cambridge University Press, 1989).

many objections to narratives of decline whether portrayed by Radical Orthodoxy or others in similar projects.[2]

While historical assessment has so frequently been pursued with motivation from such archaeological and diagnostic concerns, I wish to propose a markedly different approach to the Christian past. In this chapter retrieval is considered from a theological vantage point, inquiring after theological affirmations that compel a program of retrieval and characterize the posture of retrieval. Because claims are made regarding material principles of the gospel of Jesus Christ, this proposal will no doubt share much and distinguish itself from those proposed by theologians working within the Eastern Orthodox and Roman Catholic traditions.[3]

A Brief Dogmatics for Retrieval

A theology of retrieval follows from a host of more basic theological beliefs about matters intrinsic to the gospel of Jesus Christ. In short, retrieval—or a program and posture with which one stands in regard to the past—must be related to

---

2. For influential examples of grand narratives, see, for example, Alasdair MacIntyre, *After Virtue: A Study in Moral Theory* (2nd ed.; Notre Dame, IN: University of Notre Dame Press, 1984); Amos Funkenstein, *Theology and the Scientific Imagination from the Middle Ages to the Seventeenth Century* (Princeton, NJ: Princeton University Press, 1985); Alasdair MacIntyre, *Whose Justice? Which Rationality?* (Notre Dame, IN: University of Notre Dame Press, 1988); Charles Taylor, *Sources of the Self: The Making of Modern Identity* (Cambridge, MA: Harvard University Press, 1989); John Milbank, *Theology and Social Theory: Beyond Secular Reason* (Oxford: Blackwell, 1990); J. B. Schneewind, *The Invention of Autonomy: A History of Modern Moral Philosophy* (Cambridge: Cambridge University Press, 1998); Charles Taylor, *A Secular Age* (Cambridge, MA: Belknap, 2007); Jean Bethke Elstain, *Sovereignty: God, State, and Self* (New York: Basic, 2008); Michael Allen Gillespie, *The Theological Origins of Modernity* (Chicago: University of Chicago Press, 2009); and Brad S. Gregory, *The Unintended Reformation: How a Religious Revolution Secularized Society* (Cambridge, MA: Belknap, 2012). For an example of objections to such narratives, see the essays in Lawrence Paul Hemming, (ed.), *Radical Orthodoxy—A Catholic Enquiry?* (Aldershot: Ashgate, 2000).

3. For survey of commonalities across ecumenical traditions with regard to recent retrieval or *ressourcement*, see John Webster, "Theologies of Retrieval," in *The Oxford Handbook of Systematic Theology* (ed. John Webster, Kathryn Tanner, and Iain Torrance; New York: Oxford University Press, 2007), 583-99. For an example of Webster's own judgments regarding how ecumenical differences do affect one's retrieval of the theological tradition, see his "Purity and Plenitude: Evangelical Reflections on Congar's Tradition and Traditions," *International Journal of Systematic Theology* 7 (2005), 399-413; and "Ressourcement Theology and Protestantism," in *Ressourcement: A Movement for Renewal in Twentieth Century Catholic Theology* (ed. Gabriel Flynn and Paul Murray; New York: Oxford University Press, 2012), 482-94.

basic metaphysical, soteriological, and ethical claims that compose the Christian confession.

Doctrine of God

The prompt for a theology of retrieval may be seen in the prologue to the Apocalypse: "Grace to you and peace from him who is and who was and who is to come" (Rev. 1.4). Grace and peace are granted unto his servant as the gift of God, and God is identified by this expansion of the tetragrammaton. "I am the Alpha and the Omega," says the Lord God, "who is and who was and who is to come, the Almighty" (Rev. 1.8). With this repetition of the three tenses prompted by the divine name ("I am"), the link between the burning bush and this searing apocalypse becomes more than apparent.

"Fear not, I am the first and the last, and the living one" (Rev. 1.17-18). Beginning and end. Alpha and Omega. First and the last. With these pairings, the steady possession of time comes to confession. God is the living one, Almighty with respect to limits of time. God does not grow or fulfill himself through time, nor does the Almighty suffer any change of diminution throughout time's lapse. God possesses life in and of his triune self—just so, he is the "living one." God holds eternity in his repose. God enjoys the fullness of life in his own self-sufficient movement internal to the Godhead as Father, Son, and Holy Spirit. The internal processions of the Trinity bespeak of origin and end, possessed eternally and perfectly, without any need or loss.

God's eternity does not undermine or denigrate time. Rather, time finds its reference point, amidst its own intrinsic dynamics and shiftiness, in God's constancy and faithfulness. And any attempt to connect the confession of the past with present or future attestation must first attend to the consistent identity and character of the God of this confession. The words of our speaking Savior should grip us: "Fear not." We need not fear the lapse of time for God has not evolved. We need not fear the passing of generations for death has no power over the living one. We need not fear the vanquishing of leading lights theologically for, in the land of God's limitless freedom, their witness continues.

Doctrine of Humanity

The infinite fullness of the divine life does not serve as a bound to the story of the gospel. Rather, God's perfection functions as a baseline and ballast unto the good news that this perfect life is made common or shared with others. In creation, the God who has all life and fullness in himself calls other life into being, summoning dependence, contingency, and finitude into his presence and calling them good. Having made them, God placed them in Eden. Not only does this action manifest God's superabundant goodness in granting paradise but it also witnesses to humanity's limits: they were in one place; they were in one time. They are bounded not by God's grandiose majesty but by their given nature as finite and ordered.

A remarkable dignity is conveyed upon the human creature in the scriptures of the prophets and apostles. Psalm 8 attests the grandeur and scope of creation (long before telescopes could plumb the massive character of deep space on a far greater scale) and attests "what is man that you are mindful of him?" God is mindful of this limited and ordered being, this creature who comes from the will of another and lives by the provision of that which is outside him, whether in the form of oxygen to breathe, of food and water to nourish, or of God's providence to sustain.[4]

Humanity continues to live on borrowed breath and in dependence upon those who go before them. Nothing so sharply substantiates this need as the abject and complete dependence of infants upon their parents: for protection, for provision, for cleanliness, for instruction, for love. Life returns at its end to such a state, more often than not, as the elderly again require care from their descendants. Again, basic needs of food, sanitation, medical care, and the like signal the interconnected and interdependent nature of human life. The fifth commandment calls for honoring one's father and mother. In ancient Israel, this involved not only heeding their authority but also providing for their livelihood in old age. It was a costly gift, not a cheap grace.

Generational interdependence goes hand in hand with the finite limits of any and every human being. And these realities have much to say about the nature and activity of knowing the one true God. Any individual man or woman faces severe limits in this regard owing to their weak and bounded mind, their unique perspective and experience, their own giftings and lack thereof. Any individual, man or woman, however, ought to be trained in the nurture and admonition of the Lord by those who go before them, whether from biological or spiritual family.

Doctrine of Sin

Knowing God occurs in a conflicted time and space, for those called to such knowledge have turned stubbornly and pridefully from their God to their own wisdom. In sin, humans have run from the light and made their home in the darkness. The effects of sin magnify the limits of created finitude and, by implication, cause a situation to fester where maturing in the knowledge of God occurs in a doubly constrained context. Not only individual limits but now also

---

4. Regarding the nature of this providence, I assume something along the lines of the Augustinian tradition herein as later developed in Thomistic and Reformed approaches. Thomas is instructive: "During the whole of a thing's existence, God must be present to it, and present in a way in keeping with the way in which the thing possesses its existence" (Thomas Aquinas, *Summa Theologiae*, 1a.8.1, reply). The Thomist-influenced Reformed theologian John Owen agrees: "The Holy Spirit so worketh in us as that he worketh by us, and what he doth in us is done by us." See his *Pneumatologia, or A Discourse Concerning the Holy Spirit* (Works of John Owen; Edinburgh: Banner of Truth Trust, 1965), 204.

human immorality besmirches our efforts to gaze at the light: to discern the truth, to ponder the good, and to behold the beautiful.[5]

Sin operates at multiple levels. The apostle Paul attests to multiple facets of sinful causality:

> And you were dead in the trespasses and sins in which you once walked, following the course of this world, following the prince of the power of the air, the spirit that is now at work in the sons of disobedience—among whom we all once lived in the passions of our flesh, carrying out the desires of the body and the mind, and were by nature children of wrath, like the rest of mankind.
>
> (Eph. 2.1-3)

This thick description of sin's influence takes in the distortion of human nature ("by nature children of wrath"), the diabolical efforts of spiritual forces ("the prince of the power of the air, the spirit that is now at work"), the disorder of human desire and passion ("in the passions of our flesh, carrying out the desires of the body and the mind"), and the social malformations of society ("following the course of this world").

Given the malformations of social groupings, any closed set finds itself more limited and endangered than an open set. While there may be generational progress in certain areas, it is invariably offset by other moral and social losses. For example, recent decades in the United States have managed to include both an increasing awareness and appreciation of equality across racial lines (since the civil rights movement of the 1960s) and a decreasing concern for spiritual matters, that is, of transcendent significance (and even polling data that shows the continuing religiosity in the United States also exemplifies the naturalizing of those religions, as in what sociologist Christian Smith has termed "moral therapeutic deism").[6] While a narrow frame of reference may not harm racial reconciliation, it is only through expanding that frame of reference to a wider conversation with others of an earlier era and through a more transcendent hope that the secularizing of religion might be offset. Blind spots can be systemic precisely because of our social interrelationships.

Doctrine of Grace

The reparative work of the gospel brings grace and peace into a wasteland of history. Sin has cut off men and women from their origin, as they have been sent

---

5. More than ignorance or misdirection affects the individual in this regard, contrary to the claims of Eduardo Echeverria, *Berkouwer and Catholicism: Disputed Questions* (Studies in Reformed Theology; Leiden: Brill, 2013), 212-19. While Echeverria rightly notes the limits of knowledge acknowledged by Thomas, he does not demonstrate that these limits parallel those sketched by Berkouwer's confessional tradition.

6. Christian Smith with Melina Lundquist Denton, *Soul Searching: The Religious and Spiritual Lives of American Teenagers* (New York: Oxford University Press, 2009).

out from the paradisal presence of God. Sin has also severed their grasp upon their end, for which they have been rendered incompetent. To that distance and disorder, the gospel offers a promise of reprieve. The old is made new again in Jesus Christ.

First, grace brings the restoration of humanity's relation to its past in the person and life of Jesus of Nazareth. In this one, through the sanctifying work of the Holy Spirit, a posture of resolute and personal agreement with the faithful of the past and the testimony of God's self-revelation finds its ultimate expression. As "author and perfector of faith" (Heb. 12.2), Jesus exemplifies human excellence in embracing his Father's care through the vicissitudes of history, even embodying his calling as "man of sorrows," by remembering the testimony of faithful confession from centuries past. By faith, he proclaims deliverance with the prophetic call of Isaiah 61. By faith, he laments with the words of Psalm 22. And he not only reverences the scriptural heritage of Israel's law and prophets but also embraces the formation found in the liturgical patterns of God's people. He savors time in the Lord's house in holy season (Lk. 2.49). He sets his eye so regularly and determinatively upon Jerusalem (Lk. 9.51).

Second, grace brings the renewal of humanity's relation to its past in Christ's body, the communion of those made holy in him. While sin takes the form of many things, either an attempted manipulation of others by way of the path of social and even religious conformity or by means of auto-creativity and self-stylization, grace brings peace again between the self and human nature and Christian society. In Christ, humanity finds reconciliation with God as well as restoration of its disordered nature. John Calvin referred to this as the "twofold grace" (*duplex gratia*) of the gospel, meaning to keep us alert to its relational and moral facets without allowing them to be reduced one to the other.

In terms of restoring the knowledge of God, that is, of the theological task, we can speak with the traditional language of the principles of theology and in so doing mark the ways that our minds are restored to their intended function. The triune God is the ontological principle of theology. The Holy Scriptures are the external cognitive principle of theology. The regenerated heart and illumined mind are the internal cognitive principle of theology. We do well to consider each principle in turn.

First, the triune God is the ontological principle of theology. That is, God is not only the content but also the context for the practice of theology. Theology focuses upon knowing God and, in so doing, it is beholden to God: to divine self-disclosure, to divine gift, to divine presence. God is not approached as a postulate or as a hypothesis. Theology is a realist enterprise premised on tracing the presence of God in the divine economy. Thus, theology is an a posteriori discipline and eschews any a priori temptations.

Second, the Holy Scriptures are the external cognitive principle of theology. God's gracious self-disclosure has taken place in Christ, in covenant with Israel and now the whole church of Jews and Gentiles, and in various episodes of the divine economy. However, the revelatory provisions of the divine economy repeatedly culminate, epoch after epoch, with a prophetic or apostolic word delivered not only to God's people but also in written form. Thus, the self-disclosing presence of God, which alone gives light and wisdom, has been made available from generation unto generation with the promise of God's presence therein. The Scriptures are not merely a repository of ancient religious reflection (though they do contain evidence of ancient faith and practice). They are a living Word, active with the communicative and spiritual power of the triune God (Heb. 4.12-13).

Third, the regenerated heart and illumined mind are the internal cognitive principle of theology. A Word from God results in many things. In the parable of the soils, Jesus points to four possible results, only one of which proves life giving and beneficial in the long run (Mk. 4.3-9 and 13-20). One fundamental observation from this episode relates to the need for not only an external self-revelation from God, that is, a real or objective communication outside of us, but also for an internal renewal from God, that is, a real or subjective reception of that communication within us. Unless the word be received in faith, it does not bless the hearer.

The traditional exposition of divine revelation by means of the principles of theology has been meant to highlight grace as not only the cherished content of theology but also the essential context for its practice. By bringing together the doctrines of God, of Holy Scripture, and of sanctification, these principles seek to locate growth in theological knowledge within the gospel.

Doctrine of Church

In our recent manifesto regarding the promise of retrieval for renewing theology today, Scott Swain and I suggest a fourth theological principle to pair with the ontological and cognitive principles mentioned above. We argue that tradition is the elicitive principle (*principium elicitivum*), that is, the temporally extended, socially mediated activity of renewed reason.[7] Our concern remains the same as that behind the other three principles, namely, to locate theological knowledge within the gospel and to attend to the particular ways in which the news of God's life-giving work in Christ takes hold of human reality this side of the Fall. We believe that another facet must be considered—the ecclesial—if we are to appreciate the nature and necessity of the gospel for knowing God. Before we can consider this fourth principle, we must attend to matters ecclesiastical in their own terms.

"Jesus Christ is Lord of the Church." These are the first words of Reformed polity, as illustrated in the various books of church order in the Presbyterian tradition. The claim is not genealogical: Jesus as creator of the church. The claim is also not metaphysical: Jesus as God over the church. The claim includes but subsumes such matters under its functional, present-tense focus: Jesus as the chief shepherd, the king, the warrior, the teacher, the great high priest of the church.

---

7. Michael Allen and Scott R. Swain, *Reformed Catholicity: The Promise of Retrieval for Theology and Biblical Interpretation* (Grand Rapids, MI: Baker Academic, 2015), 36.

The heavenly session of the risen Lord finds extensive exposition in the Reformed tradition, inasmuch as Christ is viewed as being as personally involved in applying his salvation to his people as he was in accomplishing that salvation in his own person.

The ongoing agency of the risen Christ means that grace continues to be given to the church generation after generation.[8] This grace no longer takes the form of discrete new revelation. The canon for the covenant of grace has now been closed. But this grace takes the form of lordly address through those Holy Scriptures to ever-new situations of need. And with that grace comes not only illumination and insight but also wisdom and confession. The church has been brought to hear and to attest the gospel, and even to order its thinking around that gospel, by the lordly exercise of Christ's kingly office.

The church does not experience this refreshing without remainder, however, for indwelling sin persists in her members and her society. The distinction between the invisible and the visible church has been intended through the reformed confessions to make plain the eschatological tension experienced as the church has already heard the gospel afresh by Christ's life-giving grace, though she has not yet fully heard the gospel with clarity and comprehension. That gap between promise and reality marks the church not only in that some of her members are nominal Christians (and will prove to be like unto the second and third soils in Jesus' parable) but also in that all members are shy of glory at this point. The imagery of the pilgrimage has been definitive for the Reformed tradition at this point, locating the church on the way to glory and no longer mired in sin. But her present location in grace continues to experience the tug and pull of both that past in sin and that promised hope in glory.

A Reformed Ethic of Retrieval

This irregular dogmatics (to use Karl Barth's term) has sought to locate retrieval within the orbit of the Christian confession, asking what significance the Christian past might have within the lived drama of the present. Without decrying archaeological or anthropological accounts of attending to the past, we have sought to inquire after what gospel hope might be offered specifically to Christian retrieval of the heritage of the saints. Diagnostic analysis of the agonies and exigencies of human social formation may or may not prove fruitful, case by case, based on little more than the availability of causal evidence in each circumstance. But we have

---

8. Mark Bowald has helpfully traced the "Deistic" turn in modern biblical criticism owing to a metaphysics noninclusive of divine missions in his *Rendering the Word in Theological Hermeneutics: Mapping Divine and Human Agency* (Aldershot: Ashgate, 2007), 173; see Herman Bavinck, *Reformed Dogmatics*, Volume 1, (*Prolegomena*; ed. John Bolt; Grand Rapids, MI: Baker Academic, 2003), 384–5. A similar argument could be made regarding the deistic analysis of much modern ecclesiology (especially that influenced by so-called postliberalism).

sought to ask whether fundamental claims about the oneness and constancy of the triune God, the character of humanity created after his image, and the nature of the economy of grace in response to human sin do not leave us with good news for historical retrieval regarding the confession of the gospel.

Specifically, we have sought to explain how Reformed theological method is itself shaped by the material content of the gospel. Knowing God flows completely from God's own action on our behalf, or it occurs not at all. Whereas the classic threefold distinction of the principles of theology was meant to attest this reality that grace is not only the content but also the context of theology, we have tried to affirm and amplify that confession by noting its ecclesiastical implications. Thus, we return to our fourth principle, namely, that tradition is the elicitive principle of theology (*principium elicitivum*). In so doing, we must comment on tradition itself (as an eliciting principle) and upon the posture of retrieval (as a corresponding ethical principle).

First, tradition represents the temporally extended, socially mediated activity of renewed reason within the communion of the saints. Tradition may take the form of many social activities, whether they be creeds or confessions, treatises or catechisms, rubrics for worship or sacramental practice, disciplines for daily piety and spiritual exercise, authority structures, musical accompaniments to personal or corporate worship, architectural or artistic structures that mark the space of Christian practice, and so forth.

And yet tradition is the result not only of the accumulation of human social formation in its intellectual, liturgical, educational, and other forms. Tradition is, first and foremost, the result of the risen Christ's continued lordship over and through his church. The fundamental basis for tradition is Christological: "Jesus Christ is the same yesterday, today, and forever" (Heb. 13.8). But the Christological claim is regarding not only identity but also office: he is now also "the great shepherd of the sheep" (Heb. 13.20). That the risen one continues to exist and to minister faithfully undergirds a "great cloud of witnesses" (Heb. 12.1) as well as the value of imitating the faith of his undershepherds whose life outcomes we have discerned (Heb. 13.7; notice that the famous Christological teaching of 13.8 follows as an explanatory basis for this practice of imitating church leaders, evidencing a link between Christ and his body).[9]

---

9. The most fundamental matter shaping the ecclesiology of Hebrews is Christological: "Jesus Christ is the same yesterday, today, and forever" (Heb. 13.8); see Ceslas Spicq, *L'Epitre aux Hébreux II—Commentaire* (Paris: Gabalda, 1953), 2; George Hunsinger, "The Same Only Different: Karl Barth's Interpretation of Hebrews 13:8," in *Thy Word Is Truth: Barth on Scripture* (ed. George Hunsinger; Grand Rapids, MI: Eerdmans, 2012), 112–24. And this Jesus who is unchanging is a speaker: see Tomasz Lewicki, "*Weist nicht ab den Sprechenden!*": *Wort Gottes und Paraklese im Hebräerbrief* (Paderborner Theologische Studien; Paderborn: Schöningh, 2004), chap. 3; as well as B. F. Westcott, *The Epistle to the Hebrews: The Greek Text with Notes and Essays* (3rd ed.; London: Macmillan, 1903), 4. Surely the insistence that "he upholds all things by his powerful word" (Heb. 1.3) applies to the church as well.

Tradition cannot be defined reductively, then, as the artifacts and accumulations of religious history alone, as if it were simply the relics of spiritual hoarding through the centuries. Tradition must be defined spiritually—as a reality in the divine economy, traced to the life-giving work of the triune God—and perceived by the eyes of faith. In this regard, it is crucial to remember that the ontological principle of theology serves an axiomatic role with respect to the cognitive or elicitive principles. All the other principles are instruments and signs of that triune God's gracious provision for his people's intellectual and theological nurture.

We might elaborate on this priority of the ontological principle over all other epistemological principles by means of Trinitarian theology. Not only Thomas Aquinas but also the Reformed doctrinal tradition has made use of the doctrine of the divine missions of the Son and Spirit here to affirm the link between the God, himself full of grace and truth, who has shed abroad in our hearts the knowledge of his glory and light. "In his light do we see light" (Ps. 36.7-9).[10] Theology has hope, precisely because we have an evangel and, more fundamentally, because the God we have been given to know is the God of the Gospel. Though he has all wisdom in and of himself, he has seen fit to share with us that wisdom in creation and again, decisively, in Jesus Christ and with the communion of saints united to him. Tradition has hope, then, for evangelical and Trinitarian reasons.

Second, Christian moral theology seeks to consider the implications of doctrinal claims and to root proverbial, legal, or casuistic reasoning in the theological order of the Gospel. In speaking of a posture of retrieval, we are attesting the necessary ethic of receiving gratefully and humbly from those who have gone before us in the Christian pilgrimage. While this ethic may be identified with obedience to the fifth commandment (honoring one's spiritual parents), it is crucial to note that its logic does not exhaust itself in that legal command. Rather, it fits the warp and woof of Christian anthropology, wherein human experience and human knowledge are located within the divine economy of the gospel.

A Reformed ethic of retrieval will refuse to locate those who have gone before us as existing in any other strata than that which we now share. In other words, the past is not pristine and bears no more promise for perfection than do we at present. Thus, the task of critical appropriation becomes absolutely necessary, as is made so apparent by the distinction between the visible and the invisible church. We are not called to look elsewhere than the real church or to look only to its spiritual moments. We are, however, summoned to look to the church with the eyes of faith. Calvin reminded us that we confess that we "*believe* one, holy, catholic, and apostolic church" rather than that we "believe *in*" such a church.[11] In so doing, he reminds us that the church is an instrument of God, not to be confused with God himself. Tradition is not inerrant or indefectible, then, and we do well to view tradition as a reality brought by grace but not yet glorified.

---

10. On the gospel hope for ongoing theology, see Chapter 1 in this volume.
11. John Calvin, *Institutes of the Christian Religion* (Library of Christian Classics; ed. John T. McNeill; Louisville: Westminster John Knox, 2004), 1013 (IV.i.2).

In recent Roman Catholic accounts of tradition, notably those provided by Lewis Ayres and Matthew Levering, tradition finds description in Christological and pneumatological forms. Ayres suggests that we must grasp the economy of God's speech as one "in which the mystery of God is spoken among us, through the interaction of Word and Spirit, word and answering word."[12] And Levering adds that "the way to understand the active place of the Church in divine revelation is to reflect upon the missions of the Son and Spirit."[13] This is very promising. Yet tradition—whether in the form of the history of biblical exegesis (in Ayres) or of liturgy (in Levering)—is described in ideal terms. So Ayres: "we may conceive of these later 'ecclesial' readings of the New Testament as truer, deeper readings of the literal sense."[14] And Levering: "The liturgy is the true home for the reading of Scripture … it is in and through the liturgy that revelation is truly proclaimed, interpreted, and enacted for the life of the world."[15]

Reformed retrieval will demur from assuming the ideal or expounding the church only in terms of divine grace. Reformed ecclesiology, and its consideration of tradition as one key element in this broader topic, will also consider the church's tradition in an eschatological hue, graced out of darkness but not yet glorified into undimming light.[16] With Ayres, Reformed retrieval will focus upon church tradition in its various forms as lineaments of the history of the Word and,

---

12. Lewis Ayres, "The Word Answering the Word: Opening the Space of Catholic Biblical Interpretation," in *Theological Theology: Essays in Honour of John Webster* (ed. R. David Nelson, Darren Sarisky, and Justin Stratis; London: T&T Clark, 2015), 49. For further reflections on Scripture and tradition and a posture of critically receptive theology as a way forward for modern Roman Catholic theology, see also Lewis Ayres, *Nicaea and Its Legacy: An Approach to Fourth Century Trinitarian Theology* (New York: Oxford University Press, 2004), 384–429.

13. Matthew Levering, *Engaging the Doctrine of Revelation: The Mediation of the Gospel through Church and Scripture* (Grand Rapids, MI: Baker Academic, 2014), 56. For further reflection upon the missions of Son and Spirit and a graced participation of human mediating figures within those missions, see also Matthew Levering, *Christ and the Catholic Priesthood: Ecclesial Hierarchy and the Pattern of the Trinity* (Chicago: Hillenbrand, 2010); idem, *Participatory Biblical Exegesis: A Theology of Biblical Interpretation* (Notre Dame, IN: University of Notre Dame Press, 2008), esp. 90–140.

14. Ayres, "Word Answering the Word," 46; italics added.

15. Levering, *Engaging the Doctrine of Revelation*, 80.

16. Levering does suggest ways in which the doctrine of the indefectibility of the church might be maintained along with an awareness of errors on nonessential matters (*Engaging the Doctrine of Revelation*, 27). For further Reformed analysis of the indefectibility of the church, see Michael Allen, "'The Church's One Foundation': The Justification of the Ungodly Church," in *Justification and the Gospel: Understanding the Contexts and the Controversies* (Grand Rapids, MI: Baker Academic, 2013), 153–78. Affirming the sinful yet holy character of the church does not thereby implicate one in claims akin to those of Ephraim Radner, who

thus, of exegetical reasoning. It will do so because such an interrogation of the tradition offers more promising grounds for hearing the Word more faithfully. Other potential interrogations—regarding the political, social, missiological, or philosophical constructions of the church—may offer benefits but do not necessarily put us in conversation with the ultimate source of authority and the promised bearer of life, the prophetic witness of the Holy Scriptures. Even in its retrieval of the tradition, Reformed Christians will remember the axiomatic words of the first thesis of Berne (1528): "The holy, Christian Church, whose only Head is Christ, is born of the Word of God, abides in the same, and does not listen to the voice of a stranger."[17]

And yet retrieval will not take the form of cynicism or of modern progress's sneer toward the past, for the agonistics of indwelling sin continue to plague us as well. We are no more glorified than the saints of days past or the councils of centuries old. Retrieval attests our remembrance of this common location and this shared vocation to know God more fully while on this journey unto the promised glory of Canaan's shore.

---

argues for the pneumatic deprivation of the Western church (so, e.g., *A Brutal Unity: The Spiritual Politics of the Christian Church* [Waco, TX: Baylor University Press, 2012]). While Radner's argument may find fit with certain prophetic texts read figurally, it cannot attend to the breadth of the apostolic witness regarding the nature of the Christian community. Whereas Levering attends too exclusively to texts attending to divine mission in defining the church and her tradition, Radner responds by focusing single-mindedly upon texts of divine abandonment. God has come to the church, but that God continues to come to the church; she is in a state of grace, but not yet in the realm of glory.

17. "The Ten Theses of Berne [1528]," in *Reformed Confessions of the Sixteenth Century* (ed. Arthur C. Cochrane; Louisville: Westminster John Knox, 2003), 49.

Chapter 11

RETRIEVAL AND THE PROPHETIC IMAGINATION

The call to repentance is the essential mark of the prophetic message and it must be dominant in the Church's teaching to-day.
(E. L. Mascall, "The New Jerusalem," 83 in Death or Dogma?)

Tradition ... cannot be inherited, and if you want it, you must obtain it by great labour.
(T. S. Eliot, "Tradition and the Individual Talent," 38)

While retrieval has been celebrated in many corners of contemporary theology, suspicion lingers regarding whether retrieval will unduly baptize the status quo theologically, ethically, ecclesiastically, and even politically. Might a theology invested in retrieval undercut the task of ongoing reform by God's own Word?[1] Given the significance of a prophetic vocation for theology in the contemporary context (and in previous times, such as the Protestant Reformation), such would be a massive weakness in the functioning of *ressourcement*. In many ways this suspicion gains its seeming strength from the fact that retrieval is often commended in wholly sociological terms. Can a case be made, however, that upholds the practice of retrieval and the pursuit of ongoing biblical reform? In this chapter I seek to address that question by, first, offering a specifically theological argument for the necessity of retrieval and, second, describing ways in which retrieval helps foster a prophetic mindset, that the theology of the people of God might always be reformed by the Word of God.

I will first describe the prominence of the prophetic not merely in recent theological convention but also in earlier Reformational episodes, not least in the self-conception of John Calvin. Second, I will look to perhaps the most influential account of prophetic theologizing in recent decades, *The Prophetic Imagination* by Walter Brueggemann, to analyze the way in which theological reflection has taken the work of reform within its own calling. If that prophetic task is ingredient in

---

1. See, e.g., the critique of encyclopedic modes of theology in Rowan Williams, "The Unity of Christian Truth," in *On Christian Theology* (Challenges in Contemporary Theology; Oxford: Blackwell, 2000), 19.

recent and Reformed theological reflection, then we do well to ask if retrieval can help or will hinder. Third, I provide a typology for three types of retrieval theology or what might be called three self-understandings of the task of *ressourcement*, noting that two of them either hinder or leave unaided the task of prophetic reform. Fourth, I sketch briefly a doctrinal account of retrieval that not only gives it promise but passing on but also for refining the church's witness, in so doing highlighting dogmatic resources to construe retrieval in a way that does not privilege the status quo and fend off the prophetic Word of God but actually gives much hope to the recipients of God's promise to shine still further light upon them in his Holy Word. By the chapter's end, I hope to not only have warded off suspicions that retrieval theology undercuts reform and to have gestured toward a confidence that it might help augment future prophetic critique having its intended effect but also to have given reason for a hope—hope of a better future and a better Christian witness and confession—that other accounts of the prophetic imagination might not be capable of sustaining on their own.

I

The *status confessionis* has sometimes seemed to become the constant state of theological existence. That language came to prominence in the setting of Nazi Germany when confessing church members believed themselves to be impelled to speak not merely for Jesus but also against National Socialism. Since then, the term has been applied to the apartheid situation in South Africa, to the Vietnam War, and to the civil rights movement. While some theological traditions show reserve in voicing authoritative judgments about sociocultural particularities (WCF 20.2 and 31.4), the need for occasional and pointed discernments has been increasingly recognized.

At the same time there has been an emphasis upon the need to maintain a prophetic posture in Christin theology. Abraham Joshua Heschel bore witness to the role of prophetic rhetoric which threw into relief the death-dealing shape of the status quo and helped reframe culture, politics, and spirituality into a form that gave life.[2] Protestant theologians such as Jürgen Moltmann, Cornel West, Douglas John Hall, and Kathryn Tanner similarly turned to the prophet as a barometer for their own theological vocation.[3] Language of the revolution and the counterculture

---

2. Abraham Joshua Heschel, *The Prophets* (New York: Harper & Row, 1962); idem, *Prophetic Inspiration after the Prophets* (Jersey City, NJ: Ktav, 1996).

3. See, e.g., Jürgen Moltmann, *Theology of Hope* (trans. James Leitch; London: SCM Press, 1967); Cornel West, *Prophesy Deliverance! An Afro-American Revolutionary Christianity* (2nd ed.; Louisville: Westminster John Knox, 2002); Douglas John Hall, *Lighten Our Darkness: Toward an Indigenous Theology of the Cross* (Philadelphia: Westminster, 1976); and Kathryn Tanner, *The Politics of God: Christian Theologies and Social Justice* (Minneapolis: Fortress, 1992).

has only grown since becoming a major feature in the 1970s. More recently, events such as Watergate and the clergy sex crisis have heightened the suspicion of power and institutions, alerting us all to the need for whistleblowers to inform us and of the need for prophets to speak truth to power.

The prophetic vocation bears a much deeper pedigree, however, than these theologians of crisis and that hermeneutic of suspicion. For centuries, Christian theologians have looked to the prophetic office as one crucial barometer for doctrinal fidelity. The Genevan reformer John Calvin prioritized the prophetic calling in his own sense of "self-identity." Over against the radical reformers and their preference for New Testament prophets, whose praxis tilted spontaneous and disruptive in the name of charisma, Calvin fell into a line of theologians and reformers who looked to the prophets of Israel for inspiration.[4] And Calvin did not simply fall into line in this regard as a matter of course; he ardently and carefully defined and argued for the appropriate conception of the prophet.

Jon Balserak's recent study on *John Calvin as Sixteenth-Century Prophet* ranges not only through his sermons and letters to argue this approach to Calvin's own sense of vocation but also its public consequences. Calvin, says Balserak, believed that the ordinary ministry had so failed the French people that prophets did well to stir up action—even military or coercive action—so as to bring about reform in France. The purportedly "subversive" or "aggressive" anti-monarchialism lies beyond our purposes here, though Balserak's account shows how enmeshed prophetic rhetoric marked the call for ecclesiastical and even political reform in the sixteenth century.[5] Calvin did not call or identify himself as a prophet explicitly, but he would infer such by using prophetic images, narratives, and texts to frame the challenge of his own day and the action of his own ministry.

Calvin's penchant for the exegetical prophet was not idiosyncratic either. He believed it was a common calling, and others took up the mantle as well.[6] Balserak's study not only surveys widely in the Genevan's corpus, but shows how his self-identity sits alongside other members of the broader Christian body of reformers. Calvin believed himself to be a "covenant prosecutor" who hearkened the church back to its own laws given to her by God, over against, on the one hand, those who refused to speak truth to the powerful status quo and, on the other hand, those who claimed to wield a new revelation of God as the club of their reform project.[7] His was an exegetical activism, then, with charged covenantal fervor. Precisely because Calvin believed God had granted an inscripturated and authoritative Word, he had

---

4. Jon Balserak, *John Calvin as Sixteenth-Century Prophet* (Oxford: Oxford University Press, 2014), 8 and *passim*.

5. Balserak, *John Calvin as Sixteenth-Century Prophet*, 157 (see also 89 and 177 on the prophet's place and authority relative to that of the monarch and the state).

6. On Calvin's pedagogical aims and protocols in extending this prophetic work, see Balserak, *John Calvin as Sixteenth-Century Prophet*, 144–5.

7. On the concept of a "covenant prosecutor," see Balserak, *John Calvin as Sixteenth-Century Prophet*, 57, 74–7.

confidence that prophetic remembrance and reapplication of that Word in new settings might take effect in cutting off malignancies from the ecclesiastical body.

In the early Reformed tradition, this prophetic calling not only marks exceptional figures like Calvin but manifests itself more broadly in confessional expectations for normal Christian life, lay as well as minister. The moderate posture of the Heidelberg Catechism emphasized the significance of sharing in Christ's own calling in this regard:

> Q. 32 "But why are you called a Christian? A. Because by faith I am a member of Christ and so I share in his anointing. I am anointed to confess his name, to present myself to him as a living sacrifice of thanks, to strive with a free conscience against sin and the devil in this life, and afterward to reign with Christ over all creation for eternity."

That twofold claim—that one is a "member of Christ" and thus "share[s] in his anointing"—refers backward to the previous question (Q. 31) where it defines the anointing of Christ himself in this regard: "has been anointed with the Holy Spirit to be our chief prophet and teacher." Heidelberg professes that Christ's anointing involves his being set apart to speak and teach as prophet, a calling into which we are now given a share as members of his own body. The Augustinian doctrine of the *totus Christus* here takes a vocational shape, namely, that the Christian (and, by specification, especially the Christian theologian) has a prophetic anointing by means of being united to the prophet named Jesus Christ. Both Calvin's own pastoral vocation and Heidelberg's analysis of Christian identity (both lay and clerical) highlight the significance of prophetic existence today. Later Puritans continued to view Christian and confessional vocations in this sort of prophetic calling as well, even later in the seventeenth century when their proximity to political power waned; even in their most apocalyptic calls for divine intervention, John Owen and Puritan preaches continued to function as "prophetic preachers" calling a nation and her churches back to Scriptural purity.[8]

The term "prophetic" may mean many different things, and it can be used in varied religious settings as well as in all sorts of social and political contexts that do or do not involve religion overtly. While it has become something of a watchword for responsible intellectual life in recent decades, Christians have had a deeper commitment to a prophetic vocation, not only for particular office-bearers or gifts of divine intervention but also for laypersons who share in the threefold offices (*triplex mundi*) of Jesus Christ. Before we ask whether and how retrieval might help in that vocation, we do well to assess the way in which prophetic theology has been developed in recent decades, cognizant that elements of the prophetic vocation may have been recontextualized for good or ill.

---

8. Martyn Calvin Cowan, *John Owen and the Civil War Apocalypse: Preaching, Prophecy and Politics* (Religious Cultures in the Early Modern World; London: Routledge, 2017), esp. 8–36 which refutes the typical bifurcation of apocalyptic and prophetic preaching in the history of homiletics.

II

Walter Brueggemann's *The Prophetic Imagination* serves as something of a bellwether for recent reflection on theology's prophetic task (and has filled that role since its publication initially in 1978).[9] Brueggemann has addressed the prophets in a range of other books, but this small volume offers a manifesto for the task of prophetic speech today.[10] Prophets address not merely happenstance crises but an enduring challenge, namely, the co-opting of faith due to cultural pressures. "The task of prophetic ministry is to nurture, nourish, and evoke a consciousness and perception alternative to the consciousness and perception of the dominant culture around us."[11] The book begins by assessing that dominant culture, which Brueggemann terms the "royal consciousness." Over against that dominant frame, the prophet will seek to speak to criticize and to energize. To grasp prophetic action, then, one has to catch the character of life in the dominant ethos (and in spaces influenced or pressured by it) before one can think about sustaining minority communities of protest or subversion.[12]

The "royal consciousness" is terminology employed by Brueggemann to describe the dominant mindset. This ethos shapes expectations and assumptions about what reality must be like. What are ideals? What are virtues? What are problems? What resources exist? These questions all bring into relief that sort of governing philosophy that permeates the intellectual and cultural marketplace. The prophet does not batter or assault that consciousness, at least not directly, but works by way of irony and counter-persuasion. Moses is paradigmatic here; "He was not engaged in a struggle to transform a regime; rather, his concern was with

---

9. Walter Brueggemann, *The Prophetic Imagination* (2nd ed.; Minneapolis: Fortress, 2001).

10. His reflections on prophecy and prophetic ministry are voluminous, though the following texts are most pertinent (beyond his biblical commentaries on Isaiah and Jeremiah): Walter Brueggemann, *Hopeful Imagination: Prophetic Voices in Exile* (Philadelphia: Fortress, 1986); idem, *Theology of the Old Testament: Testimony, Dispute, Advocacy* (Minneapolis: Fortress, 1997); idem, *Texts That Linger, Words That Explode: Listening to Prophetic Voices* (ed. Patrick J. Miller Jr.; Minneapolis: Fortress, 2000); idem, *Deep Memory, Exuberant Hope: Contested Truth in a Post-Christian World* (ed. Patrick J. Miller Jr.; Minneapolis: Fortress, 2000); idem, *Like Fire in the Bones: Listening for the Prophetic Word in Jeremiah* (Minneapolis: Fortress, 2006); idem, *The Practice of Prophetic Imagination: Preaching an Emancipating Word* (Minneapolis: Fortress, 2012); idem, *Truth Speaks to Power: The Countercultural Nature of Scripture* (Louisville: Westminster John Knox, 2013); idem, *Reality, Grief, Hope: Three Urgent Prophetic Tasks* (Grand Rapids: Eerdmans, 2014); idem, *Interrupting Silence: God's Command to Speak Out* (Louisville: Westminster John Knox, 2018).

11. Brueggemann, *Prophetic Imagination*, 3.

12. In this regard Brueggemann is influenced by Robert Wilson, *Prophecy and Society in Ancient Israel* (Philadelphia: Fortress, 1980), 69–83 (cited on xvi n. 17).

the consciousness that undergirded and made such a regime possible."[13] The book shows that this kind of royal consciousness can seep into the religious community; indeed, the better part of a chapter traces the Solomonic downward spiral toward Israelite syncretism by way of unchecked "affluence," "oppressive state policy," and "static religion."[14] Interestingly—though unstated by Brueggemann here—these are the three great temptations of which Israel is warned in Deuteronomy 7–11 (see 7.17 on military might, 8.17 on affluence, 9.4 on presumptive religion); they may well also be descriptions of the three temptations of Christ (Mt. 4.1-11 with 4.3-4 on affluence, 4.5-7 on military might, and 4.8-10 on presumptive religion).

Criticizing does not involve carping, Brueggemann says, or simple denunciation.[15] Rather it moves by way of immanent critique, seeking to bring into relief that doomed insufficiencies of the regnant culture. It cannot possibly deliver on its promises—it has not proven itself worthy of one's trust and allegiance. The prophet beats the dominant system at its own game, much as the Lord battled and bested the gods of Egypt through the plague cycle. Much of this critical endeavor takes the form of "bringing hurt to public expression," so it is no wonder that lamentation plays such a role canonically (not least in its signal place within the Psalter).[16] Giving voice to pain plays such an enlivening role because "numbness" manifests as a symptom of the royal consciousness.[17] Numbness takes the form of failing to register hurt but also of ceasing to catch its happenstance or accidental character, indeed failing to note the passing of time at all. The royal consciousness or status quo leads to a sort of fatalism along the lines of "this is just the way it is," as participants are numbed into a loss of timeliness like casino-goers or mall shoppers in a space with no visible clocks.[18]

Energizing marks the second mood of the prophetic rhetoric. In energizing speech, the prophet helps cast a vision, sometimes literally, for new or alternative reality. Again the royal consciousness numbs, in this case numbing one to the real possibility, even promise, of transformation and change; here diminished expectations are paired with a sort of realized eschatology ("this is just the way it is" becomes "this is the just way it will be").[19] To activate such hopes afresh, the prophet must draw on ground motifs of the people's history (preferably covenant language), employ powerful metaphors paired with concrete language about its terminus, and must turn especially to remember the language of divine enthronement where power and hope are manifest.

An example helps give definition to these emphases sketched by Brueggemann. He argues that Jeremiah is the consummate prophet, so the call of Jeremiah not

---

13. Brueggemann, *Prophetic Imagination*, 21.
14. Ibid., 26–30.
15. Ibid., 11.
16. Ibid., 12.
17. Ibid., 41.
18. Ibid., 48.
19. Ibid., 60, 63.

surprisingly informs our grasp of prophetic action.[20] In Jeremiah 1, God calls the prophet, and the emphasis there falls upon the divine action in summoning this one to speech. "Behold, I have put my words in your mouth. See, I have set you this day over nations and over kingdoms, to pluck up and to break down, to destroy and to overthrow, to build and to plant" (Jer. 1.9-10). The words are God's, as is the initiative. But the action will be taken by Jeremiah, and the effect will be twofold in the creaturely sphere: first deconstruction or mortification (plucking up, breaking down, destroying, and overthrowing), and second reconstruction or vivification (building and planting). Jeremiah is sent with God's own words precisely for the purpose of tearing down that royal consciousness, the regnant status quo, and to rebuild a covenantally shaped hope based on God's promise of a new future.

The call, then, is twofold: to lament and then to doxology. The language of lament and the singing of the blues provides a space for feeling the pain of the present, the disappointment of the status quo, and the ways in which the people of God fall short of the *eschaton*. The doxology draws our eyes up again to the heavens, from which our hope comes and to which our gaze returns in joy and longing. Those genres—lament and doxology—perhaps elide what have been more common tonalities for prophetic protest in recent years. Indeed, this issue of tonality appears on the first page of the preface to the revised edition, where Brueggemann reflects on the legacy of *The Prophetic Imagination*. He notes that "the practical use of prophetic texts in 'prophetic ministry' meant rather regularly, direct confrontational encounter with established power in the way Amos seemed to confront Amaziah (Amos 7.10-17)," though he has later deemed that approach to be "somewhat simplistic."[21] Over against the angry jeremiad, he calls for an ironic rhetoric and a textured presentation of lyric and poetry and of remembrance.

Brueggemann also describes the tradition-laden character of prophetic remembrance and of prophetic imagination.

> That is, the prophet is called to be a child of the tradition, one who has taken it seriously in the shaping of his or her own field of perception and system of language, who is so at home in that memory that the points of contact and incongruity with the situation of the church in culture can be discerned and articulated with proper urgency.[22]

In this book he does not take up the image of improvisation, but one can see how that moral and hermeneutical metaphor might be serviceable in this account: having learned the scales of scriptural imagination, the prophet will know just what lyrical note—whether in the major or minor keys of doxology or lamentation, respectively—will be fitting.

---

20. Ibid., 46–57.
21. Ibid., ix–x.
22. Ibid., 2.

In these ways, then, Brueggemann sketched and rehearses a prophetic imagination that is far more than mere denunciatory protest but takes in the task of deep counter-apologetic to the dominant discourse, showing its incapacities according to its own standards and leads the numb to lament its pains, and then treads on to the task of a poetic revisioning, that rehearsing promises of old and employs symbolic resources to cultivate renewed hope and doxological cries from the otherwise numbed. The prophet has far more to say, then, than might be assumed. But the prophet, perhaps, has far less too, for Brueggemann offers an account of prophetic imagination and action—of "prophetic ministry"—that is all rhetoric and speech. It is forceful and life-giving; numerous other adjectives evoke transformation and change too. Yet it is rather devoid of divine action in the present tense; the prophet acts, the prophetic community comes to cognizance and even amazement, and the subdominant culture upholds certain values or practices; the symbols evoke wonder.

Without decrying any of these textured, causal depictions, it is simply worth observation that God is not the subject of many verbs in this account. For all his emphasis on prophetic rhetoric finding its vitality in being theological language, Brueggemann's own account of prophetic work does rather little theologically, if by "theological" we mean speech about God and God's works. Brueggemann offers a theological set of ideals or principles, we might say, wherein rhetoric is measured by its ability to match and evoke concern for that which God apparently values. Yet the action is all creaturely and textual and sociological, which is a problem not for what is said but for the miracle that goes unsaid, not only for its content as also for its flimsy emphases. So we may ask: if this is a noble goal—to stir the prophetic imagination—is there a more promising pathway to sustain it theologically? And why on earth would we ever think retrieval theology a promising instrument in that regard?

III

Retrieval theology has garnered a good bit of attention in recent decades, manifesting itself in a number of otherwise divergent ecclesiastical and academic locales and now calling for assessment.[23] Retrieval has reconnected Christians with resources, figures, and texts that help reorient their posture before Holy

---

23. See especially Rowan Williams, *Why Study the Past? The Quest for the Historical Church* (London: Darton, Longman, and Todd, 2005); Michael Allen and Scott R. Swain, *Reformed Catholicity: The Place of Retrieval in Theology and Biblical Interpretation* (Grand Rapids: Baker Academic, 2015); David Buschart and Kent Eilers, *Theology as Retrieval: Receiving the Past, Renewing the Church* (Downers Grove, IL: IVP Academic, 2015); Darren Sarisky (ed.), *Theologies of Retrieval: An Exploration and Appraisal* (London: T&T Clark, 2017). A shorter analysis still proves helpful: John Webster, "Theologies of Retrieval," in *The Oxford Handbook of Systematic Theology* (ed. John Webster, Kathryn Tanner, and Iain Torrance; Oxford: Oxford University Press, 2007), 583–99.

Scripture. Retrieval may also throw into relief some of the challenges of modernity as, perhaps, being idiosyncratic, accidental, and something less than fated, as Solzhenitsyn said, modern theology exhibits "a stubborn tendency to grow not higher but to the side."[24] Yet it may seem ill suited to help lend a hand to that other development, namely, the furtherance of theology's prophetic impulse. Does *ressourcement* theology uphold the ecclesial and theological status quo? Does it allow one to avoid the process of intellectual and moral repentance by contenting itself with repristination? One theologian who argues constructively by way of retrieval notes the danger here: "As Niebuhr's own shift from socialist to official establishment theologian demonstrates, the danger of a theological program like mine is its tendency to drift from a radical politics to a qualified affirmation of the status quo."[25] Irrespective of the validity of socialism as a test case, the concern warrants attention (and has yet to be addressed in all the literature on retrieval). This chapter seeks to commend a portrayal of *ressourcement* that in no wise forgets the principle *semper reformanda*.

Is there any hope for a morally responsible retrieval theology? First we must devote some care to defining retrieval, parsing out divergent approaches and adopting the most theologically viable one. Then, second, we can turn to ways in which the practice of retrieval operates in a spiritual setting that is charged with divine action and aimed at our constant transformation.[26] In so doing, we will seek to show that attention to one's ancestors in Christian theology may underwrite rather than offset a commitment to ongoing repentance. Now, in assessing the live options available regarding retrieval theology in the contemporary setting, three categories of retrieval theology will be sketched, drawing on a typology first offered by John Webster in the late 1990s.[27]

First, perhaps the most dominant version of retrieval theology in the Protestant world has been captivated by insights from the world of social anthropology. The so-called Yale School or postliberal movement has been influential in this regard, and the work of contributors (from Lindbeck to Hauerwas) has often involved reappropriating insights from social anthropologists such as Clifford Geertz or philosophers of science like Thomas Kuhn and from the philosopher Alasdair MacIntyre.[28] In each of these cases, traditioned reasoning has been deemed natural,

---

24. "The Relentless Cult of Novelty," Catholic Education Resource Center, 1993, http://www.catholiceducation.org/articles/arts/a10001.html.

25. Tanner, *The Politics of God*, ix–x.

26. For analysis of the subjectivity of retrieval, see Simeon Zahl, "Tradition and Its 'Use': The Ethics of Theological Retrieval," *Scottish Journal of Theology* 71, no. 3 (2018), 308–23.

27. John Webster, "Traditions: Theology and the Public Covenant," *Stimulus* 6, no. 4 (1998), 18–19 (17–23); repr. as idem, *The Culture of Theology* (ed. Ivor J. Davidson and Alden C. McCray; Grand Rapids: Baker Academic, 2019), 84–6.

28. For further analysis, see especially Paul J. DeHart, *The Trial of the Witnesses: The Rise and Fall of Postliberal Theology* (Challenges in Contemporary Theology; Oxford: Blackwell, 2006).

typical, and thus necessary for theology. Geertz and Kuhn have described cultural and intellectual traditioning in a way that might be focal for looking at Christian theology. MacIntyre's *After Virtue* shows, by way of contrast, what remains after the loss of traditioned inquiry, providing an argument by way of contrariety.

Tradition thus becomes a grammar for speech and habits for practice. It serves to shape cultural animals by developing virtues and verbal intuitions that fit with the grain of the Christian universe. John Webster raised concern not so much for what is said but for how little is said here: "The greatest problem is that a certain doctrinal configuration tends to be presupposed in some post-liberal theology, one in which ecclesiology shifts to the center, and in which language about the presence of Christ and of the agency of the Holy Spirit tends to be occluded or accorded only background status."[29] It is not so much here that ecclesiology is not a pertinent theme by way of which to address tradition; indeed, Webster himself would go on to use an ecclesiological (creedal) term, "apostolicity," to derive an alternative account.[30] Rather, the danger is an ecclesiology in which human or social observation drives the agenda, whether by enlisting the works of anthropologists or of historians of philosophy and science.[31] In so doing, there is a material doctrinal loss, namely, that presence of Christ and the Spirit of which Webster makes mention. Centering church while backgrounding or dismissing the church's God turns the tradition of the church into a merely human stratagem. Doing so also endangers reflection upon tradition as being itself a testimony or witness to God's own self-revelation and, therefore, capable of revision, perhaps even likely revisable owing to the promise of divine transformation or sanctification through time.

Second, another approach toward tradition offers itself as something of a response to any such inviolability of tradition. In this regard, a more recent tilt toward *ressourcement* has taken inspiration from postmodern theory; the work of Kathryn Tanner serves as a paradigm. In her work on culture, tradition is recognized, like all human items of production, as something made or fashioned. Tradition is not a gift or a deposit but a determination, and it is thereby invested with real indeterminacy and exists accidentally. Tradition exists in an economy of power and its exercise, so that it comes into being and develops to suit certain interests with privilege. This second approach generates an ethic of caution about tradition's claims: at best they may be locally judicious; at worst they tilt in a colonialist direction.

---

29. Webster, "Traditions," 18.
30. Ibid., 20–3.
31. Webster is strident here not least because he had previously articulated such an approach methodologically and materially; see his "Locality and Catholicity: Reflections on Theology and the Church," *Scottish Journal of Theology* 45, no. 1 (1992), 1–17 (esp. 6 and 16, where he will say that "'conversation' with publics other than our own is, then, a Christological imperative"); and idem, "The Church as Theological Community," *Anglican Theological Review* 75, no. 1 (1993), 102–15 (esp. 103 fn. 4, where he admits that "My tiny sketch of 'tradition' is informed less by theological sources and more by work in philosophy… and in the human sciences").

This postmodern or critical approach toward tradition leads, in positive dogmatic terms, to accenting divine freedom and transcendence. The majesty of God can be accorded epistemological and ecclesiological significance in that he can never be strictly identified with the traditioning judgment of any creaturely congregation. Tradition takes a radically Protestant tact in Tanner's mold, and yet there is something more as well. Webster relates her postmodern vision of traditioning interpreted always as intellectual power politics to an equally extreme version of apophaticism wherein God is not only transcendent but darkness itself.[32] And yet it is difficult to consider this hard postmodern posture without observing a tendency toward epistemological and ecclesiological nihilism. Divine action may be promised but it never actually generate human life or witness or confession, at least not any with a lasting effect. Divine action exists rather like the wake off the back of a boat, vital but temporary, fleeting and not substantive. The teacher's words—"vanity, vanity, all is vanity" (Eccl. 1.2)—seem fitting for this approach.

Third, some have argued for a distinctly theological account of tradition, catholicity, and an ethic of retrieval by providing a Trinitarian and evangelical account of the church's being and life. In such an approach, overlapping concern with insights from social anthropology, philosophy of science, or philosophy may be explored and examined, yet theological categories will provide a framework and the promise of the gospel generates any real hope. In mid twentieth-century Roman Catholicism, *la nouvelle thèologie* provided not merely happenstance illustrations of retrieval but also a principled philosophy for its significance. Yves Congar and others located tradition within the work of the triune God whereby the body of Christ continues to minister the Word of Christ to the world. By linking Church and Word, and via the body metaphor Church and Christ as well, this tendency sought to give Christological imprimatur and to view tradition as an exegetical ministry of the saints.

Protestants have sometimes sought direct inspiration, claiming that these doctrinal accounts can be adopted within a Protestant theology, some even going so far as to argue that they must be enlisted for evangelical purposes. Reinhard Hütter, when still a Lutheran, argued that a social doctrine of the Trinity and a *communio* ecclesiology inspired by Vatican II-style ecumenism provided space for construing "theology as church practice" and tradition as a pneumatological gift.[33] Hans Boersma has suggested that a sacramental ontology inspired by de Lubac and Congar's approach generates a more integrative and holistic picture of Scripture and Tradition, one which may be shared in good conscience by post-Vatican II Roman Catholics (this side of *Dei Verbum*) and evangelical Protestants.[34] In this

---

32. Webster, "Traditions," 18–19.

33. Reinhard Hütter, *Suffering Divine Things: Theology as Church Practice* (trans. Doug Scott; Grand Rapids: Eerdmans, 2000).

34. Hans Boersma, *Nouvelle Thèologie and Sacramental Ontology: A Return to Mystery* (Oxford: Oxford University Press, 200); idem, *Heavenly Participation: The Weaving of a Sacramental Tapestry* (Grand Rapids: Eerdmans, 2011), esp. 120–36.

regard providence and participation serve as the most significant doctrinal terms for underwriting an account of tradition as what Boersma calls "sacramental time."

A more distinctly Protestant approach has been offered by a number of others, seeking to show distinctively Protestant concerns for appreciating tradition and catholicity. In this vein, John Webster argued that a Christological account of tradition needed to attend much more decisively to the ongoing action of the exalted Christ, rather than turning simply to his ecclesiological or Eucharistic body. Doing so, he suggested, would provide reason to expect the church to receive and bear grace, passing on tradition, as well as to receive and be reformed by grace.[35] In so doing *sola Scriptura* might be upheld as a Christological necessity. With inspiration from Webster, Kevin Vanhoozer has gone on to argue for the possibility of "biblical authority after Babel." In providing a doctrinal argument for Protestant hermeneutics, Vanhoozer has reoriented the five *solas* of the Reformation as each bearing hermeneutical significance, and he has appended a sixth *sola* drawn from Michael J. Glodo: *sola ecclesiae*, noting that the Reformers assumed that the church was the context for salvation and, by implication, for Scripture-reading.[36] In so doing, Webster and Vanhoozer present Christological and soteriological principles for a distinctly Protestant account of tradition.

A broader proposal has been offered by Michael Allen and Scott Swain in our call for *Reformed Catholicity*, specifically for the work of retrieval in theology and biblical interpretation. In that text a Trinitarian account is offered whereby not only Christology but also pneumatology situates an account of the scripture reader and the scripture reading congregation. Just as theological from Reformed Orthodoxy onward have spoken of ontological and cognitive principles of theology as a means of locating its existence in the being and work of God, so here a principled statement is made. God is the ontological principle of theology, to be sure, and God as Word and as Spirit serves as external and internal cognitive principles, respectively. All is of God, though this living and true God works in varied ways: inside and outside his people, transforming from within, to be sure, but also addressing from without. And yet Reformed Catholicity involves a claim also that God's *communio sanctorum* serves as the elicitive principle of theology, that is, the principle within which or amongst whom theology becomes real by God's doing.[37] In this regard, tradition serves as the "school of Christ" wherein women and men are guided and formed according to the "measure of the statute of the fullness of Christ" (Eph. 4.13) through the way in which the "body builds itself up in love" (4.16). In so doing, this approach wagers that "*Ressourcement*, properly conceived, is not driven merely by a traditionalist or communal sensibility

---

35. Webster, "Traditions," 19–20.

36. Kevin J. Vanhoozer, *Biblical Authority after Babel: Retrieving the Solas in the Spirit of Mere Protestant Christianity* (Grand Rapids: Brazos, 2016); see also Michael J. Glodo, "Sola Ecclesiae: The Lost Reformation Doctrine?" *Reformation & Revival* 9, no. 4 (2000), 91–7.

37. Allen and Swain, *Reformed Catholicity*, 36.

in theology. The deepest warrants for a program of retrieval are Trinitarian and Christological in nature." Specifics are then argued: "Formally stated, they concern the relationship between the principles of theology and the church, specifically, the relationship between the Spirit of Christ (the *principium cognoscendi internum* or internal cognitive principle of theology) and the renewed mind of the church (the *principium elicitivum* or elicitive principle of theology)."[38]

Two approaches to retrieval, then, operate out of a current perception of how immanent sense can be made of human knowledge, either via social anthropology regarding grammars of speech and thought or by means of critical theory about power. In both cases, however, there is no ground for hope or confidence in the notion of reform. While the first account suggests tradition as a passing on or inculcation of a deposit, the second account suggests that all reform is beholden to the well wishes of those with power or who claim power by some means. Neither approach renders reform impossible, of course, but the first incentivizes against it, while the second suggests that changes will be more akin to manipulation via the shifting identity of the powerful (whose interests alter those of the previously powerful but are no less pure or promising). The pathways of postliberalism and critical theory, then, may inform or help assess all sorts of angles regarding traditioned reasoning, but they do not provide resources for perceiving promise in this activity's pursuit of reform. At best, they leave open the possibility of prophetic critique of the status quo, much more likely and worse they stymie it or deem it mere manipulation.

While secular accounts of tradition and prompts to retrieval may well leave one without any goad to reform, a distinctly dogmatic approach to retrieval has unique resources upon which to draw. By avoiding a secular posture and adopting a spiritual sketch of the space of intellectual inquiry and construction, this third iteration of retrieval theology finds itself moved by an external force, namely, the present agency of the triune God working through the means of grace. In so doing, this third variant of Protestant *ressourcement* has notable parallels with its historical inspiration: the mid-twentieth-century movement known as *la nouvelle thèologie* in the Roman Catholic world. Like Congar, De Lubac, and Balthasar, this latest iteration of Protestant retrieval looks to a distinctly theological and uniquely Trinitarian vision of reality within which alone obedience to the fifth commandment ("Honor your father and your mother") makes intellectual sense. And yet this more recent vintage does differ notably from *la nouvelle thèologie* in the exact doctrinal matrix offered. While the apostolic character of the Christian theological tradition may play a significant role in both approaches to retrieval, the Reformed variant will turn to reflect more consistently upon the exalted singularity of the risen Christ in whose light alone we do see light (Ps. 36.9).[39]

---

38. Ibid., 18.
39. See chapter 1.

IV

May we envision a prophetic posture that acts by retrieving the riches of the theological past? What would it involve to imagine retrieval theology that serves rather than scuttles theological repentance and transformation? If we have seen reasons contemporary and classical suggesting the importance of the prophetic summons today, and, further, if we have seen that many overarching protocols for retrieval serve to pass on and, by implication, to underwrite or simply leave undisturbed the status quo, then what sort of theological matrix allows us to reimagine retrieval in a manner that feeds intellectual and spiritual reform? We will conclude by offering a minor dogmatics that helps contextualize the task of *ressourcement*, lest it become an instrument of power or a new tool of intellectual consumer taste.[40]

Tradition and resources which might be retrieved must be located, first, in light of the triune God and, second, among God's gifts and callings given to his human creatures. While a range of themes and subtopics suggest themselves (not least sacraments, office, and the like), we will confine ourselves to three major areas: trinity; the relationship of nature, grace, and glory; and, finally, the apostolicity of the church.

First, any approach to prophetic theology will only be as life-giving and truth-telling as is the living and true God of which it speaks. In beginning to reflect on a dogmatics of retrieval, the doctrine of the triune God—the only "living and true God" (WSC 5)—proves not only necessary but primary. The holy God of Israel and her prophets possesses all wisdom and goodness.

"Jesus Christ is yesterday and today and forever" (Heb. 13.8). That Christological and Trinitarian maxim proves fundamental for the task of retrieval. It is both a moral and a metaphysical statement; this one proves steadfast and implacable, faithful and immovable, just as this one is immutable and eternal. The Son, the one now known as the Christ and the bearer of that name Jesus (*Yeshua*, "Deliverer" or "Savior"), has his being from eternity past and possesses it completely, firmly, to the end of all ages.

Hebrews 13 puts this Christological and Trinitarian maxim to methodological use, however, if we read the verse within its context. "Remember your leaders, those who spoke to you the word of God. Consider the outcome of their way of life, and imitate their faith" (Heb. 13.7). The confession of Christ's eternal constancy grounds this posture of remembrance. These Hebrew Christians are summoned not merely to remember Israel's witness (Heb. 11), nor only that of Christ himself (12.1-3), but also to look to the elders and ancestors in their own locale (13.7). They are not to slavishly repeat or identically mimic their behavior, for they are inconsistent and live and move and have their being in settings only analogous to

---

40. Further arguments may be found in chapter 1 and 10; see also Michael Allen, "Confessions," in *The Cambridge Companion to Reformed Theology* (ed. David Fergusson and Paul Nimmo; Cambridge: Cambridge University Press, 2016), 28–43.

their own. They are to "run the race set before them," not their ancestors, but they are to do so with an eye to "so great a cloud of witnesses" (12.1) and specifically the testimony of their former leaders whose lives have now had a commendable outcome and whose faith can be imitated. Hebrews 13.7-8 provide a Christological and Trinitarian warrant for retrieval.

Second, retrieval theology exists with an eye to this living and true God's goodness displayed in his gifts of nature, grace, and glory. God spoke the world into being (Genesis 1) and his early beckon call serves to shape our reception of that global gift to this very day. Nature is a divine beneficence. At the right time, God also sent his Word to be born of a woman and offered up as a lamb for the slaughter and given for the sins of the world (John 1).

God's grace is shown in nature, grace, and glory alike. Various lessons can be drawn from this wide-eyed perception of God's agency. Germane to our purpose here is a perception that the Christ's work manifests itself not merely in the transition from nothingness to nature or from nature to grace but also in drawing his own—those who bear his very name—from grace to glory. There is a present tense to the gospel, and this involves a pledge of the Head of the Church to be with always, even to the end of the age (Mt. 28.20). According to John Webster, "Theologically construed, tradition is a function of the encounter of the risen Jesus and his people."[41]

Third, retrieval theology ought to be considered as a characteristic of the communion of saints, who are known as bearing an apostolic gift and calling. The Nicene-Constantinopolitan Creed declares that the true church is one, holy, catholic, and apostolic; more can be said of this church, but less may not be. Apostolicity deserves our attention, as it involves both backward and forward movements. It points backward first by rooting their church's place in the word of Christ, who sends; its testimony and its task are both granted from him. Apostolicity also points forward, however, in that its very being is purposive or telic. If it is centered in Christ, then it proceeds centripetally toward the ends of the earth, to be sure, and to the totality of the gospel or what might otherwise be called the "whole counsel of God" (Acts 20.26). The church is sent geographically, temporally, and materially to bear witness: that testimony resounds to the ends of the earth, to the end of this age, and to the relation of all things to God himself.

In speaking of the apostolic sending of the church, we continued to speak of the doctrine of the living and true God. The church's action and history is not mere history and no superficial or merely immanent agency. As argued in *Reformed Catholicity*, "a Reformed theology of retrieval must help us perceive the processes and products by which the church receives and transmits apostolic teaching not simply as human cultural activities and artifacts but also as fruits of the Spirit."[42] Tradition, therefore, exists as a set or range of products or testimonies from

---

41. John Webster, "Reading Theology," *Toronto Journal of Theology* 13, no. 1 (1997), 56 (53–63).

42. Allen and Swain, *Reformed Catholicity*, 25.

Christian individuals and churches which are rooted in God's ongoing sending and equipping generosity. The promise of the exalted Christ to "equip the saints" for "building up the body" (Eph. 4.7-12) offers not merely space for tradition but real promise, because it connects divine agency to ecclesial tradents.

John Webster spoke of two ways in which a theology that invested in reading theological classics might serve the church's life and witness: first, "theology serves the Word of God by assisting the Church to remain faithful to the gospel as it is manifest in Holy Scripture"; and second, "Theology serves the Word of God by assisting the Church to remain alert to the challenge of the gospel as it is manifest in Holy Scripture."[43] We can and should expand what it means to employ tradition or to read theology, taking in liturgy and rites and architecture and polity and art as well as commentaries and sermons and treatises and *summae*. But we dare not shrink Webster's depiction of how theology serves the church. Like the prophet Jeremiah, theology does help the church pluck up and tear down and then to build and to plant (Jer. 1.10). And immersion in the imaginative world of the Christian tradition and its thick and diverse manifestations aids in both the task of passing on and of purifying further. Calvin viewed the prophet as a covenantal prosecutor, one so enamored and convinced of the law's principles that he might bear righteous anger when pointing to instances where the people of God fall perilously short of its demands. Such a witness demands familiarity, deep and intimate knowledge, of that tradition and its previous applications (for any prosecutor needs to pay attention to their case law).[44]

That posture for theology depends ultimately upon more than Webster gave in that inaugural lecture. It demands what he soon thereafter sketched as an account of the exalted Christ as teacher of the church and of the church's theological task as an apostolic calling. It demands, further, a Trinitarian and Christological rooting that locates that postexistence of Christ within the full sweep of his ministry and his eternal life, as in texts such as Heb. 12-13.

So retrieval may well play quite the substantive role in prophetic address. Thinking doctrinally, one might wonder how prophetic reform might otherwise occur. Surveying the canon, it could be asked if prophetic transformation ever happens apart from remembering roots and seeing their ever-fresh application. And yet we must also note that prophetic reform oftentimes brings not only a change of the status quo but also a transformation of what we believe is needed. Prophetic ministry or speech cannot be aligned with any particular program or movement, at least nothing other than our witness to the movement of God's life-giving Word and Spirit.

---

43. Webster, "Reading Theology," 56, 59.
44. See especially Jaroslav Pelikan, *Interpreting the Bible and the Constitution* (New Haven: Yale University Press, 2004).

ACKNOWLEDGMENTS

Chapter 1 appeared previously as "'In Your Light Do We See Light': The Self-Revealing God and the Future of Theology," in *Theology and the Future: Evangelical Assertions and Explorations* (ed. David Starling and Trevor Cairney; London: T&T Clark, 2014), 13–26.

Chapter 2 appeared previously as "Living and Active: The Prophetic Ministry of the Exalted Christ," in *So Great A Salvation: Atonement in the Epistle to the Hebrews* (ed. Jon Laansma, et al; Library of New Testament Studies; London: T&T Clark, 2019), 144–56.

Chapter 3 appeared previously as "The Creature of the Word," *Reformed Faith & Practice* 3, no. 1 (Spring 2018), 4–12.

Chapter 4 appeared previously as "Divine Transcendence and the Reading of Scripture," *Scottish Bulletin of Evangelical Theology* 26, no. 1 (2008), 32–56.

Chapter 5 appeared previously as "Systematic Theology and Biblical Theology (Part 1)," *Journal of Reformed Theology* 14, no. 1–2 (2020), 52–72; and "Systematic Theology and Biblical Theology (Part 2)," *Journal of Reformed Theology* 14, no. 4 (2020), 344–57.

Chapter 6 appeared previously as "Review Article on *Militant Grace* by Philip Ziegler," *International Journal of Systematic Theology* 22, no. 3 (2020), 287–99.

Chapter 7 appeared previously as "Disputation *for* Scholastic Theology," *Themelios* 44, no. 1 (2019), 105–19.

Chapter 8 appeared previously as "Dogmatics as Ascetics," in *The Task of Dogmatics: Explorations in Theological Method* (ed. Oliver D. Crisp and Fred Sanders; Grand Rapids: Zondervan Academic, 2017), 189–209.

Chapter 9 appeared previously as "On Theology: The Active and Contemplative Life," in *Aquinas among the Protestants* (ed. Carl Manfred Svensson and David VanDrunen; Oxford: Blackwell, 2017), 189–206.

Chapter 10 appeared previously as "Reformed Retrieval," in *Theologies of Retrieval: Exploration and Appraisal* (ed. Darren Sarisky; London: T&T Clark, 2017), 67–80.

Thanks to the various publishers, journals, and editors for help and for permission to reprint.

INDEX

abiding in Christ 38–42
Abraham, looked toward the resurrection 16–17
active life 161, 163–4
Adams, Edward 23
agnosticism, about the resurrection 17
Albert 131
Allen, Michael 196
Alpha and Omega 174
analogia entis 53
Anfechtung 125
animality, and life of pleasure 161
Anizor, Uche 25
anti-speculative approach to biblical reasoning 153
apartheid 186
apocalyptic reading of Paul 96n86, 97n89
apocalyptic theology 103–15
apophaticism 139
apostolicity 194, 199
archetypal theology 160
Aristotle 119, 131
ascension 17, 67
ascetical dogmatics vii, 137, 145–53
atonement, and resurrection 18
Augustine 93, 117, 126, 147
    on beatific vision 163
    on *totus Christus* 188
author's intention 51, 59, 61
autonomy 39
Averroes 131
Avicenna 131
Ayres, Lewis 44–5, 182

Balserak, Jon 187
Balthasar, Hans Urs von 197
baptism 6, 38, 39
Barth, Karl 2, 6–7, 15, 54, 103, 106, 167, 179
Bauerschmidt, Frederick Christian 151, 168

Bavinck, Herman 2, 4, 32, 33–4, 78n20, 86, 148–9, 151, 169
Bayer, Oswald 125
Beal, Gabriel 119
beatific vision 69, 158–61, 163, 164, 167, 169
beatitude 131
Behr, John 146n53
Berkouwer, G. C. 176n5
biblical reasoning 6
biblical theology 73–80, 98, 101
    mainstream 92–3
    as regulative of exegesis 84, 87
    serves systematic theology 80–1, 83, 87
    tendency to imbalance and overreaction 91
biblical traditioning 8–10
Biel, Gabriel 126
Billings, Todd 32
bodily well-being 160
Boersma, Hans 29, 30, 139n22, 195–6
Bonaventure 101
Bonhoeffer, Dietrich 3–4, 52
Bowald, Mark 11, 40n33, 179n8
Braaten, Carl 96, 109
Brazos Theological Commentary on the Bible series 94n82
Bruce, F. F. 17
Brueggemann, Walter 63n83, 185, 189–92
Bucer, Martin 42, 93
Bultmann, Rudolf 103
burning bush 174

Cajetan, Cardinal 119, 122
Calvin, John ix, 29, 44, 93, 101, 107, 118, 168
    on the church 181
    on divine transcendence 64
    on prophet as covenant prosecutor 200
    on prophetic calling 185, 187–8
    and scholasticism 127
    on twofold grace 177

Campbell, Douglas 107
Carson, Donald A. 91n79, 92
causality, competitive view of 49n1
central dogma 149
Chadwick, Henry 147
Charry, Ellen 67n97
Christian burials 171
Christian life
    "impossible newness" of 108, 110
    militant discipleship in 106
Christian pragmatism 50
Christology
    of apocalyptic theology 107
    in Hebrews 15
    priority over bibliology 56
church
    as creature of the Word 32, 34–46
    holiness of 38
    as instrument of God 44
    and reading of Scripture 57–8
    visible and invisible 179, 181
church *in via* 69
church tradition 44
civil rights movement 186
Clement of Alexandria 43
Coakley, Sarah 118n3, 137–40, 144, 145–6, 151–2
Cocceius 92
communio ecclesiology 195
communion with God vii, 169
communion of saints 196, 199
community 68
compatibilism 65
conformed to the world 135
Congar, Yves 195, 197
Congdon, David 103–4n1
constructive theology 10
contemplation
    Coakley on 138
    of divine effects 162–3
    of divine truth 162–3
contemplative life 159–61, 162–4
conversational approach to theology 52, 136, 143, 152
Council of Chalcedon 53n15
covenant fellowship 149
covenant theology 92
Cowan, Martyn Calvin 188n8
creativity 10

Creator-creature distinction 74
creatureliness, precedes creativity 55
critical theory 32, 197
Cyril 93

"dark corners" of the church 143, 144, 148, 152
Davis, Joshua 107
de Lubac, Henri 195, 197
De Rijk, L. M. 126
deconstructionists 67
deism, in contemporary theology 10
deistic turn in biblical criticism 40n33, 41, 179n8
desire 138
determinism 63
discernment 135
discipleship 107, 136
    and dogmatics 145
    dual purpose of 108
discipline 27
disenchantment 29
"Disputation Against Scholastic Theology" (Luther) 117–34
divine and human action 49–50, 57, 58, 62–6, 71
divine missions 40n33, 157
divine speech 22, 40
divine transcendence
    and radical immanence 65
    and reading Scripture 49, 63–6, 71
doctrine of God, and retrieval 174
doctrine of human, and retrieval 174–5
dogmatics 50, 98–101
    and sanctification 137
    serves discipleship 145
doxology 191
Duns Scotus, John 49n1, 54n18, 168
duplex gratia 177

ecclesiastical authorities 35, 43–5
Echeverria, Eduardo 176n5
economic Trinity 74
ectypal theology 160
effectual calling 107
Eglington, James 78n20
Elias 49
Eliot, T. S. 15
Emory, Gilles 166n8

Erasmus 117, 120
eschatology 67, 89, 96–7, 158–9
Eubank, Nathan 148
Eucharist 6
evolution analogies, in biblical theology 79
exalted Christ
    gives and graces 41
    as prophet 16
exalted Christology 27
exegesis 84–5, 98–101
    at core of theological task 89
exegetical reasoning 6
expressive individualism 43
external cognitive principle of theology 177–8
external goods 160

false humility, of theology 54
fear of the Lord vi, 98
feminist theology 138, 172
fifth commandment 181, 197
figural reading 59n65, 66, 70n110
finitude and sinfulness 67
    in author's self-knowledge 59
Finnish reading of Luther 103
first commandment 35–6
first- and second-order language 3
Fish, Stanley 69
foolishness to the Greeks 132
Ford, David 52
Forde, Gerhard 131
Fowl, Stephen 50–2, 54, 58–62, 70
Frei, Hans 104
French Confession of Faith (1559) 11–12
Freud, Sigmund 138
friendship 121
frui and *uti* 147
fruitfulness 47

Gabler, J. P. 79n24, 85, 87
Gaffin, Richard 85–90, 91, 95–6, 97
Geertz, Clifford 193–4
generational interdependence 175
Glodo, Michael J. 42, 196
God
    ad intra life shapes *ad extra* life 78n20
    as completely other 64
    constancy and faithfulness of 174
    as fountain of life 2
    as living and true God 198, 199
    militancy of 106
    as mystery 150–1
    as ontological principle of theology 177
    perfection of 148–9
    presence as the Word 55
"god of the gaps" 64
grace 2, 11, 176–8
    in apocalyptic theology 105, 109, 114
    Luther on 120–1
    restores nature 167–9
grammars of speech 197
Gregory, Brad 29
Gregory the Great 161, 163
Gregory of Nyssa 139
Gregory of Rimini 121n7

Hall, Douglas John 186
Hamilton, Victor P. 63n84
happiness 158–60
Harink, Douglas 107
Hauerwas, Stanley 31, 56n33, 193
Hays, Richard 132n39
head and the body image 36–7
Healy, Nicholas 69
Hector, Kevin 151
Hegel, G. W. F. 78n20
Heidelberg Catechism 20, 188
hermeneutical naturalism 94, 98
Heschel, Abraham Joshua 186
Hilkert, Mary Catherine 152n76
Hill, Wesley 111n7
historicism 96–7
Hodge, A. A. 86
Hodge, Charles 86
holiness 141–2, 153
Holy Spirit
    and call of the gospel 107–8
    Coakley on 139–40, 152
    and development of Christian doctrine 82, 84–5
    ministry with the Word 67
    "unfitting gift" of 108, 110
homosexuals in the church 61n76
Houseman, A. E. 123
Hugh of St. Victor 166
Hughes, Graham 24
human dignity 175
human flourishing 67

humanity 174–5
  finite limits of 175
Hütter, Reinhard 195

identity politics 32
idolatry vii, 3, 6, 35–6, 43, 141, 142
imago Dei 52
immanent frame 40
immanent Trinity 74
incarnation 65
incorporation 146
indestructible life 17, 18, 20
individualism 31
indwelling sin 45, 50, 68–9
innovation 10
intellectual asceticism 118, 168
intellectual discipleship viii, 136n3, 168
internal cognitive principle of theology 177, 178
interpretive pluralism 51, 59, 68
inventiveness 10
inwelling sin 179
Irenaeus 29, 93, 146n53

Jenson, Robert 96, 110
Jeremiah 190–1
Jesus Christ
  anointing of 188
  as apostle 21
  ascension of 19–20
  as author and perfector of life 17
  divine and human agencies of 65
  as great shepherd of the sheep 4, 37, 180
  heavenly session of 20
  as high priest 17, 21
  humanity of 157
  as king 107
  lordship of 35–6, 180
  ongoing prophetic work 20
  prayer of 17
  resurrection of 2, 16–20
  session of 19
  speech of 21
  union with the church 36
  as unsurpassable eschatological act of redemption 105
  as Word of God 56
Jobes, Karen 24n30
Johnson, Luke Timothy 21

Joseph 62
Jüngel, Eberhard 52
justification, distortion of 130–1

Kafka, Franz 5
Kähler, Martin 96
Kant, Immanuel 11
Karlstad, Andreas von 119n4
Käsemann, Ernst 96, 103, 105, 107, 112n12, 114
Kelsey, David 38
kenosis 108n4
Kerr, Nathan R. 107, 112
Kibbe, Michael H. 19n14, 28
Kilwardy, Robert 166
Kingdom, coming of 108
knowledge of God 98
Korthaus, Michael 124
Kroeker, Travis 107
Krötke, Wold 113
Kuhn, Thomas 193–4
Kuyper, Abraham 86, 169

la nouvelle théologie 195, 197
Lamb, Matthew 167
lamentation 190, 191
Lane, William 17
Lash, Nicholas 3, 6
law, and love 121–2
law-gospel distinction 110–11
Legaspi, Michael C. 86
Levering, Matthew 44–5, 50n3, 146, 165, 182, 182–3n16
Levinas, Emmanuel 52
Lindbeck, George 58, 69n107, 104, 193
Logos ensarkos 56
Lord's Supper 39
love 121–2, 162
Lowe, Walter 112
Luther, Martin ix, 26, 29, 38, 93, 103, 117–18, 168, 169

Macaskill, Grant 96n86, 111n8
MacIntyre, Alasdair 31, 60, 193
McCabe, Herbert 168
McCormack, Bruce 53n17, 111
McFarland, Ian 36–7
magisterium, and reading Scripture 50, 67, 68, 69, 70

Mangina, Joseph 111–12
Manicheans 120
Marcion 129
marketing 43
Marshall, I. Howard 9
Martyn, J. Louis 97n89, 103, 106, 107, 111, 112, 114
Mascall, E. F. 185
means of grace, and theology 11–12
mediator 122
meditatio 125
Melanchthon, Philipp 131
Melchizedek 16, 17, 19
"mere Protestant Christianity" 30–1
merismos 26
methodology 67
Milbank, John 53–4
Milgrom, Jacob 18
Miller, Patrick 100
miracles 64n89
modern theology, restating and resituating of epistemology 29
Moffitt, David 16–20, 27
Moltmann, Jürgen 53n15, 96, 186
monophysitism 65
monothelitism 65
moral autonomy 166–7
moral formation 123
moral virtues 162
moralistic therapeutic deism 43, 176
mortification and vivification, in reading 57
Muller, Richard A. 70n110, 127
Murray, John 81–5, 86, 87, 89, 90, 97
mystery 151

Nadab and Abihu 36
narrative 167
  as reductive 97
narratives of decline 173
National Socialism 186
natural theology 4
neo-Calvinism 169
New Criticism 51
new heavens and new earth 169
new perspective(s) on Paul 88, 97n89, 103
New Studies in Biblical Theology series 91n79, 93
Nicene-Constantinopolitan Creed 199

Nietzsche 133
no resurrection approach 17
nominalism 49n1, 50n3
numbness, from royal consciousness 190, 192

Ockham 119
O'Donovan, Oliver 132n41
oikonomia 74
ontological principle of theology 177, 181
ontology, and divine economy 167
order of being and of authority 10
order of knowing 10
ordo salutis 88
Otto, R. 142
over-realized eschatology 50, 67
Overtures to Biblical Theology series 91n79
Owen, John 7, 92, 167, 175n4, 188

Packer, J. I. 137n4
Pannenberg, Wolfhard 96
participation 149
past, critical appropriation of 181–3
pastoral eschatology 27
Pelagianism 65, 118, 120, 123
Pelagius 119
"pervasive interpretive pluralism" 29
Pesch, Otto Hermann 124n18, 147
Peter Lombard 166
Pickstock, Catherine 53, 54n18, 61n79
pilgrim theology, and scholasticism 133
pilgrimage 179
Platonic philosophy, in Hebrews 23
pneuma 26
Pneumatology 107–8
Porphyry 119
positive psychology 93
postliberalism 40n33, 69n107, 104, 179n8, 193–4
postmodern theory 58n56
post-structuralism 51
power 186–7, 197
pragmatism 61, 69
prayer, in apocalyptic theology 108
pre-glorified human activity, and indwelling sin 68–9
priesthood of all believers 31
Princeton Theological Seminary 74, 79

principium cognoscendi externum 4–5
principium cognoscendi internum 5, 197
principium elicitivum 178, 180, 197
principium essendi 4
progressive revelation 77
prophet, as covenant prosecutor 187, 200
prophetic calling 185–8
prophetic imagination 189–92
prophetic speech 109
prophetic vocation 185–7
prosopological exegesis 24n30
Protestant Scholastics 167
providence 7n22, 175
psychē 26
purgation and desire 137
Puritans, on prophetic calling 188

racial reconciliation 176
Radical Lutherans 110, 131
Radical Orthodoxy 53n13, 54n18, 59n65, 140
Radical Reformation 42
radicality, of the gospel 105
Radner, Ephraim 45n51, 182–3n16
Ramsey, Michael 41
rationalism 79, 87
rationality 161–2, 168
reader-response criticism 57
reading
    with docility and humility 98–9
    as receptive of divine action 51
    requires patience, care, and compassion 67
reading vs. interpretation 57
realized eschatology 190
redemptive history 88, 90, 96–7
reformational anthropology 134
reformed and catholic 30
Reformed ecclesiology 45
Reformed orthodox 70n110
Reformed polity 178–9
Reformed retrieval 45, 179–83
Reformed theology, doctrine of sin 107
Reformed Thomism 156, 166–9
regenerated heart and illuminated mind, internal cognitive principle of theology 177, 178
regula fidei 61–2, 68–9
renewed reason 178

ressourcement vi, viii, ix, 173n3, 185–6, 193, 194, 196–7, 198
resurrection 16–17, 169
retrieval viii, 8
    anthropological approach 172–3
    and communion of saints 199
    in contemporary theological conversation 171–83
    and critical approach to tradition 193–5
    and goodness of God 199
    as prophetic address 200
    and prophetic imagination 185–6, 192–200
    and reform 185–6
    and theological account of tradition 195
    theological approach 173, 197
    and triune God 198–9
revelation, organic character of 77–8, 88
Ribbens, Benjamin J. 19n14, 28n40
Ricouer, Paul 52
Ridderbos, Herman 96
Rieff, Philip 35
Rogers, Eugene 60, 152
Romanticist theory 51
Rorty, Richard 69
royal consciousness 189–91
ruled reading 67

sacra doctrina 165
sacramental ontology 195
salvation-historical development for Christian reading of Scripture 61n76
sanctification of reason 125, 140–2, 148, 151–3
sapiential and existential theology 147
Sarisky, Darren 94
Schaff, Philip 33, 34, 78n20
Schenk, Ken 24
scholasticism, 118, 132
    and breadth of God's Word 129–30
    defines a method 126–8
    employment of philosophical terms 131–2
    and theological priorities 130–1
Schweitzer, Albert 96, 103
scientific method 32
Scripture

clarity of 57
  as external cognitive principle of theology 177–8
  as instrument of divine action 56
  as living Word of God viii, 56
secularism 31
secularization 29
self-denial vii
semi-Pelagianism 118, 123
sense of the self 35
sensus literas 60
shema 43
sick and dying, care for 171
Siggelkow, Ry O. 109n5, 112n12
sin 175–6
Sinai 22–3
sinfulness, stranglehold of 120–3
Sklar, Jay 18
Smith, Christian 29, 176
Smythe, Shannon Nicole 108n4
social anthropology 193, 195, 197
Socinians, on Hebrews 19n14
sola ecclesia 42
sola fide 30, 31
sola gratia 30
sola Scriptura 11–12, 30, 33, 136n3, 196
soli Deo gloria 30
solus Christus 30, 33
Son
  priestly role of 22
  speech of 15
  suffering of 21
Sonderegger, Katherine 150, 152n76
Song of Songs, erotic imagery of 132
speculation 110, 113–14
speech-act 51
spiritual worship 135
status confessionis 186
Stoic fatalism 65
Stout, Jeffrey 69
stranger, voice of 43–4
structures of texts 51
Studies in Biblical Theology series 91n79
Studies in Theological Interpretation series 94n82
Summa theologiae 155–6
supernatural revelation 76–8
Swain, Scott R. viii, 32, 178, 196

Synge, F. 24
systematic theology
  John Murray on 81–5
  missionary importance of vii

Tanner, Kathryn 186, 194–5
Taylor, Charles 29, 35, 40, 166
tentatio 125
Ten Theses of Berne 24, 45, 183
tetragrammaton 174
textual ontology 51
theologia 75
theologian of the cross 124–5
theologian of glory 124
theologians, captivity to philosophy 53
theological discipleship 118
theological exegesis 94
theological interpretation of Scripture viii, 94–5, 98, 101
theological *principia* 147
théologie totale 137, 138, 140, 143
"theology and ... " 136
theology
  duty to its time and place 83
  as ecclesially bounded 12
  in economy of the gospel 157
  as exercise in the fellowship of the saints 143
  as "fundamentally purgative of idolatry" 137
  phallocentric form 138
  purgative character 137, 140, 144
  as *scientia* 166
  serves spiritual purposes 135
  in wake of God's agency 11
theology of exaltation 20
theology of holiness 141–3
therapeutic ideal 43
Theresa of Lisieux 52
"thick description," of reading Scripture 50, 63, 65–6, 70–1
Thomas Aquinas 101, 124n18, 131
  on beatitude 158–61
  definition of theology 1
  on divine missions 181
  on divine transcendence 64
  eschatology of 158–9
  ethics of 161

intellectual asceticism of 155–6
  on limits to knowledge 176n5
  on sanctity of mind 151
  theocentric focus of 169
  on theological method 164–6
  on the theological task 156–8
Thompson, James 23
Timmermann, Daniël 26
totus Christus 166, 188
tradition 44–5, 126–7, 180–1
  as elictive principle of theology 178, 180
  as grammar for speech 194
  serves as the "school of Christ" 196
Treier, Daniel J. 24
trinitarian order 146
Trinity 145–6
  Coakley on 139–40
  "reflective" model of 139
triune economy 30–1, 150, 153
T&T Clark International Theological Commentary series 94n82
Turner, Denys 168
Turretin, Francis 168–9

union with Christ 89
universale bonum 159
universale verum 159
University of St. Andrews 95
univocity of being 64
Ursinus, Zacharias 10

Van Driel, Edwin Chr. 113
Vanhoozer, Kevin J. 30–2, 34, 42, 196
Vermigli, Peter Martyr 167
via moderna 126
Vietnam War 186
virtue in reading 67–8
vocation 188
Vos, Geerhardus 73–81, 86, 87, 89, 90, 96, 97, 100

Warfield, B. B. 86
wayfaring knowledge 160
Webster, John 2, 32, 40, 99, 167
  on biblical reasoning 6
  on divine and human actions in revelation 55–8, 70
  on holiness 51, 137, 140–5
  on immensity of God 65
  on postliberal theology 194, 195
  on reading Scripture 50–2, 69n109
  on retrieval 173
  on theology serving the church 200
  on tradition 195–6
West, Cornel 186
Westminster Standards 85, 88
Westminster Theological Seminary 81
Wheaton College 95
whole counsel of God vii, 99, 101, 129–30, 132
will 122
William of Ockham 49n1
wisdom eschatology 167
Witsius, Hermann 92
Wood, Donald 9n27
Word of God 4
  abides in us unto the goal of flourishing 47
  breadth of 129–30
  guidance in language 132
  as living and active 25–8
Workgroup on Constructive Theology 100, 143
world, object of divine salvation 105–6
worship 135

Yale School 193
Yeago, David 32n16, 43

Ziegler, Philip 104–6, 107, 112, 113, 114
Zion 22–3
Zwingli, Huldrych 25, 27

www.ingramcontent.com/pod-product-compliance
Lightning Source LLC
Chambersburg PA
CBHW062227300426
44115CB00012BA/2249